RECONCILIATION

in RELIGION *and* SOCIETY

Published by the Institute of Irish Studies, 1994.

Grateful acknowledgement for financial assistance is made to the
Community Relations Council and to
the University of Ulster.

ISBN: 0 85389 508 2

British Library Cataloguing-in-Publication Data. A catalogue record for this
book is available from the British Library.

Printed by W. & G. Baird Ltd., Antrim
Cover design by Rodney Miller Associates

Reconciliation
in Religion *and* Society

**Proceedings of a conference organised by the
Irish School of Ecumenics and the University of Ulster**

Edited by
Michael Hurley, SJ

Institute of Irish Studies
The Queen's University of Belfast
in association with the University of Ulster

For   The Columbanus Community of Reconciliation

CONTENTS

THE CONTRIBUTORS

W. DENNIS COOKE, BA,BD,MTh, PhD is a Minister of the Methodist Church in Ireland and Principal of Edgehill Theological College, Belfast.

THOMAS CORBETT, BSc, DD, DipScMed is Professor of Dogmatic Theology at St Patrick's College, Maynooth.

REDMOND FITZMAURICE, OP, STL, PhL, MA, a Dominican priest who ministers at St Catherine's Newry, lectures on Islam and Christian-Muslim relations at the Irish School of Ecumenics and on World Religions at the Milltown Institute of Theology & Philosophy, Dublin.

DUNCAN B FORRESTER, is Professor of Christian Ethics and Practical Theology and Principal of New College in the University of Edinburgh.

JULIAN GREENWOOD, BSc, PhD is Senior Lecturer in Science at Stranmillis College, Belfast.

ROISIN HANNAWAY, BSc, HDipEd is a St Louis Sister and Leader of the Columbanus Community of Reconciliation, Belfast.

RUPERT WILLIAM NOEL HOARE, PhD was Principal of Westcott House, Cambridge until his recent consecration as Bishop of Dudley in the Church of England.

MICHAEL HURLEY, SJ, STD, LLD was Lecturer in Continuing Education in the Irish School of Ecumenics until his recent retirement.

KATHERINE VIRGINIA (GINNIE) KENNERLEY, MA is a priest of the Church of Ireland, formerly Lecturer in Applied Theology at the Church of Ireland Theological College, Dublin, recently appointed Rector of Narraghmore and Castledermot in Co. Kildare.

PHIL KILROY, PhD is a Sacred Heart Sister who has worked in the Centre for Research on Women in the University of Ulster at Coleraine and is now engaged in historical research.

GEMMA LOUGHRAN, MA,BL was until recently Lecturer in Religious Studies, St Mary's College of Education, Belfast.

CARMEL McCARTHY, MA, STD is a Mercy Sister who is Lecturer in Near Eastern Languages, University College Dublin.

J.CECIL McCULLOUGH, BA,BD,PhD is Professor of New Testament, Union Theological College, Belfast.

CELINE MANGAN, BA,MA,LSS is a Dominican Sister who lectures in Scripture at the Milltown Institute of Theology and Philosophy, Dublin.

JOHN D'ARCY MAY, Dr Theol., Dr Phil., lectures in Interfaith Dialogue and in Social Ethics at the Irish School of Ecumenics in Dublin.

CARMEL NILAND BEd, MA is a Sister of Sion who specializes in Jewish-Christian relations.

GERARD O'HANLON, SJ, MA,PhD is Lecturer in Systematic Theology and Dean of Theology at the Milltown Institute of Theology and Philosophy, Dublin.

TERENCE O'KEEFFE is Dean of Humanities at the University of Ulster and was until recently Head of the Department of Philosophy and Politics at the University.

JOHN PETTY, MA has been Provost of Coventry Cathedral since 1988.

HELGA ROBINSON-HAMMERSTEIN, MA, Dr Phil., is Senior Lecturer in History and, until December 1993, Dean of Graduate Studies at Trinity College Dublin and an ordained assistant in the Lutheran Church in Ireland.

PAM STOTTER, BA,M.Phil (Ecumenics) is Lecturer in Adult and Continuing Education at the Irish School of Ecumenics in Dublin.

GEOFFREY WAINWRIGHT, MA, BD, DD, Dr Theol., a British Methodist Minister, is Robert Earl Cushman Professor of Christian Theology in the Divinity School, Duke University, Durham, USA.

FLORA JANE LOUISE WINFIELD, BA is a deacon in the Church of England (who will be priested in May 1994) and Ecumenical Officer for Gloucestershire.

PREFACE

Trevor Smith

I am writing this shortly after the two awful events that occurred on consecutive weekends in late October 1993. The slaughter occasioned by the bombing in the Shankill Road, which was swiftly followed by the reprisal shootings in the *Rising Sun* public house in Greysteel, brings home very forcefully how desperately reconciliation is needed but equally illustrates what evil forces are doing to widen the divisions between the two communities in Northern Ireland. Such atrocities momentarily stall us in our tracks but we are presented with no choice – we have to redouble our efforts for reconciliation.

The contributors to this volume seek therefore to address one of the most pressing issues confronting the agenda of post-secular society. From different perspectives – disciplinary, confessional and experiential – the authors endeavour to explore how and in what way the churches and other religious institutions might more successfully pursue the quest for greater reconciliation in Ireland and beyond.

It is clear that for some time now we have been witnessing the emergence of post-secular society and it is one which will characterise much of the next century. We are witnessing the awakening of a greater concern for spiritual values that were either ignored or suppressed for most of the twentieth century, where the emphasis in both capitalist and collectivist regimes has been on the pursuit of materialist goals. In the transition from the secular to the post-secular society it is already apparent that the revival of religious interest is something of a mixed blessing: on the one hand, there is a growing attraction for a return to basic orthodoxy, which is often referred to as fundamentalist, and, on the other hand, more promisingly, some tentative moves towards a more universalistic approach to revealed truth. In many areas of the world the former appears to be serving both as a precursor and a concomitant to narrow nationalistic or tribal sentiments which will hardly further the cause of reconciliation. The latter, however, offer a real promise. As yet it is only at an embryonic stage but one can see in the writings of Karen Armstrong, Keith Ward, Hans Küng, Raimundo Pannikar, Ewart H. Cousins and others how the major religions might be regarded in such a way that they may become vehicles for better mutual understanding and tolerance. It needs intensive and empathetic understanding to reach across from one's own tradition to comprehend both the unique insights and complementarities to be found in others. In the words of Ewart H. Cousins such an exercise has to attempt to come up with 'neither a narrow fundamentalism nor a bland universalism'. The search, that is to say, is not for some middle way where various creeds are translated into a kind of spiritual esperanto, but rather for a sensitive dovetailing of the thrusts, nuances and visions of the main religions of the world without diluting the strength of one's own spiritual convictions. Indeed, such an exercise may well produce not only a greater appreciation of revealed truth to be found in religions different from one's own but may well strengthen and deepen one's own spiritual identity and quest.

It is earnestly to be hoped that these early and tentative advances towards a new 'spirituality of reconciliation', to use Fr. Michael Hurley's terminology, will gather momentum. Even more difficult will be the second stage when the insights of the new theology are broadcast more fully to the wider world. This process cannot simply be left to an evangelism which seeks to influence the individual man or woman of religious disposition and goodwill, for it has also to permeate the institutions of society and policy-making in general. A spirituality of reconciliation, that is to say, requires to be manifested not only in our personal devotions and behaviour but also in innovatory and purposive structural change. The University of Ulster has recently taken two initiatives of the sort of thing I have in mind and I cite them simply by way of example. Out of its own applied research experience, especially that emanating from its Centre for the Study of Conflict, it developed the idea of creating INCORE – the joint University of Ulster/United Nations University programme for an international centre for conflict resolution and ethnicity. This is now established and functioning and will be physically located in due course on the Magee campus in London/Derry. It will seek to undertake applied research into the causes of ethnic conflict and to develop practical training programmes for those involved in the mediation and management of such conflicts. Within the next five years INCORE plans to have spawned four associated centres in Southern Africa, Southern Asia, Eastern Europe and Latin America. Closer to home the University has embarked on a major feasibility study to establish a new campus on the peaceline in Belfast. Magee College has assisted in the economic development and more positive outlook emanating in London/Derry and it is hoped to replicate this in the Springvale development area of Belfast. These two examples are taken from higher education, which is my own field of interest, but I am aware that in the voluntary sector in Northern Ireland much courageous, imaginative and sheer hard work is going on to initiate and build up cross-community projects. I equally admire the work of many of the clergy and their congregations in fostering reconciliation. During my time in Northern Ireland, however, it has been borne in on me time and again how extensively the words 'Protestant' and 'Catholic' are used by religious spokesmen and how relatively little used is the more generic term 'Christian'. It is a sad commentary and reinforces one of the main motives behind the research project, the reports of which are contained in the present volume, about what Fr. Hurley refers to as 'the ineffectual character generally of the churches' work for reconciliation in Ireland and elsewhere'. It may well be that the churches as corporate entities have failed to rise to the challenge and are in real need of an effusion of the new theology.

INTRODUCTION

The Editor

This book began life as a research project which I had the opportunity of directing as Lecturer in Continuing Education in the Irish School of Ecumenics. The findings of the project were presented to a residential seminar held in Belfast from 30 April to 3 May 1992 under the joint auspices of the University of Ulster and the School of Ecumenics. This book brings the findings to a wider audience.

The background to the project was the growing malaise and concern of so many at what is felt to be the ineffectual character generally of the Church's work for reconciliation in Ireland and elsewhere. Like the disciples on the road to Emmaus (cf Luke 24) many Christians and others 'had hoped' that the Churches would have a greater impact in situations of conflict and be part of the solution more than part of the problem; that the Churches would not have to be so apologetic and defend themselves by stressing how, without their ministry of reconciliation, things might be so much worse.

The research project chose nine aspects of the topic for special consideration. Two specialists were invited to concentrate on each of eight of these aspects:one to prepare a paper, the other to prepare a response; four others agreed to concentrate on the 'Other Religions and Reconciliation' aspect, which perhaps was particularly appropriate as we approached the centenary year of the Chicago Parliament of World Religions in 1893. In addition, because two celebrations of the eucharist were planned for the residential seminar, two addresses were also commissioned on 'The Eucharist and Reconciliation'.

Of the twenty two specialists thus involved, ten were women, twelve men. Twelve were Roman Catholic, ten were Anglican, Lutheran, Methodist or Presbyterian. Nine were from academic institutions in the south of Ireland, eight from Northern Ireland

and five from Britain and the USA. In other words the research
project was conceived not just as a study of reconciliation but as
itself an exercise in reconciliation.

In the course of the project the pairs consulted with each other
as much as possible and the foursome dealing with 'Other Religions and Reconciliation' met together on a number of occasions.
Two general meetings were also held:one in Belfast on 24 October
1991, the other in Dublin on 16 January 1992. The primary aim was
not so much to further understanding of each aspect in isolation
but rather to seek an overview and in the process to deepen and
develop our understanding of the meaning of reconciliation and,
by so doing, to make a significant contribution towards a more
fruitful, effectual ministry of reconciliation.

What the project did for me and what I hope the book will do
for many others is, in the first place, to give me a deeper appreciation of the inclusive, comprehensive nature of reconciliation. Just
as the eye cannot say to the hand 'I have no need of you', nor the
head to the feet 'I have no need of you' (cf 1 Cor 12:21), so
ecumenists cannot say to evangelicals nor feminists to ecologists,
nor politicians to preachers, nor historians to theologians and *vice
versa* 'We have no need of you'. Perhaps too many of us in our
work for reconciliation fail to see the wood for the individual trees.
As a result one reason why the Churches are so ineffectual in their
reconciliation ministry may well be because bishops and their
counterparts, all those who have oversight in the Church, either
lack an inclusive overview of reconciliation or fail to follow it
through with appropriate strategy and planning, so that a serious
imbalance develops in the ministry at a given level with some
aspects (eg prayer among Evangelicals and work for justice among
Catholics)being overemphasized and other aspects being over-
looked.

The project has also given me a new appreciation of the
religious character of reconciliation. It has helped me to sketch
in outline for myself what I would call a 'spirituality of
reconciliation'. Reconciliation for me is primarily about persons,
people, parties, groups; only secondarily about issues:showing,
making conflicting facts, statements, positions, doctrines to be
compatible with each other. It assumes the existence of a state of
estrangement, alienation, excommunication: people have quar-
relled, fallen out, are no longer talking to each other but rather
fighting against each other; there is a bone of contention, a rock

of offence, a cause real or imaginary. A spirituality of reconciliation judges such a situation to be unacceptable, intolerable, unChristian, evil. It rejects any continuation of it, any worsening of it, any progression into violence, war, oppression, destruction. It also rejects any unilateral imposition of a solution to the cause of the quarrel, the conflict. It wants an end to the estrangement, the resumption of a relationship of friendship, of unity and peace.

A spirituality of reconciliation emphasizes forgiveness. Forgiving persons have no wish to harbour any animosity or anger; any bitterness or bad blood; any ill-feeling or ill-will; any resentment or hatred; any desire for satisfaction, revenge, retaliation. They also forgo, give up all rights to recompense or retribution. The fact of the offence, of the sin committed, does of course remain: they recognize the fact, do not close their eyes to it, much less condone it; they continue to hate the sin but overlook it in the sense that they abandon the natural path of justice, the logic of law, seek no remedy or redress but want to continue in love with the offender, to wish this person or group well, despite the offence, the sin which they would prefer to forget as well as to forgive.

With a spirituality of reconciliation forgiving persons acquire a more comprehensive view of the situation, they begin to see things less partially, to see them as others see them, to accept that responsibility may well be shared. They want to resume contact and conversation, to fall back in love again.

A spirituality of reconciliation involves the will to change things for good. The forgiveness of one party facilitates a change of heart on the part of the other, a change of mind on the part of each, of both. The ensuing dialogue is sincere and honest; it is not superficial, it is not satisfied with patching over or covering up; it goes to the roots, it is radical. Reconciliation is not cheap; it is no soft option; it does not mean peace at any price, unity at any cost. There is no reconciliation without repentance, reparation, without change, without the making of amends; there is no at-one-ment without atonement of some sort. The cause of the estrangement – the act or habit or structure – has to be looked at and remedied; an accommodation has to be mutually agreed to re-establish a right relationship.

A spirituality of reconciliation recognizes the sacredness of the other, the primacy of love and the existence of God revealed in Christ as one who forgives, who forgives without condoning, whose forgiveness inspires our repentance and whose example moves us to be in our turn ministers of reconciliation, forgiving those who offend us and making amends to whose whom we ourselves offend.

Against the background of such a spirituality I am forced to conclude that the secularization of reconciliation, the increasing use of the term in secular contexts, is not all gain; that some serious loss is also entailed.

Reconciliation focuses on people and on problems. In religious contexts, in the Christian context at least, the emphasis is more on people. Here it is the unilateral, unconditional expression of forgiveness by one party – the miracle of forgiveness – which breaks the logjam evoking a response which can lead to a change in the whole situation. In secular contexts however the emphasis is more on issues. The logic seems to be this:remove the obstacle, the alienating factor, and the relationshsip will heal. But this methodology can involve confrontation between the conflicting parties. The primary aim seems to be a change of mind more than a change of heart. The main emphasis is on justice and, according to some thinkers and theologians at least, justice is a virtue which of itself may only divide and alienate unless it is animated by love and charity. As a secular ethic reconciliation seems severely handicapped. How can it be based on forgiveness insofar as this forgoes all rights and seeks no redress in justice and so makes a gesture which is superhuman and divine in its generosity? A secular ethic of reconciliation seems too impersonal. It seeks to reconcile differences, differing positions rather than differing people. It attempts, on a basis of justice, to reach a solution of these differences. But perhaps differences as such are 'irreconcilable'? Perhaps it is only differing people, insofar as they have the capacity to love and trust and forgive, who are in fact 'reconcilable'? Happily this capacity is not confined to the members of any one Church or any one religion: it is given by God to all.

It remains for me to renew my thanks to my distinguished colleagues, the contributors to this volume, for their kind collaboration in the project; to the Vice-Chancellor of the University of Ulster, Professor Trevor Smith, for the honour of his presence and address at the opening of the seminar, for the reception he hosted that evening and for his Preface to this volume; to the Provost of Trinity College, Dublin, and the Head of the Central Community Relations Unit at Stormont Castle for the receptions they also hosted during the seminar; to the secretary and his staff of the

Department of Adult and Continuing Education of the University of Ulster at Jordanstown for the administrative assistance which they afforded so expertly and without which the seminar could not have taken place; to the authorities and staff of St. Clement's Retreat and Conference Centre in Belfast for their warm welcome and generous hospitality during the days of the seminar; to Ms Janet Barcroft who in the absence of Sr Carmel Niland kindly presented her paper; to the Abbot of Glenstal, the Right Reverend Christopher Dillon, OSB, who travelled from Limerick to preside at our evening eucharist on the Saturday of the seminar; to Dr Brian Walker of the Institute of Irish Studies at The Queen's University of Belfast for his practical interest in the publication of the papers and to Ms Kate Newmann, the Institute Assistant Editor and the printers for the skill and care with which they have produced this volume; to Cyril Barrett, SJ and Roisin Hannaway, SSL for advice on illustrations; and finally to Eddie FitzGerald, SJ and Ray Lawler, SJ for help with proof-reading.

I wish to express a special word of thanks to the Director of the School of Ecumenics, the Rev. A. D. Falconer, for his encouragement and support of the project, for his expert chairing of the seminar and for presiding at the celebration of the Lima Liturgy on the Sunday morning of the seminar. News of his appointment to the World Council of Churches in Geneva has come just as this book goes to press. All of us offer him our heartiest congratulations and very best wishes.

My special thanks are also due to the Columbanus Community. It was my life in Belfast as a member of Columbanus since 1983 which brought home to me how much reconciliation in Ireland and elsewhere is suffering because the word is at once both too much used and too little studied. The inspiration and the energy to undertake the project and to persevere at it I owe to the members of the Columbanus Community and to them I gladly and gratefully dedicate this volume as a belated gift for their tenth birthday in September 1993.

The publishers join me in expressing both to the University of Ulster and to the Community Relations Council our deep appreciation and gratitude for financial assistance.

HISTORY AND RECONCILIATION

Helga Robinson-Hammerstein

What is the place of historical reflections in a conference on *Reconciliation in Religion and Society* which endeavours to arrive at a 'deeper, fuller understanding of the meaning of reconciliation in a Christian context as a contribution towards a more fruitful, effective ministry of reconciliation'? [1] It flatters historians, particularly those with a specialisation in the early modern period of European history, to be recognised as capable of making a useful contribution to something. However, I needed the assistance of the observations by two eminent historians on the subject of relevance to encourage me to venture into the sphere of 'useful history'. My first witness is William J. Bouwsma who in the introduction to his collection of essays entitled *A Usable Past* likens history to water and electricity as a 'public utility'. He argues that 'like other professional groups, historians are properly the servants of a public that needs historical perspective to understand itself and its values, and perhaps also to acknowledge its limitations and its guilt. Historians have an obligation . . . to meet public needs of this kind'.[2] My second witness, J.R. Hale, has urged that 'relevance . . . is not so much to be found in looking to the past for situations analogous to our own or, still less, for solutions to present problems, as in making it possible to compare our own attitudes to questions of basic concern . . . with those of past ages, and, vice versa, to review past attitudes in order to wonder afresh about our own'.[3] These opinions reassured me that the historian's role in the conference was merely to offer a review of the nature and circumstances of past reconciliation attempts. There was no need to make them artificially relevant; the other participants would have to determine to what extent they were helpful.

Historical investigations must be guided by an impeccable sense of honesty to be useful. In some respects the task is easier for the early modernist, since one is far less likely to be emotionally involved in the conditions or events one reviews (although there is no absolute guarantee of this either). In the context of the present conference, however, the task may be considerably more difficult. There may be the temptation to ignore blemishes for the sake of establishing a more respectable ecumenical ancestry for the ministry of reconciliation. To lay bare all the cracks is nevertheless absolutely imperative in order to gain a true perspective on what Jean Delumeau has called 'Oecuménisme d'autrefois'.[4] Hatred and atrocities as well as the creative imagination and intellectual integrity mobilised in the past in defence of true religion must be carefully identified and named to enable us usefully to check up on our own attitudes.

Fully aware that meaning and usage of words change over time, there is now the need to establish the current meaning and usage of the word reconciliation in the Christian context before a historical search can be conducted. In this century there has been a relative Christian consensus on the concept of reconciliation. This consensus is inspired by the scripturally-directed conviction that reconciliation is initiated by the Creator-God who offered His Son to restore mankind from enmity to friendship with himself.[5] This God reconciles universally: *objectively,* reconciliation has been effected by Christ once and for all; *subjectively,* it has to be practised by the divinely-reconciled persons on earth in order to be complete.[6] One such *subjective* response in the early twentieth century was the founding of IFOR, the International Fellowship of Reconciliation, which was started in Cambridge in 1914 by two theology professors, F. Siegmund-Schultze and H. Hodgkin. IFOR bore fruit in the peace movement, in effective support for conscientious objectors and the international peace service, *Eirene.*[7] The entry under reconciliation in the *Dictionary of the Ecumenical Movement* stresses the role of 'the church' as offering in word and sacraments the renewal of the believer's relationship with the Triune God.[8] Nowhere does there appear in this consensus definition any reference to a search for agreement between Christian churches. *Objectively,* 'the church' is represented as mediator (potentially problematical for Protestants) of the message of reconciliation. *Subjectively,* reconciliation seems to be confined to private initiatives of Christian individuals or groups, although churches show an interest and occasionally send representatives to meetings of such groups.[9]

The historical exploration of the theme might usefully evolve as a search (albeit a somewhat eclectic one) for the meaning and application of the word or concept (when the word was not used but the aim was the same) of reconciliation in the early modern period. The most notorious instance of the use of the word reconciliation in the early modern period belongs – hard as it may be to accept this – to the context of the history of the Spanish Inquisition.

The kingdoms of Castile and Aragon were united by the marriage of their rulers, Ferdinand and Isabella, in 1474. To achieve cohesion within this union of crowns and to develop the image and substance of a truly Christian monarchy, official policy abandoned the previous *convivienca* of the different socio-religious communities of Christians, Jews and Muslims with broadly shared cultural assumptions and traditions.[10] It replaced them with a dubious procedure of Christian assimilation. Cohesion of the *corpus christianum* was, however, difficult to sustain. The threat to the integrity of this construct arose from the doubtful orthodoxy of the *conversos* and fed on the watchful paranoia of the indigenous Christian nobility whose traditional crusading ideals assumed a sinister inward direction. Systematically from 1492 onwards, the Inquisition, the only instrument at the government's disposal, was used to cope with the crisis of the government's own creation; created that is, by the rushed and superficial conversion to Christianity of Muslims and Jews. It was generally recognised at the time and later in the sixteenth century that 'the main purpose of the trial and execution is not to save the soul of the accused, but to achieve the public good and to put fear into others'.[11] The procedures of the Inquisition were indeed shrouded in fear and secrecy. The nature of this policy of engendering fear by secrecy can be highlighted by reference to the implementation of the *Edict of Grace* from the 1480s onwards. Issued by the Inquisition, the *Edict* purported to admit self-confessed heretics, that is those who came forward of their own volition without ever having been testified against, to *reconciliación* with the church without grievous punishment or confiscation of goods.[12] But that was not the end of the story. Henry Kamen suspects, probably correctly, a devastating effect of the *Edict* on the fearful minds of the recently converted Christian population. He observes that around 1500 the *Edict* was a 'welcome opportunity for people in this frame of mind to unburden themselves of fear rather than guilt'.[13] A version of the *Edict*, issued in Mexico in 1571, makes it quite clear that this type of *reconciliación* was considered the key to the stability and integrity of the Spanish commonweal.[14] Henry Charles Lea cites many cases which confirm that *reconciliación* was indeed often followed by arrest, condemnation and execution of the penitent, since he was under the absolute obligation to reveal 'the names of all accomplices'. These were then more than likely to implicate the self-confessed penitent and reconciled heretic in some misdemeanour previously concealed by him; and *reconciliación* proved his actual undoing.[15]

At the height of the Counter-Reformation (in the later sixteenth century) when Spain was locked in conflict with 'the Turkish infidel', suspected of enjoying the support of lapsed Muslim-Christians in Spain, and Calvinist rebels in the Netherlands, the Holy Office had no hesitation in giving *reconciliación* its true character as the extremest form of punishment.[17] It referred to culprits who were 'condemned to reconciliation'. The punishments that were the precondition of *reconciliación* spelt ruin to the person thus reconciled.

The utter perversion of the church's original calling to welcome penitent sinners back into the fold was the direct result of the all too close intertwining of the fortunes of state and church. Such a close interdependence was, of course, the norm in contemporary Europe wherever states sought to achieve the consolidation and integrity of their own national territories. The crucial preservation of *one faith* was the core principle of such coordination. Spain differed from the rest in the fact that the state possessed the structures and the instrument of coercion and was without difficulty able to enlist the services of a fanaticised church doing its duty. The policy of the extreme punishment of fearful rather than guilty subjects was the most manifest sign of disorientation in the face of a dilemma: to safeguard the perceived interests of the commonweal by being true to its divinely prescribed goal of protecting the *one faith*. The government, however, while pursuing its aim and indulging the predilections of the nobility, did manage to keep control of the religious fervour among the population at large. The ceremonies of reconciliation, the *auto de fe*, constituted an impressively choreographed spectacle to feed the minds of the ordinary Christians, but their destructive energies, religious 'rites of violence' were not called for in the process. The government may have been aware that, once unleashed, these destructive energies would be difficult to rein in again; a lesson other governments had to learn from the bitter experience of faction fighting.[18]

The search for a type of reconciliation that was truer to the spirit of Christianity was, however, not absent from the Later Middle Ages and the early modern period. The word itself was not used; different terms, notably that of *concordantia* were substituted. It operated in a realm inhabited by a number of theological intellectuals. There was never any attempt to apply these ideas to the practical socio-political realities of the day. The focus of attention was a vision of the 'harmonization', from a Christian perspective, of the *different world religions* that were aggressively offending each other and the will of God whom they all claimed to worship. An emblematic example to explore in our context is the vision of the peaceful coexistence of the world religions of Nicholas Cusanus. It is the subject of his utopian tract *De Pace Fide*, written in response to the fall of Constantinople into the hands of the Turks in 1453.[19] The model of 'syncretism' he developed was inspired by his concept of *docta ignorantia* as the 'knowledgeable understanding of the unattainability of (total) knowledge (of the truth)'.[20] As an extension of this he argued that each religion contained something of the truth which was wholly known only to God alone. The learned cardinal advanced the ideal of a universal concordat – not a written treaty – as a target to be pursued with conviction although unattainable in the reality of earthly conditions. He envisaged a council of wise men from all religions meeting in the presence of God. Standing back from their mundane preoccupations, they are able to hear the Word of God which reveals God's will to them: 'All religious differences must, by common consent of man, be reduced to one single religion, from then never to be violated'. The wise men appeal to God to assist them in overcoming the enmity and hatred which the existence of different religions generates among the nations.[21]

In particular the issue of the diversity of religious rites is elaborated when the wise man of the Tartars attributes divisions and wars to the continued observance of these diversified religious rites. His intervention gives St Paul the opportunity to express what must have been Cusanus' sincerest conviction: since the soul depends on salvation, rites should not be overrated in their significance; they had evolved, not as a hindrance but as enablers of faith, as specific expressions of the truth of the faith. Cusanus, like Marsilio Ficino, even referred to the enriching beauty of such diversity.[22] While the signs change, the object which they signify does not change. Cusanus demanded a changed perspective to appreciate the true significance of rites, to help people to separate what is essential from what are indifferent matters. In order to change perceptions and perspective most decisively, 'a religious concordat is concluded in Heaven where *reason* rules'. In the light of what follows below, it is instructive to note that Nicholas Cusanus emphasised the diversity of rites as enriching people's faith, whereas rites and their specific symbolism became the irreconcilable issue on which later Christian reconciliation attempts foundered. Cusanus offered a discourse which was not only not taken up at the time, it was also deemed utterly irrelevant later. He had idealistically probed the problem of reconciliation posed by the existence of antagonistic world religions at a time when there was merely 'sporadic heresy' but no alternative church within Christendom, when heresy, real or imagined, could be dealt with by more or less stringent persecution.

After 1520 a different reconciliation policy was called for to cope with the ecclesiastical revolution of the Lutheran reformation in Germany. Again, the word reconciliation was not used, the word *concordia* appears instead in the debates and meetings. The policy was designed as a response – albeit a very inadequate one – to what sixteenth century Catholics were bound to recognise as successful schism. What spirit animated this policy, what did it seek to achieve and who championed it?

Even in the face of manifest divisions within Christendom, the focus of attention was on bringing about *unity*. In fact, the concept of unity of the Christian faith was the common ground on which the antagonistic parties failed to meet. Lutherans were just as convinced as Catholics of the essential value of unity as wholeness; neither Catholics nor Lutherans saw themselves as schismatics, although each accused the other of having departed from the original truth.[23] Each claimed to possess within its own concept of unity the exclusive access to the divinely revealed truth.

There was, however, at least initially, a supreme endeavour on all sides to avoid coercion as a means of bringing about commitment to the exclusive faith of either. Luther, for one, was at pains throughout his career, with growing verbal venom as time went on, to discredit the Catholic religion as a fear-engendered 'false faith' born out of coercion and operated as a manipulative sacramental system.[24] In this context he argued that force could never achieve conviction and insight into the truth which must simply be preached and communicated by all available media. The rest was

God's work.[25] When Luther encouraged his followers to adopt the new concept of 'freedom of conscience', he was referring to the liberation of the gospel. The conscience freed from Law was sustained by the belief in free grace.[26] Freedom of conscience was not a right to be conceded to all believers whatever their Christian orientation. In order that this 'evangelical truth' should be firmly established, once it had been preached freely for a time, the protection of legitimate secular authority was enlisted. With time, this led to the establishment of the Schmalkaldic League for the defence of the true faith, if necessary by force of arms.

The defence of the faith lay exclusively in the hands of those who had authority over subjects; it never fell to the people's lot. While Lutheranism was undoubtedly popular and a matter of personal conviction, the people were right from the start discouraged from resorting to 'rites of violence' in the name of religion. Iconoclasm, the usual popular defence, was nipped in the bud in the Wittenberg Movement of 1522.[27] This policy was not just a rigorous assertion of secular authority, it also possessed its inner logic. Luther had concentrated his theology on the rejection of 'works-righteousness'. Luther had never condoned attacks on the material objects of 'idolatry'. What mattered was not the existence of the object itself but people's inner attitude to it. The idol must be removed from people's hearts.[28] He thus guarded against the justification of social acts of violence in the name of religion.

In the face of Luther's rebellion, the universal Catholic church was at first quite reluctant to develop a policy for the defence of its claim to unity. However, the curia was at least prepared to condone the conciliation attempts made by Catholic German princes and the Catholic emperor. They developed an official peace policy to avoid public discord and civil war of the politico-religious defence leagues from the 1530s onwards.[29] Pursued by rulers out of evident necessity, this policy was lifted from pragmatism to the more idealist plane of humanist convictions of Erasmus of Rotterdam. He was convinced that some form of unity could be reestablished, if the contending parties agreed to pin his *philosophia Christi* to their banners.[30] He placed emphasis on the teaching of Christ as an expression of love of peace. Agreement could be achieved if the parties learnt to concentrate on what they had in common and forgot about the dogmas that divided them, aware at all times that Christianity was not merely a faith but also a distinctive way of life.[31] For the rulers it was a practical issue. They worked from the generally held assumption that heterodoxy, 'false faith', prompted sedition and treason; therefore a state was not safe if it tolerated religious minorities within its borders. Rulers like Duke George of Saxony, however, were grateful to have Erasmus' ideals at their disposal for their practical purposes.[32] The conciliation policy, despite several colloquies with Lutheran representatives, was unsuccessful in the terms adopted between 1530 and 1555. Military confrontation was not avoided either. One had under-rated the nature and strength of the Lutheran theological posi-tion which fuelled the ecclesiological controversies. The princely aspirations were too complex and narrowly self-interested to be reduced to the simplistic adoption of the debased currency of Christian charity. The situation became particularly fraught when the much advocated reform-from-within the universal church proved a figment of scholars' imagination.

In 1555 a different kind of arrangement was worked out and legalised. The Religious Peace of Augsburg, recognising the free-dom of worship of princes, conceded to rulers the right to deter-mine the uniform religion of their subjects within their own terri-tories. Since the Holy Roman Empire of the German Nation was divided into some 350 political units of varying sizes, emigration of dissidents became the norm. At best, therefore, Germany pre-sented the picture of a patchwork of largely peaceful Catholic and Lutheran states, where the proximity of the heterodox views in the neighbouring territory provided the welcome safety-valve of emi-gration; ultimately a doubtful guarantee of overall social stability.[33]

The Augsburg Religious Peace did not provide a suitable model for other countries in Europe where religious divisions existed under more large-scale territorial conditions. Our eclectic search for useful evidence of attempts at Christian reconciliation must now turn to the second half of the sixteenth century in order to explore the circumstances which led to the adoption of a policy of accommodating religious minorities within the confines of a larger state. The issue itself was encapsulated in the word toleration. The word was used in the sense of sufferance, of the concession of religious liberty to clearly defined minorities which were allowed to live within a state that officially adhered to a dominant religion. Toleration was offered at the conclusion of decades of internecine warfare and unspeakable atrocities perpetrated in the name of 'the true religion'. Its legal recognition involved a significant shift in state policy. The principle of religious unity as the axiomatic basis of order in the state was abandoned, and the toleration of religious minorities rather than their persecution became a question of survival of a more secularised society.

Nowhere in Europe was the basic right of freedom of conscience conceded without bloody strife, except in Poland. There Stephen Bathory, a fervent Catholic and a cautiously calculating elected ruler faced with a determined Calvinist nobility offered religious freedom, accepting the Calvinists' *Pacta Conventa* (1573) in 1576 as a measure of securing his political control of the country. This concession turned out to be a temporary expedient (at first denounced by the pope) that ultimately enabled the Counter-Reformation championed by the Jesuits to take root and re-establish Catholic unity within a generation.[34]

Things certainly took a different course in the Netherlands. In 1555 the 17 Provinces constituted Philip II of Spain's legitimate inheritance. He had already come to see it as his *damnosa hereditas* by 1559.[35] Not only did the Netherlands present the confusing picture of a conglomerate of diversified and largely incompatible political and constitutional privileges utterly at variance with the monarchical system of Spain, but the political leaders thus privileged had also discovered their common destiny in the preservation of their cherished diversity. This diversity was enhanced by a profusion of religious practices which no self-respecting ruler, particularly not one of Philip's Catholic principles, could countenance. There were Lutherans, Calvinists and Anabaptists, all organised illicitly; and there were also, especially among the higher nobility and the merchant-oligarchs of the self-governing towns, Catholics who were emphatically not at all enamoured with Counter-Reformation militancy. Philip's regent faced the impossible task of persecuting heresy and curtailing privileges in the process in order to gain some form of control over the country. A policy of streamlining the church and introducing the decrees of the Council of Trent suggested itself as a logical beginning consistent with Philip's innermost convictions. This was instantly opposed by the Catholic nobility who stood to lose most by such measures. While they naturally agreed that heresy was a destabilising pollutant in a state, they were also acutely aware of the need to broaden the platform of their protest by gaining the support of the population at large. The population at large, however, could only be won over by a cessation of persecution of their diversified forms of religious worship.

When reviewing the struggle for and the nature of toleration in the Netherlands it is imperative not to detach its consideration from the larger context of the defence of the liberties of the 'political nation' which was made up of the higher nobility, most of them Catholics, the younger, fervently Calvinist nobility and the city fathers of mixed religious but utterly non-militant persuasions. This struggle developed eventually into the war of independence from the 'tyrannical yoke' of Philip II and resulted in 1581 in the *Abjuration* of the Northern Provinces. William of Orange, the foremost rebel leader, managed to project the opposition that was growing into rebellion as true obedience to the legitimate ruler who was kept in the dark about the real problems of his inheritance by wicked counsellors. This was a much-favoured device to allow the ruler a face-saving way out of 'wrong policies'. Born a Lutheran, turned Catholic in order to fulfil the conditions of inheriting estates in the Northern Netherlands, William eventually adopted Calvinism as the religion that best suited his political interests. However, even while he was still officially a loyal son of the Catholic church he put his name to texts which advanced arguments in favour of toleration formulated under the ideological influence of Calvinists.[36] At the beginning of 'the troubles' William announced in the name of the Catholic nobility that a policy of persecution in the interest of establishing Catholic unity was simply not safe. He warned that the ruler would be held responsible for provoking the outbreak of rebellion if he persisted in the pursuit of his injurious policy of persecution. Persecution was inadvisable at a time of bad harvests, at a time furthermore when the Dutch as a trading nation had extensive commercial contacts with 'heretics' in other countries; and in particular when the proximity of Germany with its different kind of religious peace could not be ignored.[37] The cleverest defence of toleration, even while Philip considered the practice a total anathema, was to conjure up the spectre of atheism as a result of non-toleration. Such arguments were advanced in *A Brief Discourse,* anonymously addressed to the king, written by the Calvinist minister at Antwerp in 1566. He was in close consultation with William of Orange's younger, staunchly Calvinist brother, Louis of Nassau:

. . . it is through conscience that people should recognise their errors . . . we cannot extirpate the faith which these people

[Calvinists] cherish in their hearts, it is little use (even if it were feasible) preventing them from attending their public worship. . . . For instead of being taught in their assemblies to be honest people fearing God and respecting the king and his officers, they would then become vile atheists and libertines stirring up seditions and disturbing order and peace . . . [38]

The difficulty for William of Orange who sincerely advocated religious toleration as the essential political tool to preserve the socio-political integrity (in all diversity) of the 17 Provinces, was to keep the Calvinists committed to the cause of toleration. It proved ultimately impossible to persuade them to condone something they deeply abhorred as an abomination. The convictions and actions of the Seabeggars faced him with an extreme dilemma. The Seabeggars, ardent Calvinists of the lower social orders, had been instrumental in achieving the first military breakthrough for the 'rebels'. True to the premise on which they had started they sought to establish the exclusive observance of their Calvinist religion by the violent means of iconoclasm, 'of destroying the idols', as Calvin's theology (unlike Luther's) demanded.[39] Already in 1566 they had smashed up churches, ransacked monasteries and killed priests in the process. The same actions were furiously repeated in 1572.

Regardless of William of Orange's more secularised intentions for the greater good of the whole commonweal, the toleration advocated by Calvinist preachers was for them and their followers merely a means to achieving the exclusive practice of their own religion, *not* co-existence with Catholics. As the war of independence developed, the promise of freedom of worship for Protestants and Catholics, to which the Estates of liberated Holland agreed, was rescinded to placate the Calvinists. All subsequent negotiation with 'the other side', including the Pacification of Ghent in 1576 and the Religious Peace of 1578, incurred the same fate.[40] When in 1579 the rebels established the Union of Utrecht out of Holland, Zealand, Friesland and Gelderland (in response to the pro-Spanish Union of Arras), the desire of providing a basis for closer cooperation and persuading other provinces to accede to their Union, again prompted the formulation of the principle of toleration. The rebels observed that it was 'not their opinion that one province or town should lay down the law to others in matters of religion, as they want to further peace and unity among the provinces to avoid and take away the main occasion for quarrels and discord'.[41] The expression of such aspirations proved so much highsounding rhetoric which was as unacceptable to Catholics as it was to Calvinists. The Calvinist populace in several towns almost immediately resorted to violent iconoclastic attacks. William of Orange and his entourage continued to advocate toleration for the political reasons of the greater good of the common fatherland, but the Calvinists flatly objected that 'no papist' could be a 'good patriot'. The country ended up divided into the predominantly Calvinist United Provinces in the North (with some toleration) and the Catholic South, a stronghold of the Counter-Reformation, the future Belgium.

The developments in France which led to the official recognition of Calvinism as a minority religion in the Edict of Nantes of 1598 cannot be rehearsed here in any detail. The Edict encapsulated a toleration (reconciliation) policy which sought to ensure the pacification of France after more than thirty years of civil wars that had had the most devastating effect on the integrity of the country.[42] The defence of the true Christian religion had of old been the cornerstone of the French monarchical principle, the practice of which conferred sanctity upon French kingship. It was the essential clause in the coronation oath. 'One faith, one law, one king' was the triad on which the stability of French society was assumed to rest. The existence of Calvinist strongholds in France was the result of a careful strategy of infiltration – from one noble safe house to the next – by highly trained missionaries from Geneva.[43] The Genevan reformation model sustained by its insistence on the *jus reformandi* of the 'lesser magistrate' in the case of a non-reforming king, was attractive to the nobility in the outlying areas of France who felt that their independence was being undermined by monarchical centralisation. The Catholic nobility – some, like the Guises, ardent champions of the Counter-Reformation – were clustered around the centre and exercised an effective stranglehold on the capital Paris.[44] Noble factions with the capacity for recruiting private armies among their retainers and the population under their manorial jurisdiction asserted themselves and sought to establish their influence over the crown. The Catholic faction gained its profile and essential justification of its oppositional activities by criticising the king for tolerating heretics, thus breaking his coronation oath and undermining the stability of the French state. The Calvinist/Huguenot faction, the

heretics in question, well versed in the Calvinist theory of resistance, accused the ruler of condoning the abomination of idolatry,
thus calling down the wrath of God upon the French monarchy.
Both sides were supported by crowds which engaged in 'rites of
violence'[45]. As for the Dutch Calvinists, the issue for the French
Huguenots was the utterly uncompromising defence of the once-
discovered exclusive truth; and this defence called for the violent
physical destruction of the objects of Catholic devotion.[46]

While a Calvinist pastor might incite his congregation to go out
and destroy the idols of the ungodly, a Catholic preacher in Paris
could be sure of a strong reaction when he encouraged his parish-
ioners to smite the children of Belial who were seeking to infiltrate
the city.[47] Huguenot and Catholic crowds, although adopting somewhat different styles, were only too ready to fight in defence of their
true doctrine, since the sufferance of such pollutants in society was
bound to incur divine retribution. Crowds were particularly dangerous when they adopted the argument that, since the lawful
magistrates were not doing their job properly, they had to do it for
them. Such crowds were on the whole not motivated by any rich-
poor antagonism; apart from some members of the clergy, there
was always a cross-section of townspeople involved. Natalie Zemon
Davis has convincingly established that the occasions for rites of
violence were frequently public religious events such as pilgrimages
or services in connection with the rites of passage. The Huguenots
emerged primarily as the champions of the destruction and vile
vandalisation of sacred objects of Catholic devotion. The Catholic
crowds, on account of their 'greater sense of the persons of heretics
as sources of danger and defilement', engaged more readily in
bloodshed. To them 'injury and murder (with desecration of
corpses) were the preferred mode of purifying the body social'.[48]
The Massacre of St. Bartholomew's Day stands out among these
attacks: on that 23 August 1572 and the following two weeks 3000
Huguenots were killed in Paris and 8000 in the provinces.

How all these atrocities could be performed in the name of a
faith that enjoins love of the neighbour and condemns killing,
finds at least a partial explanation in the 'conditions for guilt-free
massacre'.[49] In the eyes of the perpetrators the victims had been
transformed into dehumanised devils. Such a form of 'rationalisa-
tion' of utterly aberrant behaviour conferred an aura of legitimacy
upon the actions of the crowds that were in any case instigated by
the most sinister propaganda compaign on both sides.[50]

Throughout these years there were frequent attempts made by French statesmen to defuse the volatile religious situation by arranging colloquies to establish grounds of consensus. Since they sought to replace conviction politics by pragmatic political compromise, their efforts were doomed to failure from the start. There were also many highminded and logically persuasive advocates of toleration. They were able to point to the evident fallacy of the assumption that the stringent defence of the one religion guaranteed the preservation of the state. The opposite could obviously be seen to be true. From the early 1560s onwards toleration as a means of staving off corrosive atheism was promoted in high places. As early as 1561/2 the Queen Mother's Chancellor, Michel de l'Hôpital, was convinced that civil wars were caused by political corruption rather than religious dissent; and he proffered the nation the first of many edicts of pacification which gave freedom of worship to the Huguenots in safeplaces.[51] Such edicts periodically and temporarily halted the hostilities, but their stipulations could never be fully enforced. French society was not yet ready to accept the principle and practice of freedom of worship. Such an acceptance was only brought about by the policies of Henry IV, the former Huguenot leader whose marriage had occasioned the Massacre of St. Bartholomew's Day. Henry converted to Catholicism in 1593 in order to liberate his capital from the stranglehold of the Catholic nobility. From a position of relative strength he could make the Edict of Nantes work in the interest of peace in France. In the first instance the Edict represented a pact between Catholics and Calvinists promising to respect each other in their demarcated spheres of influence. The Calvinist minority was thus protected by the law of the land and the Catholics could glory in the fact that they belonged to the dominant religion. By this means Henry had also managed to detach noble factions from the possibility of recourse to religious justification of the defence of sectional interests.[52]

The course of violence in the name of the 'one true religion' could only be reversed when the political will of the ruler was strong enough to enforce the toleration that had long been recognized as the obvious way to save lives. The idea of 'toleration' as 'reconciliation by mutual acceptance of differences' to which God was supremely indifferent only came into its own when the political situation was amenable to being stabilized by legitimate political action.

NOTES

1   Rev. Michael Hurley *Memo for Participants,* 18 June 1992.
2   W J Bouwsma *The Usable Past,* Berkeley, Los Angeles, Oxford, University of California Press, 1990, pp 1–16 here p.1
3   J R Hale *Renaissance Europe,* 1480–1520, London, Collins 1971, p.8 (The Fontana History of Europe).
4   Jean Delumeau *Naissance et Affirmation de la Réforme,* Paris, Presses Universitaires de France, pp. 335–381. (Nouvelle Clio, l'Histoire et ses Problèmes, vol. 30)
5   The biblical texts most frequently cited are: 2 Cor.5, 18–20; Romans 5, 10–12; Col. 1, 20–22; Eph.2, 11–16; Acts 2, 38.
6   *New Catholic Encyclopedia* vol. 12, New York, McGraw-Hill Books Company, 1967, pp. 129–130: Reconciliation with God.
7   *Religion in Geschichte und Gegenwart* 3. ed., vol.6, Tübingen, C.B. Mohr, 1962, col. 1370–1380: Versöhnungsbund.
8   *Dictionary of the Ecumenical Movement,* ed. by Nicholas Lossky et al. Geneva, WCC Publications, London, Council of Churches for Britain and Ireland, Grand Rapids, Mich. Eerdmans, 1991: Reconciliation.
9   *Reconciliation. Steps for Action.* Conference for World Mission (BCC), National Missionary Council of England and Wales, London, March 1987.
10 What follows draws on the researches by H.C. Lea *A History of the Inquisition of Spain,* 4 vols., New York, The Macmillan Company, 1906–08; Henry Kamen *Inquisition and Society in Spain in the Sixteenth and Seventeenth Centuries,* London, Weidenfeld & Nicolson, 1985; John Lynch *Spain under the Habsburgs,* 2 vols. Oxford, Basil Blackwell, 1964 & 1969.
11 Kamen, *Inquisition,* p. 161.
12 Lea, *A History,* vol. 1, p. 165.
13 Kamen, *Inquisition,* p. 163.
14 Lea, *A History* vol. 2, Appendix of Documents: 1. *Edict of Faith* = 'the simplest and oldest formula at the installation of the Inquisition there'.
15 Lea, *A History,* vol. 2, p. 460.
16 Kamen, *Inquisition,* p.186.
17 Lea, *A History,* vol. 3, pp.146 ff.
18 On the social controls policy during the reign of Philip II cf. Geoffrey Parker *Philip II,* London, Sphere Books, 1988 (2.ed.) pp.96 ff.
19 Excerpts of the text are reprinted in *Religiöse Toleranz. Dokumente zur Geschichte einer Forderung* ed. by H. R. Guggisberg, Stuttgart-Bad Cannstatt, frommann-holzbog, 1984, pp.35–45; see also Joseph Lecler *Toleration and the Reformation* (English Transl.) London, Longmans, vol. 1, 1959, pp. 107–110.
20 Lecler, *Toleration,* vol. 1, p. 107.
21 *Religiöse Toleranz,* p.41.
22 Lecler, *Toleration,* vol. 1, p. 111.
23 Heinrich Bornkamm, 'Die religiöse and politische Problematik im Verhältnis der Konfessionen im Reich' in *Zur Geschichte der Toleranz und Religionsfreiheit* ed. by Heinrich Lutz, Darmstadt, Wissenschaftliche Buchgesellschaft, 1977, pp. 252–262, here p. 253.
24 H. A. Oberman *Luther. Man between God and the Devil,* New Haven & London, Yale University Press, 1989, pp. 67–81.
25 This was the issue that caused the rift between Luther and Karlstadt in the course of the Wittenberg Movement 1521/2. Luther preached his Invocavit Sermons, March 1522, in that spirit; cf. Martin Luther. *Studienausgabe* ed. by

Hans-Ulrich Delius, vol, 2, Berlin, Evangelische Verlagsanstalt, 1982, pp. 520–558.

26 Ernst Wolf, 'Toleranz nach evangelischem Verständnis' in *Zur Geschichte der Toleranz und Religionsfreiheit*, pp.135–154.

27 C. M. N. Eire *War against the idols. The Reformation of Worship from Erasmus to Calvin*, Cambridge, Cambridge University Press, 1986, pp. 65–73.

28 Martin Luther. *Studienausgabe*, vol.2, p.537.

29 Nikolaus Paulus, 'Religionsfreiheit und Augsburger Religionsfriede' in *Zur Geschichte der Toleranz und Religionsfreiheit*, pp. 17–41; W.D.J. Cargill Thompson, *The Political Thought of Martin Luther*, Brighton, Harvester Press, 1984, pp. 91–95; Heinz Scheible, *Das Widerstandsrecht als Problem des deutschen Protestantismus, 1523–1546*, Gütersloh, G. Mohn, 1969. A solid brief overview of compromise in German politics to 1555 can be found in Euan Cameron *The European Reformation*, Oxford, Clarendon Press, 1991, pp. 339–360.

30 *Religiöse Toleranz*, pp.69–76: *Erasmus* ed. by Richard L. DeMolen, London, Edward Arnold, 1973, pp.98–134.

31 R. H. Bainton *Erasmus of Christendom*, London, Collins, 1970, pp. 313–315. Erasmus retained his belief that the schism could be healed until the end of his life, cf. his most pertinent tract *De Sarcienda Ecclesiae Concordia*, 1533 referred to by Lecler, *Toleration*, vol.1, pp. 121–123.

32 Lecler, *Toleration*, vol. 1, pp. 226, 228, 236.

33 Fritz Dickmann, 'Das Problem der Gleichberechtigung der Konfessionen im Reich im 16. und 17. Jahrhundert' in *Zur Geschichte der Toleranz und Religionsfreiheit*, pp. 203–251; H. Tüchle, 'The Peace of Augsburg: New Order or Lull in the Fighting?' in *Government in Reformation Europe*, 1520–1560 ed. by H.J. Cohn, London, Macmillan 1971, pp. 145–160; W.D.J. Cargill Thompson, 'Luther and the Right of Resistance to the Emperor' in *Studies in the Reformation: Luther to Hooker*, ed. by C. W. Dugmore, London, Athlone Press, 1980, pp. 3–41.

34 Karl Völker, 'Stefan Bathorys Kirchenpolitik in Polen' in *Zur Geschichte der Toleranz und Religionsfreiheit*, pp. 64–92; Gottfried Schramm *Der Polnische Adel und die Reformation*, Wiesbaden, Franz Steiner, 1965, pp. 271–281.

35 Marvin R. O'Connell, *The Counter-Reformation, 1560–1610*, New York, etc., Harper and Row, 1974, pp. 54–67. On the development in the Netherlands cf. Geoffrey Parker, *Spain and the Netherlands*, Glasgow, Collins, 1979; Geoffrey Parker, *The Dutch Revolt* 2. ed., Harmondsworth Middlesex, Penguin, 1985.

36 *The Low Countries in Early Modern Times* ed. by H.H. Rowen, London, Macmillan, 1972, pp.37–39.

37 *Ibid.*

38 *Texts concerning the Revolt of the Netherlands*, ed. by E.H. Kossman and A.F. Mellinck, Cambridge, Cambridge University Press, 1974, pp. 56–59.

39 Eire, *War against the Idols*, pp. 279–281.

40 Parker, *Revolt*, pp. 76–78, 176–178; *Texts concerning the Revolt of the Netherlands*, pp. 173 ff.

41 *Texts concerning the Revolt of the Netherlands*, pp. 165. ff.

42 Mark Greengrass, *France in the Age of Henri IV. The Struggle for Stability*, London, Longmans, 1984, pp. 75 ff.

43 N.M. Sutherland, *The Huguenot Struggle for Recognition*, New York & London, Yale University Press, 1980, pp.35 ff; R. M. Kingdon, *Geneva and the Coming of the Wars of Religion in France (1555–1563)*, Geneva, Droz, 1956.

44 Barbara Diefendorf, *Beneath the Cross: Catholics and Huguenots in Sixteenth*

Century Paris, New York, Oxford, OUP, 1991; J.H.M. Salmon, *Society in Crisis, France in the Sixteenth Century,* London, E. Benn, 1979; E. Schalk, 'The appearance and reality of nobility in France during the wars of religion: an example of how collective attitudes were changed', *Journal of Modern History* 48, 1976, pp. 19–31.

45   Natalie Z. Davis, 'The Rites of Violence' in *Society and Culture in Early Modern France* by N.Z. Davis, Cambridge, Polity Press, 1987, pp. 152–187.

46   Eire, *War against the Idols,* p.3.

47   Davis, *Society and Culture,* p. 152/3.

48   *The Massacre of St Bartholomew: Reappraisals and Documents* ed. by A. Soman, The Hague, M. Nijhoff, 1974; Davis, *Society and Culture,* p.174.

49   Davis, *Society and Culture,* p 181.

50   Greengrass, *France in the Age of Henri IV,* pp.58–62.

51   *Religiöse Toleranz,* pp. 102–112.

52   Henri Lapeyre, *Les Monarchies Européennes du Seizième Siècle,* Paris, Presses Universitaires de France, 1967, pp.178–182. (= Nouvelle Clio, l'Histoire et ses Problèmes, vol. 31).

A RESPONSE

Phil Kilroy

While aspects of reconciliation in 15th and 16th century continental Europe are mirrored in Ireland, its context was different: any overtures taken were mainly between the several reformation traditions which had taken root in Ireland by the 17th century. Indeed in the early years of the Ulster Plantation some Church of Ireland bishops were sympathetic towards the demands of Scottish Presbyterian ministers in their dioceses. A form of ordination was negotiated and accepted which allowed such ministers to be ordained according to their own theological tradition.[1] The motivation for such comprehension was quite pragmatic: ministers were needed in the dioceses and the 1615 Irish Articles of the Church of Ireland, deliberately vague on the issue of ordination, more than justified this stance.[2] Primate James Ussher and bishops such as Robert Echlin of Down and Connor and Andrew Knox of Raphoe hoped for a broad, comprehensive church in Ireland, strong enough to withstand the Church of Rome.

On the other hand, William Bedell, Church of Ireland bishop of Kilmore and Ardagh, took quite a different view. He accepted the Roman Church as a church, though in deep error. He considered it his duty to persuade and win over the native population in his diocese to the reformed church. To this purpose he tried as far as possible to get ministers who could preach in Irish; Bedell himself set to translating the Old Testament, and he had a catechism printed in Irish in 1631.[3] Such a view cost him dearly within his own church, more used to controversies with the Church of Rome. Nevertheless, Bedell's attitude and activities did effect some form of reconciliation in his diocese to the extent that in 1642 he was given both safe burial and warm tributes from the rebel Irish.

During the disturbing times of 1641–1660 in Ireland new religious traditions were added to the country: Independents (Congregationalists), English Presbyterians, Baptists and Quakers as well as the refounding of Scottish Presbyterianism in Ulster. With monarchy and episcopacy restored in 1660 Protestant dissenters had to find ways of surviving the new realities. Very soon Independents, English Presbyterians and Baptists moved towards some type of association. Samuel Mather, minister of the Independent Church at New Row in Dublin proposed his *Irenicum or an essay for union wherein are humbly tendered some proposals in order to some nearer union among the godly of different judgements* (1680). Although published after his death, the document certainly dates from the early years of the Restoration[4] and reflects his efforts to find some form of union between Scottish Presbyterians, English Presbyterians, Independents and Baptists, citing the confessions of the several traditions as the basis for such agreement. He outlined the areas of disagreement and sought ways to accommodate them. It is clear that the Baptists created the greatest difficulty and that on very few counts could either the Church of Ireland, or the Quakers be included in this search for some form of agreement. In effect, an association was created by the ministers of the Scottish Presbyterian, the English Presbyterian and the Independent churches in Dublin which enabled them to act as a body when necessary.[5] This was not so much an effort towards reconciliation of doctrine and religious traditions for its own sake as a pragmatic arrangement for mutual survival.

On the other hand, William King, Dean of St. Patrick's in Dublin in the years prior to the 1688 Revolution, tried to find some form of accommodation between the Church of Ireland and Protestant dissenters.[6] Such overtures were occasioned by the fear of a resurgence of Roman Catholicism, justified indeed by the experience of Tyrconnell's power in Ireland at this time. Yet it was very much a theory on paper, for King denounced the dissenters when replying to Peter Manby, former Dean of Derry, who converted to Roman Catholicism in 1686.[7] Later on as bishop of Derry, King rejected the English Presbyterian and the Independent Churches even though Joseph Boyse, English Presbyterian minister in Wood Street, Dublin, had indicated that both traditions could reach some accommodation.[8] For his part King thought a form of agreement could be made with the Scottish Presbyterian Church because of similarities in church order.[9] But in fact the differences between the two churches in terms of theology, forms of worship as well as church order and discipline, were very real as King was to discover to his cost. Robert Craghead, Scottish Presbyterian minister in Derry since the Cromwellian period, responded to King several times and suggested a way forward: 'we cannot see with their (Church of Ireland) eyes nor they with ours'.[10] By this time the Scottish Presbyterians were seeking toleration of their religion, not accommodation. But in the political climate of the time such a situation was unthinkable for the Church of Ireland.

While theological debates between the Church of Ireland and the Scottish Presbyterians tended to polarise these reformation traditions, there were occasional efforts at agreement on a practical level. For example, Lord Massereene's chaplain, the English Presbyterian minister, John Howe,[11] was given permission both by the bishop of Down and Connor and by the Primate, to preach in Antrim parish church on Sunday afternoons 'after the liturgy had been read'.[12] When Thomas Gowan, Scottish Presbyterian minister, succeeded Howe at Antrim in 1673 he tried without success to get a meeting house built. Though he held services in the parish church, his congregation resisted the practice and three years later they built a meeting house themselves.[13] What was possible for an English Presbyterian minister was in the end impossible for a Scottish Presbyterian minister to sustain: the distance between traditions could not be reconciled.

While there was at least some basis for discussion within the several reformed traditions in Ireland, none of them felt they could accept the Quakers as in any sense truly Christian. Indeed from the time of their arrival in Ireland in 1655 Quakers had been heavily criticised and controversies arose concerning, for example, the nature of Christ, the Trinity, the inner light of conscience, the status of the Bible, role of ministry, the use of sacraments, payment of tithes, use of oaths. Edward Wetenhall, bishop of Cork, in his debate with William Penn in 1698 concluded that the Quakers could not be called Christians at all.[14] Even Richard Lawrence, a prominent Baptist, insisted in 1682 that some form of agreement could be found within all the religious traditions in Ireland excepting Roman Catholics, Quakers and Muggletonians.[15]

Thus during this period efforts at accommodation were made in several directions: between the Church of Ireland and the Scottish Presbyterians; between the Scottish Presbyterians, the English Presbyterians and the Independents; within Scottish Presbyterianism itself also, in the struggle between Resolutioners and Remonstrants.[16] The motivations for such efforts to reach some agreement were quite pragmatic and political, often arising out of fears of Rome. So current understanding of reconciliation, perhaps, is not a term to apply to 17th century Ireland. Whatever we may mean today, the concept then did not intend the coming together of churches in theological harmony, for the express purpose of fulfilling some divine call to union. Rather each tradition tried to survive as best it could: the Church of Ireland expected conformity of all; the Scottish Presbyterians aspired to be the Church of Ireland and when this was not possible hoped for toleration; the English Presbyterian and Independent churches, while differing theologically themselves, worked in association in Dublin and the south of Ireland. None of them reached out in any way towards the Quakers or Roman Catholics, though there was a rite for the reconciliation of Roman Catholics to the Church of Ireland.

Certainly there were shafts of light in works like Jeremy Taylor's *The Liberty of Prophesying* (1647), James Ussher's *Reduction of Episcopacy*, the *Heads of Agreement* in 1682, and in William Penn's plea for Liberty of Conscience. But there was no paradigm available for viewing several traditions differently and so direct theological reconciliation could not be realised at this time. However, there was room for a sideways journey towards reconciliation by way of culture and education, as seen in the work of the Irish Jesuit, William Bathe,[17] and the Moravian, Amos Comenius.[18] Indeed Comenius was greatly influenced by Bathe's work and though both Cromwell and Lord Clandeboye invited Comenius to settle in Ireland,[19] he declined both offers. Nevertheless, both Bathe and Comenius gave a hint of hope for the future and a possible way forward on the journey towards reconciliation.

NOTES

1 Robert Blair, *The life of Mr Robert Blair . . . his autobiography from 1593–1636 with supplement to his life and continuation of the history of the times to 1680, by . . . Mr William Row,* ed. Thomas McCrie, The Wodrow Society (Edinburgh, 1848), 58–9; John Livingstone, *A brief historical relation of the life of Mr John Livingstone . . . written by himself,* ed. Thomas Houston (Edinburgh, 1848), 76–7.

2 Aidan Clarke, 'Varieties of Uniformity: The first century of the Church of Ireland' in W.D. Sheils and Diane Woods (ed.), *The Churches, Ireland and the Irish. Studies in Church History xxv* (Oxford, 1989), 107; R.B. Knox, *James Ussher Archbishop of Armagh* (Cardiff, 1967), 14–15.

3 E.S. Shuckburgh, *Two biographies of William Bedell, bishop of Kilmore* (Cambridge, 1902), 131, 300, 317.

4 Mather, *Irenicum*, pp. 2–7

5 Joseph Boyse, *Vindicae Calvinisticae or some impartial reflections on the Dean of*

Londonderry's considerations . . . and Mr Chancellor King's answer thereto Dublin, 1687), p. 17.

6 Archbishop King's Treatise and Principals of Church Government (c. 1685–88), T.C.D., MSS 865; (William King), The present state of the Church. 'Notes for a design for union' (1688), T.C.D., Mss 1995–2008, no. 69a Correspondence of William King, ff 1–14.

7 William King, *An answer to the considerations which obliged Peter Manby, late Dean of Londonderry in Ireland, to embrace what he calls the catholic religion* (Dublin, 1687), pp. 6, 29.

8 Joseph Boyse, *Remarks on a late discourse of William lord bishop of Derry, concerning the inventions of men in the worship of God* (n.p., [1694]), pp. 69–74, 77, 114.

9 William King, *A discourse concerning the inventions of men in the worship of God* (London, 1694).

10 Robert Craghead, *A modest apology occasioned by the importunity of the bishop of Derry who presses for an answer to a query stated by himself in his second admonition concerning joining in the public worship established by law* (Glasgow, 1696), To the Christian reader.

11 J.T. Carson, 'John Howe: Chaplain to Lord Massarene at Antrim Castle, 1671–1677' in *Bulletin of the Presbyterian Historical Society of Ireland*, no. 7 (Dec. 1977).

12 James Armstrong, 'An appendix containing a summary history of the presbyterian church in the city of Dublin' in *A discourse on presbyterian ordination* (Dublin, 1829), pp. 84–6. H.C. Waddell, *The Presbytery of the Route* (Belfast, 1960), p. 31.

13 P.R.O.N.I., D 1759/1A/2, Antrim minutes, 1671–1691, pp. 74, 78, 83, 88, 96, 100.

14 Edward Wetenhall, *The Testimony of the bishop of Cork*. No copy of this tract survives but it was printed in Penn's reply to Wetenhall, *A defence of a paper entitled Gospel Truths against the bishop of Cork"s Testimony* (London, 1698), pp. 6–11.

15 Richard Lawrence, *The Interest of Ireland* (Dublin, 1682) pt. ii, ch. 2, p. 96.

16 Resolutioners accepted Charles II as the 'Covenanted King'; Remonstrants recognised only the authority of the Solemn League and Covenant.

17 William Bathe, 1564–1614, wrote *Janua linguarum Latine et Hispanice ubi sententiarum xii centuriis comprehensa sunt omnia usitatoria Latinae linguae vocabula* (Salamanca, 1611). It was reprinted in Milan (1627) and in Basel (1636). The English edition was published in 1615 (London).

18 Amos Comenius (1592–1670) wrote *Janua Linguarum reseratae sive seminarium linguarum et scientiarium omnium, hoc est compendiosa Latinam (et quamlibet aliam) linguam, una cum scientiarium, artiumque omnium fundamentis, pediscendi methodus; sub titulis centum, periodis autem mille comprehensa* (Leszno, 1632).

19 R.F. Young, *Comenius in England. The visit of Jan Amos Comenius . . . to London, 1641–1642* (Oxford, 1932), p. 12; T.C. Barnard, *Cromwellian Ireland, English Government and Reform in Ireland, 1645–1660* (Oxford, 1975), p. 185.

BIBLE AND RECONCILIATION

Cecil McCullough

At the heart of the concept of reconciliation in the Bible is the notion that all is not well in the relationship between God and humankind . In the Genesis story this is portrayed as a fall into sin resulting in a rupture of husband/wife relationships (Adam and Eve), family relationships (Cain and Abel), community relationships (Tower of Babel) and even in the relationship between humanity and the natural world (Gen 3: 17b–19; 4:10–12; 9:1). God's purpose is to restore that relationship with himself. In the Old Testament this is done through the covenant, in the New Testament through the new covenant inaugurated through the death and resurrection of Jesus Christ. But the thesis of this paper is that in the Bible the restoration of a vertical relationship always was accompanied by a restoration of the horizontal relationships. When people were reconciled to God they also were reconciled to each other. You could not have one without the other. Consequently throughout the Bible there are constant impulses towards reconciliation. We hope to examine what these impulses are and how they are expressed, both within Christian communities and in the relationship between Christian communities and the world. Along with these impulses toward reconciliation, however, there are other strands in the Bible which when misused or misunderstood or dealt with carelessly can lead in the opposite direction and provide impulses towards conflict and the following paper will deal with those.

Reconciliation in the Old Testament

The Old Testament section will be dealt with in the following paper and so I will mention it only very briefly. The Old Testament is the story of God's covenant with his people and of his faithfulness to that covenant in spite of the frailties of his chosen ones.

Major events in the history of Israel, their possession of the Land, their government and sacramental life, the departure into exile and subsequent return, the rebuilding of the Temple are all told from the perspective of this covenant. Within that covenant God's people are reconciled to him and live in a reconciled community within the safe borders of the Land of Israel. Alongside a particularistic view of reconciliation – Israel called out of the nations – there was also a universal one, found especially in the prophets, and in particular Second Isaiah, with famous passages such as Isaiah 49: 6.

Reconciliation in the Life and Teaching of Jesus

It is impossible to get full consensus on anything about the Historical Jesus[1], but there is as near to a consensus as it is possible to get, given our state of knowledge, that a major theme in Jesus's self-understanding and teaching was that of the Kingdom of God. In the events surrounding the life of Jesus, God was establishing his Kingdom, his active 'reign'.[2] He was acting, however, not as an Eastern Potentate governing his people but as a human Father presiding over his extended family.[3] As a Father God was graciously inviting people to enter that family and welcoming them to it. God's 'reign', therefore, was being established on the initiative of the Father God.[4]

Jesus extended this gracious divine invitation both by his words and actions. In Luke 4:20 he took up the theme of Isaiah 61:1 and pointed out that this day the Scripture has been fulfilled . . . Good News has been announced to the poor, release has been proclaimed for the prisoner and recovery of sight for the blind. Like a shepherd searching for his lost sheep (Lk 15: 4–7), a woman searching for her lost coin (Lk 15: 8–10) and a father receiving his lost son (Lk 15: 11–24) and perhaps even a master searching for a dishonest steward (Lk 16: 1–9), God in Jesus searches for and saves the poor, the oppressed and the marginalized.

But in Jesus' teaching, when the sinner accepts this offer of reconciliation from God then the sinner must of necessity be reconciled with his/her brother and sister. I will take several examples:

In the Lord's Prayer in Luke's Gospel (Lk 11: 2–4) we as petitioners are encouraged to ask for the forgiveness of our sins, but the passage goes on 'as we herewith forgive (present tense) all who

have done us wrong'. (R.E.B.). As we receive God's offer of reconciliation we at the same time are reconciled to others. In Matthew's version, the tenses are different, as is the word for 'sin', but
there is the same stress. We ask God to forgive us our debts, as we
forgave others their debts. Then, lest we should miss the point of
the statement, Matthew drew attention to this petition by repeat-
ing it and strengthening it at the end of the Lord's Prayer (Matt 5:
14–15).

The same theme is re-enforced in a negative way in a parable,
that of the unforgiving debtor in Matthew 18: 23–34 (Lk 7: 41–47)
where a servant who refuses to offer to another debtor the same
reconciliation that he has received from his master is 'condemned
to torture until he should pay the debt in full. That is how my
Heavenly Father will deal with you, unless you each forgive your
brother from your hearts'.

But perhaps the best known example of this teaching is found in
the parable of the Prodigal Son. In the story the parallels between
the position of the younger and of the older son are clearly drawn:
both stand outside the village unable or unwilling to go in. Both
see their father go out to them to offer his love, forgiveness and an
invitation to the feast; both have to respond to the father's offer.
The younger son accepts but the older son cannot accept because
he cannot be reconciled with his younger brother and it is at this
point the parallelism in the two stories breaks down . . . the younger
son goes in to the feast, but there is an ominous silence as regards
the older son who stands outside the village and outside the feast.
The parable of the unforgiving debtor of Matthew 18 is being
repeated here in a most dramatic way.

The need for reconciliation is also taught in relation to prayer.
In Mark 11:25 prayer and forgiving others go hand in hand, 'And
when ye stand praying, forgive, if ye have ought against any: that
your Father also which is in heaven may forgive you your trespasses. (26) But if ye do not forgive, neither will your Father which
is in heaven forgive your trespasses.' This idea is repeated in Matt
5:24 where we are told that when we are going to the temple to
pray, if we have anything against our neighbour, then 'Leave there
your gift before the altar, and go your way; first be reconciled to
your neighbour, and then come and offer your gift'.[5] Prayer is a
family matter, a child talking to its parent and a prerequisite for it
is reconciliation within the family.

But it was not just by his teaching that Jesus stressed the importance of reconciliation, but also by his action, particularly by his very controversial practice of eating with sinners.

Table fellowship is even to-day of immense social importance in the Middle East but it was of particular importance in the Palestine of Jesus's day. '"To eat at the same table" is late Hebrew idiom for being a solidary member of a group whose members labor for the same ends together and whose members stand together over against other groups. Table fellowship was the litmus test of social unity in the ancient world'.[6] It became particularly important, therefore, to the Pharisees of Jesus's day, as a boundary marker to protect their society from the pressures around them. They were under intense pressure from both the political might of the Roman authorities and the cultural pressure of the Hellenistic thought forms around them. Some Jewish groups coped with this pressure by fleeing from it, into the Judaean desert for example, as did the Qumran sectaries. Others fought against it by terrorism, as did the Sicarrii and the Zealots. Still others, like the Sadducees, tried to live with the pressure and preserve Jewish institutions and practices as best they could under very difficult circumstances, usually by compromising with the Roman authorities. The Pharisees, on the other hand, tried to resist the pressures by setting up clear social boundary markers round themselves. These boundary markers were based on a rigid observance of certain aspects of the Jewish Law, for example, strict Sabbath observance and close attention to all the purity laws, especially as they concerned the consumption of food. By observing all these laws, they were able to cut themselves off from the strong influences around them. 'The pre-70 strata of the Mishnaic law bear witness to a group where food taboos were the chief mode of social differentiation by which they maintained their continued existence as a group'.[7]

Some Pharisees of the time of Jesus, however, seemed to go even further than that. They used the laws concerning table fellowship to cut themselves off from other Jews whom they considered to be undesirable. While some recent scholars have questioned the historicity of such an attitude on the part of some Pharisees, stressing that this attitude was read back from post CE70[8] by a church which saw the Pharisees as its chief enemy, and while it would undoubtedly be unfair to paint all the Pharisees with this particular brush, nevertheless it seems unlikely that all the New Testament evidence was invented.[9] It is historically very probable that a) there was a local rift between Jesus and some hard line

Pharisees ovcr table fellowship; that b) these Pharisees seem to have defined those who were sinners, and *ipso facto* those with whom they could not have table fellowship, as those who did not belong to their group or faction, rather than as those who were non-Jews. In other words, some of Jesus' contemporaries were erecting barriers to table fellowship within Judaism itself. Hence their objection to Jesus welcoming sinners and eating with them in Luke 15:1.

Jesus, however, refused to limit his table fellowship, giving as his reason (in Luke 15) that . . . if God accepts sinners and is reconciled to them, then we too must be reconciled and show our reconciliation by eating with them. And he acted on his convictions. Again and again we read of his having table fellowship with those considered to be outside the group.

Perhaps the most dramatic story was the one about his eating with the tax collector Zacchaeus. Jesus had entered Jericho and 'was passing through', in other words, as K.E. Bailey has pointed out[10] he had decided against staying in town that night and had therefore refused the hospitality of the good people of that town and was going on to the next village. He comes across a tax collector, a collaborator with the Roman authorities, hiding among the broad leaves of a sycamore tree, trying to get a glimpse of Jesus without being himself seen by the crowd. Jesus looks up and says to him:

Luke 19:5. 'Zacchaeus, come down immediately. I must [divine compulsion] stay at your house today'. 6. So he came down at once and welcomed him gladly.

He had turned down other invitations, and here he was accepting that from a sinner. No wonder that 'All the people saw this and began to mutter, "He has gone to be the guest of a sinner"'. These actions of Jesus seem to have been rather typical and to have earned him the strong disapproval of the authorities.

By his eating with sinners Jesus was therefore 'ignoring and abolishing boundaries which more sectarian attitudes had erected *within* Israel.'[11] He did this on the basis that God had broken down the barriers through the bringing in of his kingdom and that therefore, they must break them down as well. When sinners are reconciled to God it is simply impossible that they should not be reconciled to God's children.

Two problems remain, however. Firstly, what of those who refuse to be reconciled to God? Secondly, what of those outside of Israel? For an answer to the first question several passages are important. In the Sermon on the Mount Jesus gives the famous advice 'Do not throw your pearls before swine'. This seems to find its practical outworking in the command to the twelve on their mission in Matthew 10: 13ff: 'if it (the village you visit) is welcoming, let your peace descend on it, and if it is not, let your peace come back to you. If anyone will not receive you or listen to what you say, then as you leave that house or that town shake the dust of it off your feet. Truly I tell you: on the day of judgment it will be more bearable for the land of Sodom and Gemorrah that for that town.' It is also seen in his attitude to the Pharisees who are taking offence at him when he says in Matt 15:14 'Leave them alone; they are blind guides, and if one blind man guides another they will both fall into the ditch'.

This attitude of rejection may also be seen in the famous episode of the cleansing of the temple. Scholars are divided as to precisely what was symbolised by this cleansing. There was certainly more involved than simply reforming corrupt practices or even opposing commercialism in the temple. Since the temple courts which were symbolically cleansed were those of the Gentiles, there may have been a hint that the Temple was to return to its original function, that of being a light to the Gentiles as well as to Israel but, in view of the fact that it was impossible to carry out the functions of the temple without the selling of animals and the changing of money, Sanders is surely correct when he suggests that Jesus was symbolically portraying the destruction of the temple as an institution.[12] Coupled with the preceding episode of the cursing of the fig tree, (which in Mark's Gospel sandwiches it and therefore helps to interpret it)[13] the message is clear: where there is no reconciliation to God, there is judgement. There is, therefore, a sharp edge to the teaching on reconciliation in Jesus. Where he finds injustice, unfairness, the putting down of the marginalized (as in the story of the woman who anointed him in Luke 7:36ff), there is a very firm rejection. Clearly the Church must take account of this note even though at the same time she must confess that, misused in the past, it has led to some terrible atrocities committed in the name of Christ.

The second problem is that of Jesus's attitude to those outside of Historical Israel. On one level, the situation is fairly clear. Jesus

teaches reconciliation in the sense of love and concern for others,
not just with the members of one's own community but also with
the outsiders as well. In this context his teaching on love for one's
enemy and on non-retaliation must be considered. In one sense
passages on non-retaliation such as Matthew 5: 39ff (Do not resist
evil and turn the other cheek) can be understood against the
background of a people under an oppressive military regime. The
only form of resistance possible is passive resistance, which will
eventually shame the oppressor into a fairer attitude to the oppressed. Understood in this way they give practical, very sensible
advice to the oppressed in first century Palestine. The Gospels
however, go further than simply advocate non-retaliation as a
political weapon. The pericope in Matthew 5: 38–42 is followed by
one which addresses the command to 'Love your neighbour and
hate your enemy'. It rejects that advice and instead advocates
loving your enemies and praying for those who persecute you. As
Theissen [14] has pointed out, in the Gospels there are four theological motivations for this behaviour of loving and praying for enemies: imitation, differentiation, reciprocity and eschatological
reward. You are to love your enemies

- to imitate God: 'That you may be sons of   *Imitatio Dei*
  your father who is in heaven; for he makes
  his sun rise on the evil and on the good'
  (Matthew 5: 44–45)

- to set yourself apart from the groups which   *Differentiation*
  do not do this: 'For if you love those who love
  you, what reward have you? Do not even the
  tax collectors do the same?' (Matthew 5: 46f)

- in expectation of similar behaviour on the   *Reciprocity*
  part of others 'And as you wish that men
  would do to you, do so to them' (Luke 6: 31)

- and finally in anticipation of eschatological   *Eschatological*
  reward 'Give and it will be given you'   *Reward*
  (Luke 6: 36ff)

Loving others and showing practical concern for all in need is the
outcome of a relationship with God and this is reinforced in the

parable of the good Samaritan where he defines our neighbour as anyone who is in need, rather than simply one who is a compatriot.[15]

But what of the deeper sense of reconciliation, acceptance into the family of God and acceptance of each other in that family? Did Jesus envisage this process of reconciliation as going beyond the bounds of Judaism? Here we enter an area of continuing controversy, mainly because there is insufficient evidence on which to draw firm conclusions and because some of that evidence is conflicting.

On the one hand there is clear evidence that Jesus considered his own mission at that time to be restricted to the House of Israel. This is made clear both in Matthew 10 where the twelve are sent out and they are told in v. 5 'Do not take the road to Gentile lands, and do not enter any Samaritan town but go rather to the lost sheep of Israel' and in Matthew 15 where Jesus is being addressed by a woman from Phoenicia and where he says: 'I was sent only to the lost sheep of Israel'.

But, on the other hand, there are hints of a wider interest. The Jesus who said he was sent only to the lost sheep of Israel and that 'it is not right to take the children's bread and throw it to the dogs' was able to react when the woman replied 'yet the dogs eat the scraps from the master's table' and could acknowledge 'what faith you have. Let it be as you wish'. He could also be astonished at the faith of the centurion and say to his followers: 'I tell you the truth, I have not found anyone in Israel with such great faith' (Matt 8:10; Luke 7:9). He healed the Samaritan leper who returned to thank him (Luke 10: 33)[16]; in John's Gospel he talked with a Samaritan woman and through her brought good news to a Samaritan village. While many scholars would doubt the historicity of this latter passage, if Jesus had been known as one who refused to preach the Gospel outside Israel, it is unlikely that such stories would have been invented in their entirety. Similarly if he had been unconcerned about the Gentiles it is unlikely that Luke would have created or recorded Simeon's speech that Jesus was to be 'a light for revelation to the Gentiles and for glory to your people Israel' (Luke 2:32).

In fact, however, when one looks at the inauguration of Jesus' ministry it is difficult to see that Jesus did not have an interest in the reconciliation of the whole world, or at least that the Evangelists did not perceive that he did. Jesus's ministry follows on the ministry of John the Baptist who in Luke 3: 4ff quoted Isaiah 40:3–5 which has a clearly universal thrust 'all flesh shall see the Salvation of God'. Jesus's own ministry is described in Luke 4: 18ff as being founded on Isaiah 61: 1–2 which again is one of the great universal passages in the Old Testament. Luke (and Mark) tells the story of Jesus against this background and it is difficult to see that he would have told the story so programmatically if Jesus himself had not had this emphasis. Moreover the whole motivation for Jesus's ministry seems to have been based on the thought of 'God's own scandalous mercy'[17] and this led to a provocative boundary-breaking in his ministry. While Jesus, therefore, may not personally have inaugurated a widespread mission to non-Jews, certainly the germs of that mission of reconciliation to the world were contained in his own theology. While it is practically universally agreed that Jesus did not formulate his mission in the precise words that we have in Matthew 28: 18–20, nevertheless they sum up the essence of what Jesus said: 'Go therefore and make disciples of all nations, baptising them in the name of the Father and of the Son and of the Holy Spirit, teaching them to observe all that I have commanded you; and lo, I am with you always, to the close of the age.'

There seem, therefore, to be two levels of reconciliation of the world in Jesus' thought. On one level, there is the command to love and pray for all, even our enemies; this would include respect for and help for those of other faiths or none at all. At another level there is this desire to see all flesh reconciled to God, in other words, universal mission. These two levels have always sat uneasily with each other in the history of the Christian church, and perhaps, never was there greater need to recognise them than in our pluralistic society. How does one show tolerance and love to all and at the same time keep faith with the missionary vision of Jesus?

Reconciliation in Paul and his Followers

Ralph Martin in his book *Reconciliation: A Study of Paul's Theology*, quotes T.W. Manson as saying that 'Reconciliation is thus the keyword of Paul's Gospel so far as its working out in Christ is concerned. The driving-force behind the Gospel is the love of God. The *modus operandi* is reconciliation'[18]. If, however, reconciliation, is an 'interpretative key to Paul's theology' . . . the 'chief theme' or 'centre' of his missionary and pastoral thought and practice[19], then to do it justice one would have to consider all of Paul's theology. Clearly this is an impossible task for this paper. We will, therefore, for reasons of space, restrict ourselves to one passage where the term is particularly noticeable . . . 2 Cor. 5: 18–21.

This passage comes in a long section in the epistle (2 Cor 2: 14–7:4) where Paul is defending his own ministry. It is a complicated, sometimes even confusing, section where the structure is sometimes difficult, a phenomenon usually accounted for by Paul's emotional involvement in the topic. It is a section, however, which contains some of Paul's finest statements.[20]

In the context of the sharp dialogue Paul was having with the Corinthians, the passage comes at a high point where the opposition against Paul seems to have been crumbling (as later chapters show, this happier state of affairs was not to last) and where Paul is making a last appeal to those still wavering to accept his offer of reconciliation. Into this appeal for reconciliation he inserts a piece of traditional church teaching about God's reconciliation of the world to himself in Christ and the need to proclaim that reconciliation in the world.

The section is itself very well structured. An introductory statement in v. 18 that all renewal is from God is followed by a double theological statement: God in Christ reconciled us to himself and gave us the ministry of reconciliation. This statement is then repeated in two parallel lines which give more detail and add a personal appeal (a typical way to emphasise something in semitic thought): in Christ God was reconciling the world to himself (then detail: not counting their trespasses against them) and entrusting to us the message of reconciliation (detail: so we are ambassadors for Christ, God making his appeal through us. Personal application: We beseech you on behalf of Christ, be reconciled to God). Paul then returns to the first part of the statement, that God was reconciling the world and in v. 21 explains how he does that and finally in chapter 6:1ff he returns to the second part of the statement with our responsibilities.

Other very important passages to be studied with regard to reconciliation are Col 1: 19–23 and Romans 5: 1–11. Without going into any more detail, however, it is clear that for Paul humankind is estranged from God. God initiated the work of reconciliation through Jesus 'in the fullness of time' and made us agents of that reconciliation. It is particularly important that Paul should stress this in a book like 2 Corinthians which reflects a situation where reconciliation was the last thing on certain church members' minds!

Paul in this passage is making several very important points: God has initiated reconciliation; reconciliation is through Jesus Christ; we are agents of that reconciliation. But for whom was this reconciliation intended? The distinctive (though not unique) contribution of Paul is that it was for Gentiles as well as Jews. In looking back upon his experience on the Damascus road Paul in Gal 1: 16 saw it as a time when God revealed his Son to him that he might preach him among the Gentiles. 'The primary purpose of the risen Christ's appearance was to send him to the Gentiles'.[21] As Stendahl says: 'the persecutor was *called* and chosen to be apostle with a very special mission which focused on how the gospel should reach the Gentiles'.[22] From then on, this call seems to have been the dominant motivation of his life, so that the 'the Gentiles may become an offering acceptable to God' (Rom 15: 16). It was this conviction that sent him travelling throughout the Mediterranean world, suffering the loss of status which his trade as a peripatetic leather worker caused, meeting danger from shipwreck, wild animals, bad weather and of course fellow human beings, enduring the hardships associated with travel at that time ... cold, hunger, tiredness, even bed bugs.[23]. If ever a theologian put his convictions into practical action, it was Paul.

This reconciliation, however, was also offered to his own people. Paul's attitude to his own people is a very large and difficult subject and can only be dealt with briefly here. In Romans Paul deals with this issue in great detail and the theme is picked up again in the deutero-Pauline book, Ephesians 2:15ff. Although Ephesians is probably not by Paul, it is certainly Pauline in thought and is a good starting point for the discussion. Here the author says that those who once were 'separate from Christ, excluded from citizenship in Israel and foreigners to the covenants of the promise, without hope and without God in the world' (2: 12ff) are now 'brought near through the blood of Christ'. The dividing wall of hostility has been broken down and God has created 'one new person out of the two, thus making peace'. (2: 16). The question here is: what does reconciliation involve? Is the author suggesting that the differences between Jews and Gentiles are abolished in one new humanity which is the church? Does the author, in fact, envisage the church as a 'third entity' which replaces both Jews and Gentiles, so that people are no longer Jews or Gentiles but simply Christians. This has been the traditional interpretation of this passage, going back at least to Clement of Alexandria[24]. But is the author and ultimately Paul his/her teacher, really postulating that reconciliation comes through each group (Jew and Gentile) losing its identity and accepting a new identity, Christianity. Two recent scholars[25], Markus Barth and William Rader, have challenged this view and their challenge has been judged to be successful by many others working in the field.[26] Markus Barth interpreted Ephesians 2 in the context of the church's continuity with Israel. He argued that 'the new person' is not constituted by the denial or abolition of differences between Jews and Gentiles but by their common worship of the Father. For him, therefore, the 'new person' is not an individual man or woman, but instead the 'bride of Christ'. 'When in Eph 2:15 Christ is called creator and creates a person, then the term 'one new man' must mean a person distinct from Christ. No other person can be meant than the 'bride of Christ'. While this bride is never explicitly named the New Eve, she is identified as the church in 5: 23–32 or as the people or property of God in 1:14'.[27] The new creation, therefore, consists of Jews and Gentiles worshipping together in Christ. Both remain Jews and Gentiles but are reconciled to God and to each other through Christ.

This fits with Paul's thinking in Romans where in chapters 9–11 he deals in some detail with the place of his own people in God's plan. As a Jew he is heartbroken by the rejection of Jesus by his compatriots and something of this sorrow can be seen in Romans 9: 2–3. Nevertheless he clings to the hope that one day they will be saved (Romans 11:1–2) and if their temporary failure meant riches for the Gentiles, that is, their grafting into the vine, how much more will their full inclusion mean! (Romans 11: 12). For Paul, therefore, the rejection of Israel is purely temporary and he looks forward one day to the reconciliation of Jews and Gentiles but this reconciliation is always 'in Christ', that is, reconciliation and mission go hand in hand.

The reconciliation, however, had profound consequences on the ground. For Paul the community of the church is a community of people reconciled to each other. This can be seen, for example, in the images that Paul uses for the church community. It is pictured as a body, where each member has its own role to play (1 Cor 12: 12ff), as a family (Paul is often described as Father) and also as a building in Ephesians 2: 19ff. It is seen in his doctrine of the Spirit who distributes gifts in 1 Cor. 12: 1ff. What we would stress in this paper, however, is that this was no theoretical contruct in Paul's theology but something to be striven for on the ground. It was given practical expression in the collection for the saints in Jerusalem, a collection which Paul thought so important that he could not go to Rome till he had delivered it to Jerusalem. But even, more so, it was given practical expression in the untiring energy which Paul poured into the task of keeping that reconciled community together. One only has to read the two Epistles to the Corinthians, to follow Paul as he agonises over the schisms in that community to see how seriously he took his task. For those distressed by the failures to heal the divisions within Christendom, tempted to give up in despair, the Corinthian correspondence is required reading.

In Paul, therefore, there is the conviction that God was in Christ reconciling the world to Himself; that we are agents of that reconciliation and that we live in reconciled communities where people of all races, classes and countries should live in harmony. His mission in life was to bring about that reconciliation through mission and see it operate on the ground through pastoral concern and work.

Paul is, however, aware of the 'not yet' of Christian theology. He recognises with sorrow that there will be those who for one reason or another do not wish to accept God's reconciliation, as Paul understands it. He is painfully aware that this is the case with many of his own people and his experiences in cosmopolitan cities such as Athens would leave him in no doubt about the ability of Gentiles as well to reject his message. He does not deal with the problem in any detail except on the one hand to agonise over their lot and toil himself and spur others to toil to bring them into the community of the reconciled and on the other hand to take refuge in the sovereign will of God (Romans 11).[28]

Conclusion

Throughout the Bible, therefore, there is a strong emphasis on reconciliation, God's reconciliation of the world to himself, with the subsequent reconciliation of people to each other. As Ziesler said 'the horizontal aspect of reconciliation flows out of the vertical, the human from the divine'.[29] All this has been dealt with, however, in the context of the great Judaeo-Christian tradition and one of its basic assumptions is that it is through that nation 'the chosen people' in their 'chosen land' or tradition alone that reconciliation comes. There has been little attention paid to those who 'dance to a different beat'. It is in this connection that some of the passages which are open to misunderstanding and misinterpretation occur and they will be dealt within the following paper.

NOTES

1 In this short essay we will avoid as far as possible questions about the Historical Jesus, since it is the Jesus as he is portrayed in the Gospels who has had an influence on subsequent Christian thinking and therefore it is in that Jesus that we are primarily interested.

2 Cf. R. T. France, *Divine Government: God's Kingship in the Gospel of Mark*, London, SPCK, 1990 among many.

3 Hence Jesus addressed him as Abba. cf. the debate on 'Abba' beginning with J. Jeremias, *New Testament Theology*, Vol. i. London, SCM, ET1971 and the subsequent dismissal of his views by G. Vermes, *Jesus the Jew*, London, Collins, 1973.

4 In the first century Middle Eastern context in which Jesus lived, the natural image was that of 'Fatherhood'. I have therefore decided to remain faithful to the text and translate 'Father' while recognizing the problems that many scholars have with this term.

5 Cf. also Lk6 35; Mt 5:44; Mt 18: 23–35; Mt 18: 21–35.

6 Bruce J. Malina and Richard L. Rohrbaugh, *Social Science Commentary on the Synoptic Gospels*, Minneapolis, Fortress, 1992, p. 69.

7 J. D. G. Dunn, *Jesus, Paul and the Law*, London, SPCK, 1990, p. 63 quoting J. Neusner, *Judaism: the Evidence of the Mishnah*, Chicago, University of Chicago Press, 1981, p. 69.

8 Cf. E. P. Sanders *Jesus and Judaism*, London, SCM, 1985, p.174 ff. and many others.

9 Cf. J. D. G. Dunn, *Jesus, Paul and the Law*, London, SPCK, 1990, p. 61ff. among others.

10 I am indebted to K. Bailey in a lecture given in Union Theological College, Belfast in March 1993 for this point.

11 Dunn, *Jesus, Paul and the Law*, p. 80.

12 E. P. Sanders, *Jesus and Judaism*, p. 75. 'Thus we conclude that Jesus publicly predicted or threatened the destruction of the temple, that the statement was shaped by his expectation of the arrival of the eschaton, that he probably also expected a new temple to be given by God from heaven, and that he made a demonstration which prophetically symbolized the coming event'.

13 Cf. David Rhoads and Donald Mitchie, *Mark as Story*, Minneapolis: Fortress Press, 1982 for an interesting discussion of Mark's stylistic characteristics, of which this is one.

14 Gert Theissen, *Social Reality and the Early Christians*. Edinburgh, T & T Clark, 1993, pp. 117ff.

15 It is interesting that a passage such as Matthew 5:44 ('Love your enemies') is not found in the Johannine literature where there is a great deal to say about

love but it is always love *within* the community, and within the section of the community accepting the author's teaching. Do we find here, perhaps, a changing of emphasis of Jesus's teaching?

16　It is typical that it is in Luke that the fact that the leper was a Samaritan was reported.

17　Donald Senior and Carroll Stuhlmueller, *The Biblical Foundations for Mission.* London, SCM, 1983, p. 147.

18　R. P. Martin, *Reconciliation: A Study of Paul's Theology*, Grand Rapids, Zondervan, 1989 Revised Edition, p. 3f.

19　*ibid* p. 5

20　Cf. P. E. Hughes says of 5:21 that 'there is no sentence more profound in the whole of Scripture'. Quoted in R. P. Martin *Reconciliation.* p. 108.

21　J. D. G. *Dunn, Jesus Paul and the Law*, p.89

22　K. Stendahl, *Paul among Jews and Gentiles*, p.12. We are not entering into the discussion as to whether this was the *whole* significance of the Damascus Road event.

23　Cf. Ronald F. Hock, *The Social Context of Paul's Ministry.*

24　William Rader *The Church and Racial Hostility. A History of the Interpretation of Ephesians 2: 11–22*, Tübingen, Mohr, 1978, p, 16.

25　Markus Barth *Ephesians*, Anchor Bible 34, New York, 1974 and William Rader, *The Church and Racial Hostility.*

26　Cf. W. Campbell *Paul's Gospel in an Inter-cultural Context*, Frankfurt am Main, Peter Lang, 1991 for a recent discussion of this.

27　*op. cit.* p. 309.

28　There is a similar emphasis in the Johannine literature, though there is no space in this essay to deal with it.

29　J. A. Ziesler, *The Epworth Review*, 10 (1983) p. 99–100.

A RESPONSE

Carmel McCarthy

In traditional procedures for the examination of a biblical theme it is usual to begin with its OT roots and then trace its development and refinement into the NT. In the case of reconciliation however it is not only useful but even advantageous to begin with the NT, for it is there that we can see the richness of the concept and its distinctiveness, as has been so vividly portrayed for us by the first speaker. He has rightly emphasized how the teaching and actions of Jesus are not only concerned with a reconciling mission to the house of Israel, but that they also contain the challenge of a universal mission, with all the consequences and tensions that arise therefrom.

A brief glance at theological dictionaries of the Bible confirms the degree to which reconciliation is perceived as being essentially a NT term.[1] There is in fact no single specific term in Hebrew or Aramaic to express the concept of reconciliation in the OT, even though the underlying reality itself is caught in a variety of shades through terms such as *shalom*, atonement and renewal of the covenant. Through many and varied images one of the connecting threads permeating very different OT narratives, stories, psalms and laments is that the human condition is one of limitation and misunderstanding, alienation and estrangement. Not only is this the situation on the horizontal level in interpersonal relations of every kind, but the Bible makes it very clear that this situation is but symptomatic of a more fundamental disorder and estrangement between human beings and God.

By deliberately situating the stories of creation and fall at the very beginning of Genesis the architects of the Bible demonstrate that experiences of alienation and the need for reconciliation can be traced back to the very dawn of existence, and have existed since earliest memory. However, another central connecting thread in the OT has for purpose to insist that into this appalling

situation of alienation and chaos God takes the initiative and
invites human beings into reconciliation with him and with each
other.

Certain fundamental concepts lie at the heart of the shaping
and refining of the OT people of God: in particular the intercon-
nected concepts of chosen people, land and covenant. How can
one be faithful to the essence of these biblical concepts, and retain
their theological value, and at the same time honestly recognize
that some of them can be and have been misunderstood? For
instance, can one appeal to the Bible to justify what happens when
a people understands itself as 'a chosen people', with a right to a
land in such a way that the fundamental and sometimes prior
rights of others are systematically violated? Some critical reflections on Deuteronomy might be useful in this context, since this
book is centrally concerned with the key issues of election, covenant, law and land and contains powerful images of reconciliation.

Presented as the final words of Moses to the people as they
prepare to enter the promised land, Deuteronomy was edited into
its final form in post-exilic days.[2] As such it constitutes a theological reflection on Israel as a chosen people rescued by a loving God,
who is leading them into a covenant relationship in the land they
are about to inherit. While these key theological elements in
Deuteronomy are clearly presented as coming from divine initiative, a closer, more critical reading of the texts in their historical
and literary context will show that these main emphases are not
without their shadow side, and their ambiguities.

Deuteronomy is very humanitarian in its concern for the stranger,
the widow and orphan, and recurrently pleads with the Israelites
that they provide active care for the plight of the oppressed in
their society.[3] Yet, at another level the book could be described as
the expression of an intensely nationalistic faith, with its focus on
Israel living in the land in covenant with its God, and repeatedly
warned against contamination through contact with non-Israelite
peoples.[4]

Deuteronomy therefore could be described as a collection of
often quite unenforceable laws designed to inculcate religious
convictions and attitudes in the life of the people of God within
the framework of an actually existing historical Israel. The implications for what happens when the attitudes and convictions of
the Deuteronomist are reproduced, either consciously or uncon-

sciously, in uncritical and fundamentalist ways in other times and other cultures must be obvious.

In the earlier layers of the OT Israel as the covenant people of God is struggling to emerge, and the concern therefore is more with the establishing of identity and the avoiding of what would undermine its existence, as illustrated in Deuteronomy. Hand in hand with this emerging sense of identity, the seeds of universalism were being sown in some of the prophetic writings, seeds that were destined to reach their flowering in the life and teaching of Jesus, as already demonstrated in the last paper. The image in Is 2:1–5[5] of beating swords into ploughshares speaks vividly of reconciliation in a universal context, while the text of Is 49:6 describes Israel given as 'a light to the nations, that my salvation may reach to the end of the earth.' In Tobit 14:5–7 these prophetic utterances are picked up in a vision of hope in which 'all the people of the whole earth will be converted and will fear God with all sincerity.' Here, once again, Israel is seen as an agent of reconciliation to the nations.

Since reconciliation in the OT normally takes place in and through the nation, it might be useful to explore what happens when reconciliation is effected in and through 'the outsider' and 'the powerless.' Some reflections on the story of Ruth are instructive in this regard,[6] though one could also focus on the recalcitrant Jonah who was reluctant to be an agent of reconciliation for the Ninevites. In Ruth one finds the same reconciling energy that runs through the OT, but in a different context, one in which the role of the oppressed is not to have reconciliation done *for* them, but rather *by* them, as active agents (which raises questions about our use of terms like 'marginalized' or 'oppressed' which can be paralyzing in their effects).

Ruth is a true model of both 'the outsider' and 'the powerless,' for she is an absolute foreigner without land, and as a widow she is powerless and vulnerable. Yet it is through her, on the initial story level, that Naomi can perpetuate the name and family of her dead husband, and through her, in the final form of the story, that the line of David, key ancestor in the total salvation history story, finds continuity. Her role as a link in the vertical relationship should also be noted. She is one who is open to the unexpected and the uncharted. She is ready to allow providence direct her even to the point of accepting Naomi's God.[7] Thus Ruth represents and symbolizes in a very active way what the so-called outsider and alienated can effect in the real stuff of reconciliation.

Psalms of lament often include elements of cursing and invective which can embarrass the Christian who has been taught to 'turn the other cheek' and 'to pray for one's enemies.' How should one deal with these texts which can seem very unchristian? One solution can be to remember the progressive nature of revelation and the gradual refinement of moral sensitivity which takes place in the pages of the Bible. This can be illustrated particularly with reference to the concept of retaliation in which a five-stage evolution in biblical thinking on this topic can be traced as follows:[8] (i) unlimited revenge;[9] (ii) talion or limited revenge;[10] (iii) the silver rule[11] as in 'Do not do unto others what you would not have them do unto you'; (iv) the golden rule[12] and (v) Jesus' challenge to love and pray for one's enemies,[13] which is nothing less than an invitation to moral heroism and sanctity.

It should be clear from the foregoing how an uncritical acceptance of some of the terms and images from the OT can confirm rather than challenge our prejudices in the area of reconciliation. Some observations on the central thesis of the first paper: 'that in the Bible the restoration of a vertical relationship always was accompanied by a restoration of the horizontal relationships' may be a useful way to conclude this response. In terms of revelation the process of reconciliation begins with God. He is the one who takes the initiative, as was illustrated in the first paper's examination of the key Pauline text of 2 Cor 5:8–21. In human experience, however, the possibility of being genuinely open to reconciliation on the vertical level is prepared for and facilitated by human choices and attitudes that actively seek reconciliation on the horizontal level. In Paul's words we really are 'agents of reconciliation'. We bring into effect God's gift of reconciliation every time we respond in a reconciling way to the challenges of the life and teaching of Jesus. And we are enabled to do that because God has already taken the initiative.

NOTES

1   NT = New Testament, OT = Old Testament. There is no entry for the term 'reconciliation' in the recently published *Anchor Bible Dictionary* (Doubleday 1992). Cf. J. A. Fitzmyer, 'Paul's Christocentric Soteriology', *New Jerome Biblical Commentary*, New Jersey 1990, 82:24–80; J. Murphy-O'Connor, 'Reconciliation in a New Creation', *ibid*, 50:25; E. C. Blackman, 'Reconciliation', *Interpreter's Dictionary of the Bible*, Abingdon 1962, pp. 16–17 (who devotes almost the entire article to the NT).

2   Cf. R. E. Clements, *Deuteronomy*, Sheffield 1989, pp. 13–22.
3   Cf. Deut 14:29; 16:11,14; 26:11.
4   Cf. A. D. H. Mayes, *Deuteronomy* (New Century Bible Commentary), London 1981, p. 55.
5   This passage is also found paralleled in Mic 4:1–4.
6   Cf. C. McCarthy and W. Riley, *The Old Testament Short Story, Explorations into Narrative Spirituality*, Wilmington 1986, pp. 55–83 in particular.
7   Ruth 1:16–17.
8   Cf. B. Viviano, 'Retaliation', *New Jerome Biblical Commentary*, 42:34–36.
9   Gen 4:15, 24.
10 Cf. Deut 19:16–21.
11 Tob 4:15.
12 Cf. Matt 7:12, which is more positive than the silver in its expression, and urges the reaching out to do good.
13 Matt 5:44ff.

JUSTICE AND RECONCILIATION

Gerry O'Hanlon

It is right that we test the notion of reconciliation in the context of a consideration of justice. It is right because although Christians do often have some sense of the wonder involved in being ambassadors of the good news that our faults are not held against us, that we are reconciled (2 Cor, 5, 16–21), nonetheless there often persists too a niggle that this is too easy, that there must be a price to pay, that justice requires the settling of old scores. The human demand for fair play can often seem offended by the apparently unilateral Christian injunction to unconditional forgiveness and reconciliation, as we are told to turn the other cheek and are offered the story of the Prodigal Son to illustrate God's own attitude. Somehow the more contractual ethos of the Old Testament covenant relationship between Jahweh and the people seemed to allow more scope for this very human cry for retribution in the face of injustice.

This is the cry we hear often in our newspapers as convicted criminals, particularly in cases of sexual abuse, are given sentences which victims and their sympathizers consider too light. Must one not demand appropriate punishment for the so-called war crimes involving the rape of thousands of Bosnian women? One recalls the sad case in France last October when distressed relatives of haemophiliac AIDS victims demanded tougher sentences in the case of officials of the Paris Blood Transfusion Service who were found to have knowingly allowed the distribution of HIV infected products to haemophiliacs. But is this kind of demand compatible with Christian forgiveness and reconciliation? At a more structural level it surely cannot be right that the poor in our own island and in the world's South can be reconciled with the wealthy without some kind of more equitable sharing of the world's resources? Surely it is wrong to go easy on white-collar, corporate crime or to ignore the inbuilt injustices of the international economic order?

And one knows only too well in the context of the Northern Ireland situation how talk about reconciliation sounds hollow unless basic issues of justice are addressed.[1] Are the families of the victims of paramilitary murders,for example, to be asked to express unilateral forgiveness at funerals, and not be allowed to express anger and to demand punishment?[2] And yet within this same context we have already had too much experience of the destructive nature of simple retaliatory so-called justice, particularly in the case of paramilitary retaliation against often completely innocent victims.

There is need then to address this issue of the relationship between reconciliation and justice, and to see in what sense the Christian good news and the human niggle in response may be better understood. At one level the issue is conceptual. If reconciliation involves the transformation of a relationship of enmity into one of friendship then one must ask how do forgiveness and unconditional acceptance relate to notions such as conversion, repentance, reparation, amendment and justice. Already one notes here that these latter words are very much part of the Christian vocabulary, from which one may gather that the apparent clash between the notions of reconciliation and justice may not be reduced simply to a clash between what is Christian and what is human. Furthermore one notes that the original situation of enmity, whether due to blame or not, can be interpersonal or communal and structural. And it often involves a long history, and sometimes one which includes death – how does one change the past, what good is reconciliation for those who are already gone? But this issue is also existential in at least two important ways. First it is an issue which each of us has to address in our own personal lives in our relationship with God, with one another and in the context of the economic, social, political and other divisions on our island – 'What issue on this island is more important for those who want to follow the Gospel than that of just reconciliation?'[3] Secondly it is an issue on which as Church people we have been criticized as erring on the side of a falsely irenic form of reconciliation which ignores the hard justice issues. A strong form of this criticism comes in the *Kairos* document emanating from South Africa in the 1980's (1985, 1986). There a distinction is made between a State theology which supports the unjust *status quo*, a Church theology which uses the language of reconciliation to bring about peace and consensus without confronting the basic injustice, and a prophetic theology which advocates peace only on condition that it involves justice and the liberation of the oppressed. There may be elements of caricature about this analysis which cannot anyway be transferred without question to our own Irish context. But many Christians on our island do feel uneasy themselves that the notion of reconciliation conjures up a softness that is inappropriate to the hard issues that are involved. I have argued elsewhere that in particular there may be a middle-class bias towards the politics and language of consensus that is wrongly neglectful of the biblical tradition of conflict.[4]

Biblical and theological approach to Justice and Reconciliation

I want to begin by proposing the thesis that there need be no contradiction in the relationship between justice and reconciliation as expressed biblically and understood in much of the theological tradition.[5] What I want to argue for then is an intrinsically just notion of reconciliation, without in any way minimizing the refreshing shock to the human system of the Christian good news.

At the heart of the good news of course is the abiding desire of God to heal and forgive any breakdown in relationship, and to effect a full reconciliation at any cost except that of condoning evil or manipulating us by destroying our freedom. It is interesting that the classical texts which mention reconciliation in the New Testament all presuppose a real situation of rupture and all refer to the cost of healing that rupture – 2 Cor 5, 11–20 (in order to effect our reconciliation 'God made the sinless one into sin'), Rom 5, 10–11 ('when we were reconciled to God by the death of his Son'), Col 1, 20–22 (all things reconciled in the Son 'when he made peace by his death on the cross'), Eph 2, 11–16 (reconciliation is 'by the blood of Christ'), Mt 5, 23–24 (be reconciled with your brother if he has something against you before you bring your offering to the altar, come to terms with your opponent before you pay the full price in court).

There are three crucial elements here which must cohere. First there is the clear recognition of offence, sin, injustice. This is not a question of papering over cracks, of being kind at the expense ironically of robbing human beings of their dignity by denying their responsiblity and hence the value of their freedom. And in this context it is right to name injustice, protest against it, and call for its removal: Jesus confronts the establishment of his day, the

Scribes, Pharisees and Sadducees, in this way. Secondly there is an unconditional offer of forgiveness, exemplified by the story of the Prodigal Son and by Jesus himself in his dealings with so many sinners. This is central: this is gratuitous, is clearly a matter of love, and goes beyond what Vincent Brümmer refers to as a contractual model of relationship where forgiveness might be earned through reparation of one sort or another to a fellowship model where forgiveness is given freely out of love.[6] This is the kind of forgiveness God extends to us and we are asked to extend to one another (seventy times seven – Mt 18, 21–22). It is a wonderful gift, an expression of love which can remake the past that has gone wrong and create an even stronger relationship for the future. Thirdly there is a cost to forgiveness and it is only when this cost has been paid that forgiveness can flower into full reconciliation. The cost refers first to the willingness of the injured party to absorb the offence to the relationship by his or her own suffering. This is what the Scriptures refer to when they place the cross of Christ at the centre of God's gift of forgiveness, what we human beings experience in an analogous way when we swallow our pride, refuse to let our hearts harden, and truly reach out in generous love to someone who has acted to us in an unloving way. But because relationships are between persons the solution to their rupture cannot simply be one-sided. There is a cost to the injuring party too, the sinner, the oppressor. This is what the Scriptures refer to as conversion and repentance, and what later theology would discuss in terms of amendment, reparation, expiation, atonement and so on. It is what is expressed by the notion of penance in the Roman Catholic understanding of the sacrament of Reconciliation. What is at issue here is the human experience of sorrow for sin and the human desire to change the unjust situation as an expression of the desire to renew the relationship. In the context of true sorrow this is felt not so much as an imposition but rather as a natural desire to renew the relationship by making things up to the injured party – lovers who give one another flowers after a quarrel know exactly what is meant. If this sorrow and conversion are not present then the forgiveness is one-sided and since reconciliation involves a relationship there is no real reconciliation.

This language of cost and the way in which these three elements cohere can lead to the appearance of a contradiction between justice and reconciliation. Does not cost refer to something earned, and reconciliation to something free and unconditional? But the

cost referred to must be understood in an interpersonal context of
fellowship and not one primarily of contractual arrangements
such as obtain in the exchange of goods and services. The cost is
that of love, not of something that can be bought. However – and
here I would part company with Brümmer's analysis – there is also
a contractual element involved in a subsidiary way in the sense that
all relationships of fellowship take place within a context which
involves socio-economic-political relationships of more or less equitable power, and these more contractual elements of the culture
which facilitates relations of fellowship need themselves to be
addressed. Jesus clearly relates to Zaccheus in a fellowship mode,
and Zaccheus reciprocates with his delight at the offer of table-
fellowship but notes as well that he is conscious of the contractual
blocks to such fellowship by promising to share his riches with the
poor and recompense with generosity anyone he may have de-
frauded in his capacity as tax collector. It is not that in so promising he earns the fellowship of Jesus: this fellowship is entirely
freely given, a matter of love, but it generates the need on the part
of the other to act justly in a contractual sense. The only paradox
involved here is precisely the one we are all familiar with from
personal relationships all the time – viz. that we are made in such a
way that we have a need to love and be loved freely, and that it is of
the nature of love to be unconditional and yet to depend for its
survival and flourishing in a relationship on a loving response that
is true and just. My love for you may survive your rejection of it, but
our relationship will not. Similarly the coherence of the three
elements observes a certain order: it is precisely that free, unconditional offer of forgiveness which liberates the sinner to own his or
her sin and then to redress the situation of injustice. Terry
Anderson, the American jouralist held as hostage in the Lebanon,
expressed this well at a conference in Derry last September when
he told his audience that 'it is the victim who must make the first
approach towards his oppressor, signal his willingness to forgive
the man who has tortured him, if either is to have any hope of
experiencing the freedom and the peace that come with reconciliation'.[7] One does not offer forgiveness on condition of reparation
– such demands often simply lead to a hardening of hearts. But
neither does one offer forgiveness by means of condoning the sin
– this would be untrue and no basis for a relationship. Instead one
points to the evil and the required righting of it, but offers the
forgiveness unconditionally, suffers the consequence of this one-

self, but is then open to whatever appropriate expression of sorrow and reparation may come from the other in the relationship
and is necessary for offered forgiveness to become received forgiveness, thus creating that full restoration of relationship which
we mean by the term reconciliation. This delicate balance of a
forgiving love is one that calls for the conversion of the sinner not
out of a desire to retaliate but rather out of a recognition that the
sinner can only be reconciled and made whole again by taking
responsibility for his or her deed. It was illustrated very well in
November 1992 by the words of 22-years old Rosaria Schifani at
the funeral Mass in Palermo for her 27-year old police-man husband murdered by the Mafia: 'To the men of the Mafia, for they
are here too, I say there is forgiveness even for you . . . but you
must get down on your knees if you have the courage to change'.[8]
It involves repentance on the side of the guilty as well as a surrender of righteousness on the side of those who have been injured.

There are two important glosses needed to clarify what is being
said here. First, this analysis can seem somewhat static when one
prescinds from the ebb and flow of time. It is often suggested that
the biblical sense of history became somewhat undermined when
it came into contact with the more timeless truths of Greek philosophy. Nonetheless there is already present in the High-Scholas-
tic notion of act leading to habits some recognition of what our
more recent re-discovery of an historical perspective, allied to the
emergence of psychology as a human science, can tell us about the
way justice and reconciliation operate as a process, albeit one with
decisive single moments. Relationships, including the feelings
which are at their heart, are complex and require time to build,
repair and strengthen. It may take time to forgive, and the bereaved relative of the victim of a para-military killing ought be
allowed feel anger and loss and not be press-ganged at a funeral
for so-called Christian motives into hasty declarations of forgiveness.[9] Similarly it may take time to be forgiven, and one must allow
time for discernment of suitable forms of reparation. And there is
very often a time gap between the desire for reconciliation between individuals and the righting of the unjust social situation
which keeps them apart – white and black under the apartheid
system of South Africa, women and men under systems of
patriarchy, have's and have-not's in Ireland and throughout the
world. Underlying this particular time gap is the distinction between personal responsibility and situations of social sin – it is

quite possible for individuals to act responsibly and in good conscience while being unaware of or powerless to change the unjust
situation within which their actions take place. Many might agree
with Sinead O'Connor, for example, when she criticises the Roman Catholic Church for its attitude to women. But fewer would
go on to call the Pope and all male officials of that church evil –
many are surely well intentioned, good men who illustrate the
point that it takes time to bridge the gap between structural evil
and human good intentions. We are alerted here in different ways
to the eschatological nature of the search for justice and reconciliation, so that while we are careful to put no limits to the marvel-
lous work of God based on that decisive break-in to human history
by Jesus of Nazareth, nonetheless we must acknowledge with patience and realism that wheat and tares grow together till the end,
and that it is our mission to persevere in hope as we share in the
Paschal Mystery by being in the midst of a situation which offers
anticipations only of the final reconciliation of all in Christ.

Secondly what does all this say about how justice and reconciliation are experienced by God, what does it say about the nature of
God? This refers in Christian theology to the issue of soteriology.
For our present purposes the only aspect of soteriology that we
need address is that concerning the process by which God reconciles us to God's self through Christ as it impinges on the relationship between justice and reconciliation. To be more precise, is this
reconciliation by means of love alone, or is there some element of
justice as is so central to the satisfaction theory of Anselm? Once
again it seems to me that the apparent contradiction between the
two positions is not so in fact, and in soteriology too I would argue
that justice is a subsidiary but intrinsic part of love. In establishing
this position I would agree with Gabriel Daly when he warns us
that in dealing with the various metaphors or models used in
soteriology we are speaking analogously.[10] They are then not to be
taken in their univocal human sense, nor is any one to be taken on
its own. With this in mind I suggest that Gerard O'Collins is
correct when he identifies more or less the same basic three
models as Vincent Brümmer – liberation, expiation and trans-
forming love – but uses these models, unlike Brümmer, in a
mutually complementary way without choosing the third one exclusively.[11] What he wants to preserve in so doing is the sense that
love operates within a moral order which involves truth and justice, and that when the relationship of love is violated there is

need to repair this moral order in a way which does involve a suffering love taking on the cost involved in righting injustice. This cost includes being moved by God's loving anger at sin towards a restoration of justice. Concretely then Jesus suffers and dies in attempting to bring God's love and forgiveness to his contemporaries by subverting the unjust power relationships of his day – and by being raised up and by being the Son of God he has in principle effected human reconciliation with God and empowered us all to accept this reconciliation. What is involved here is not some kind of cosmic mathematics of suffering and reconciliation, a kind of eternal ledger by which justice and recon- ciliation are balanced in some abstract way by the amount of suffering endured. Rather the appeal is to our concrete experi- ence of relationship, of breakdown, and of the cost in terms of love and justice in restoring relationship. In an analogous way the 'initiating substitution' of Christ, due to the divine providential genius, means that God's 'no' to sin is transformed into a recon- ciliation between God and humanity by the loving and suffering 'yes' of Christ. This is not the placating of the offended honour of an angry God but it is a recognition that God's anger is appropri- ate in the context of a violated moral order and the havoc it wreaks on countless victims of oppression – and that suffering love is the way by which one moves from just anger to the reality of a just reconciliation, all within the process of love.[12] The just anger which has its source in violated love does not simply disappear by magic but is transformed by a costly return of love which can be called expiation if rightly understood. It is in this context that one may with great care speak from soteriology of the analogous suffering of God – Metz is right to be cautious here, right to point out that in daring to speak of a suffering God there is a danger of both romanticizing suffering and taking away its ultimate and only healer.[13] But there are good grounds in Christology, in the kataphatic events of incarnation and cross, to go beyond the apophatic denial of suffering in God to posit something like a divine suffering in love as a perfection of God's trinitarian being in which the Son is true expression of the Father and in which there occurs the ultimate triumph of love over suffering as we know it.[14] To go further than this and to rehabilitate Anselm after the manner of von Balthasar in speaking of an inner-trinitarian drama in God in which the Father in some way takes on the role of wounded justice and the Son that of making amends, albeit within a unity of purpose which is one of love, is an interesting possibility.[15] As a helpful theological speculation it can only be fruitful if one insists (as von Balthasar does) that there can be no question of the Father punishing the innocent son, if one insists on the primacy of love within the metaphysical order which also involves truth and justice (as von Balthasar also does), but if in addition one makes as close an identification between the Father and victims of evil and oppression as that between the Son and sinners (von Balthasar does not do this). This identification between the Father and victimized people makes it clear that the Father is not some despotic God touchy about offended personal honour but rather one whose enormous love especially of the victimized entails outrage at their violation. This whole approach has the great merit too of locating conflict analogously within God, in response to human evil, thus rehabilitating constructive conflict as an intrinsically Christian quality and avoiding a 'wet' notion of reconciliation and a God without teeth who is simply no comfort to victims of oppression and is justifiable only by a very selective liberal appeal to Scripture.[16]

The Kairos document is correct in noting that there is no reconciliation without justice. The human niggle that we referred to concerning fair play is warranted. Reconciliation involves the restoration of ruptured relationship and this cannot happen on the basis of unjust inequality. The remark in the 1971 Roman Catholic Synod of Bishops that justice is 'a constitutive dimension of the preaching of the gospel' has become a *locus classicus* which has deeply affected contemporary theology. Nonetheless the distinctively Christian doctrine of reconciliation does transform this concern for fair play by locating all justice talk within a logic of love, not one of equity on its own. When the demands of justice have been completely satisfied reconciliation is still a gift, not a product: it is a matter of interpersonal love, which can never be a matter simply of rights. And, equally importantly, in the necessary struggle and conflict to bring about justice the unconditionally loving offer of forgiveness at the heart of Christian reconciliation is precisely that most vital part of the process which gives the oppressor the space to change and convert. This then is the surprising good news of the Christian position on reconciliation, at right angles to human demands for fair play, and a liberation for both oppressor and oppressed.[17] It is a position which acknowledges that as well as interpersonal there are also social, economic and political aspects to this question, that a process is involved over time, and that God is engaged in this process in a very intimate and yet transcendent way. We may hope to nuance this position now by applying it to some issues of contemporary inter-personal and societal interest.

The Interpersonal Dimension

I may be brief here since this is the dimension that traditionally Christianity has felt most comfortable with and to which it has devoted considerable attention. Because persons are made to be in relationship, and because relationships go wrong, then reconciliation with its ability to restore relationship through a forgiving and costly love is clearly a most vital Christian and human reality. It is a great gift of the Christian gospel that it promises liberation from the bitterness, hurt and resentment that can warp and imprison the human spirit due to difficulties in relationships. It is also clear that since relationships are in the end a matter of love they cannot be reduced to matters of justice. But yet we know in our guts that truly loving relationships are also just – how does one work out the connection between justice and reconciliation at the interpersonal level?

I suggest that one begins with our basic, ontological equality and solidarity as human beings and as sons and daughters of God. Any relationship of love has to recognize what is due to any human being according to this basic equality. While love may go beyond what is strictly owed (and by definition always does), it may not fall short of what is owed. Justice is a necessary if not sufficient ele-ment of a loving relationship between persons. I may not treat you then as less than a human being. Of course you may waive some of your strict rights in the interests of the negotiated compromises which are intrinsic to all but the most narcissistic relationships of love, but never those rights which touch on the basic integrity of what it is to be human – otherwise we are into a relationship that is basically inhuman and manipulative.

The trouble with this rather abstract treatment of course is that it conceals the fact that we are all the time learning what it is to be human and what are considered to be inviolable human rights and those which are more secondary. Our sensibilities change, and cultural factors come into play. We need then to be quite concrete about this, and one good way to do this in our contemporary situation in the western world is to test how these abstract considerations apply to the concrete position of marriage.

With the development of feminist consciousness the focus has sharpened on the question of how justice and love may be respected in relationships between women and men, and specifically in marital relationships. There is occuring a cultural time-lag between the recognition of the basic equality of women and the personal and institutional resistances which attempt consciously or not to reinforce the dominant patriarchy. In particular, as the novels of Joanna Trollope illustrate so well,[18] women are made to bear the burden of nurturing and being defined in a reductionist way by relationships at the cost of a fuller sense of self through participation in other areas of life, while men wield power in the public realm at the expense of their more personal and relational selves. What is needed here is a stronger recognition among Christians in particular that conflict, which involves anger at injustice, is an eminently Christian way to proceed.[19] It is not enough to say that unconditional love imposes no demands. Rather love presupposes a basic equality and where that is not there it is right to assert it and struggle towards it for the sake of both partners. The biblical motif of Jacob wrestling with the angel is one among many others which encourages what we as Christians have been slow to recognize – that change towards a more just and more loving situation occurs over time and with struggle. Of course conflict can be destructive, and great skill is needed within a relationship to ensure that it is handled well and in such a way that unconditional love, forgiveness and reconciliation continue to be the foundation of the relationship. But it is also true that there is no real intimacy without conflict and anger, and that this is how we break through from habits of pacifying toleration to honest love. Guilty repression of anger at basic injustice is both psychologically damaging and is a misunderstanding of the Christian teaching on reconciliation and justice. Again, the recognition of wrong and the struggle towards a more just situation do not of themselves bring about that situation – the eschatological motif in Christianity urges patience and the primacy of love in the struggle for justice. But it is a great step forward to understand that it is right to name and protest injustice, within marriage and elsewhere, and that in doing so one is responding faithfully to the call of the kingdom of God which is based on unconditional love. There is no contradiction between justice and love.

The socio-political dimension

The socio-political dimension requries more attention since as
Christians we are less accustomed to using categories like reconciliation to apply to this area. Yet there has been a growing willingness in recent years in different quarters to recognize the social
dimension of grace and to speak in terms of a politics of forgiveness and reconciliation.[20] Clearly this kind of talk is likely to be of
interest in a world of great economic, social and political divisions.
But can the language of grace, forgiveness and reconciliation
really have any purchase in the world of *Realpolitik*? And if one
introduces the language of justice to ensure this purchase how
does one preserve the distinctively Christian content?

In deference to a healthy realist scepticism let us begin by
acknowledging some of the limitations of a politics of reconciliation and justice. One moves by analogy from the interpersonal to
the communal and societal, so that while one may indeed speak of
the social embodiment of reconciliation, still one can never com-
pel individuals within a particular society to appropriate that reconciliation for themselves.[21] So, while politics inevitably involves
conflict and the giving of offence, and political action can produce symbols of forgiveness, there is no guarantee that any individual will as a result open him or herself up to true reconciliation,
with its transcendental character of forgiving offence. Of course,
as we shall see below, this does not detract from the real if limited
value of political reconciliation, which includes its facilitative empowerment of interpersonal reconciliation. A further limitation of
political reconciliation occurs in that because the interests of
many are at stake, and because these many share very different
beliefs, there will be strong elements of coercion involved. By
coercion here I refer to legal provisions, the back-up of police, the
acceptance of some form of majority rule and so on. Accordingly
the more obviously gratuitous, loving side of reconciliation can
seem blurred in a way which is not true when there is question of
the relationship between two individuals, which can often be
settled without the more coercive elements which are needed to
ensure that justice is done. As a private individual I can more easily
waive my strict rights provided of course I do not sacrifice personal
integrity: but as a leader of a community I am not in the same
position of relative ease in waiving the rights of others. Underlying
this point is the recognition that our world is shot-through with

what traditional theology referred to as grace, nature and sin.[22] One needs the safety-net and restraints advised by the imperfections of nature and the evil of sin, even while one hopes to grow in the perfction and freedom of grace. And this further example of eschatological tension is even more pronounced in the public realm. Still, as illustrated by the use of excommunication in the early Church, such coercive elements may indeed be understood as ordered towards the more ultimate goal of reconciliation. And this too can be said of the criminal and legal examples we referred to in the introduction to this paper – the whole legal system can be seen as a necessary protection of justice but as ordered ultimately to the transcending of justice in reconciliation. This is likely to occur realistically only when the penal part of the system integrates rehabilitation as central to its goal, whether in prison or through other forms of punishment.

I have acknowledged some of the real limitations of a politics of reconciliation. Nonetheless, running through this acknowledgement was an equally realistic assertion of the values involved, and I turn now to explore these values a little more fully.

What is at issue is the creation of structures and symbols in the public domain which facilitate communities and individuals to live together in greater peace and justice. I begin with some instructive examples from the world of *Realpolitik* to indicate the reality of what is involved as well as its great potential. Last Autumn President De Clerk ordered the release of political prisoners in South Africa. He did so, as he himself said, 'to take the term retribution out of the political vocabulary in order to pave the way for reconciliation'. Around the same time he also said he was sorry that the apartheid system had existed – up to then he had insisted that the need was to concentrate on the future and stop dwelling on the past. The ANC welcomed his apology, while noting that he needed to match actions with words. At that conference last September in Derry's Guildhall which was addressed by four of the men who had been held hostage in the Lebanon a video was shown in which former US president Jimmy Carter spoke about the meetings between Presidents Sadat and Begin which led to the Camp David accords. According to Carter neither Sadat nor Begin were able to overcome the deep personal hostility and mistrust they felt for the other and all that he represented in terms of a shared history. Nonetheless 'what each man possessed was the vision and courage to understand that, although they could not overcome their mutual personal antipathy, it was essential to deliver peace and the possibility of a new relationship between Israel and Egypt to their peoples'.[23] So the accord was signed and they embraced in an image of reconciliation shown all over the world. A third example comes from an account by the former West German chancellor Helmut Schmidt of a meeting with the former Soviet President Brezhnev in 1972. Before the official talks the two men met for a social evening at the home of Willy Brandt. In the course of that evening they shared their memories of World War II and Schmidt notes: 'Probably it was this exchange of bitter war memories that significantly contibuted to the mutual respect which has characterized our relationship between 1972 and up to his death . . .'[24]. Fourthly it has been argued very persuasively by Donald W. Shriver that justice and reconciliation were together present in the American Black Civil Rights Movement of the 1950's and 1960's. Shriver criticises the tendency of political theories to focus on justice alone and speaks of the need for a 'serious attempt to interpret forgiveness as a term appropriate for political ethics and political strategy', arguing that there is 'a political form of the forgiveness of sins' and noting how blacks were engaged in 'not forgetting the past . . . but seeking to overcome it . . . through the creation of a new future'.[25] One might finally instance the change in tone of the 1992 Referendum on The Right to Life in the Republic of Ireland from that prevailing in 1983 as an instance of political reconciliation, albeit obviously one that is incomplete.

These examples illustrate in different ways the possibility of political reconciliation and justice. What is involved is a transcending of the logic of strict justice in that the language of blame and retribution beomes subservient to the desire for reconciliation, and indeed the correction of the unjust situation is itself justified by its contribution to reconciliation.[26] There are interesting parallels between this position and one which offers a critique of the prevailing Liberal political culture in many western countries on the grounds that in pursuing self-interest at all costs not only are minorities treated badly but in fact one's own interest also suffers as a result.[27] In the examples given above blacks in America did not close their eyes to the injustice they suffered: rather they called whites to conversion but did so in a forgiving way which gave space for movement. Similarly De Clerk called for an end to the language of retribution, and made this possible by confessing past guilt and indicating a clear intention to change in the future. Other lessons may be drawn from these examples which indicate the partial nature of what remains always an incomplete but valuable process. So, one may have leadership which reconciles peoples without the personal chemistry which comes from interpersonal reconciliation (Sadat and Begin). Or one may have this personal chemistry with limited political reconciliation (Schmidt and Brezhnev). I note in this respect that while ultimately all reconciliation has to be personally appropriated it is surely the case that political reconciliation is a powerful facilitator of this personal appropriation and therefore is of tremendous value. So, for example, the civil rights movement in the USA and moves towards ending apartheid in South Africa allow individual whites and blacks to relate to one another not just in a personally loving, if unequal, way, but to do so within new structures which make more possible that basic equality necessary to all human relationships.

A common thread running through the discussion of political reconciliation is the need to cope with the past and to envisage a new future. Irish people are sometimes accused of having an overly-developed sense of the past, but, as Bishop Mark Santer points out, this is common to communities which have a history of oppression.[28] What needs to happen is not that we forget the past or undervalue it – there is a rightful 'anamnestic solidarity' with the past of which the forgetful oppressor must also be reminded. But there is a call to become free from an imprisoning hold of the past, a freedom which is promised in the biblical notion of forgiveness. This is what changing the past involves[30] – we know that things happen which are 'unforgiveable', that people are killed and that there is no possiblility of a just reparation which would restore their lives. What is required here is a forgiveness which bears the terrible pain of past loss without poisoning the present and future. This is what the 'reconciling of memories' involves[31] – an 'imaginative exchange of subjectivities'[32] by which I become aware of the pain of the other side as well as my own and bear the burden of both by a forgiveness which calls to conversion. One way of doing this at a group level is to look for those tangential, apparently unimportant events of history which show attempts to break out of hostility, and build these into our self-understanding.[33] Another is to pay attention to the liberating aspects of the myths which often control our understanding of the past in a negative way.[34] Recent attempts in Ireland to retell and celebrate key historical events which have assumed mythic proportions (1641, 1916, the Siege of Derry, the Battle of the Boyne) in a reconciling way are instances of what is meant.[35] Similarly the utopian role of myth in opening up a reconciling future ought not to be underestimated. We have need of the imaginative as well as the rational. In addition to detailed programmes for government with specific policy proposals we need an overall vision which would give coherence to these programmes. Of course vision without policy will be utopian in the pejorative sense: but policy on its own will not move a people to a better future. Arguably as well as good policy what we need most in Ireland today is a vision of solidarity, articulated in secular myth-form and expressed in appropriate symbols as well as conceptually, which would capture our imagination and minds, and harness our energies in addressing the great divisions which characterize our society north and south.

Coming closer to home, from what has been said so far it will be clear that reconciliation and justice in the political sphere cannot mean a simple neglect of past or present injustices with respect to the Northern Ireland situation. Nonetheless it is correct to seek for ways of reconciling our memories and forgiving one another: and to look for political solutions which will admit the kind of just compromise which is involved in political reconciliation. If this justice is really subservient to love and reconciliation even in the tough world of *Realpolitik*, as I have argued, then it cannot simply be assumed on both sides of the nationalist divide (i.e. by Nationalists and Unionists) that justice is served only by the capitulation of the other side. The 'no surrender' of traditional Ulster Unionism, with its mirror image in the nationalist insistence on a united Ireland as the only solution, are arguably examples of a demand for justice that is devoid of a feel for real reconciliation.[36]

Conversely, with regard to the economic divide both north and south within Ireland, it will not do to advocate class reconciliation without that call to real solidarity which will require middle-class people to share what they have in terms of the good life with those who are effectively marginalized. The poor are right to want a better material standard of living, and would be wrong only if they pursued this as an end in itself without thought to the spiritual values of freedom and reconciliation which should accompany it. Nonetheless if democratic government in Ghandi's terms is judged on how well minorities are treated then there is clear legitimation of a conflict, not consensus, model of politics in Ireland to address the imbalance of economic and social power which has been the consequence of social policy particularly in the Republic of Ireland.[37] But the conflict is one which many middle-class people might well want to engage in on the side of the poor if they are given the space which is the fruit of the gospel call to liberation and reconciliation and are not trapped by a guilt-ridden, moralistic preaching of the gospel.

Finally it should be noted that the *Kairos* critique of the Church version of reconciliation as neglecting the unjust *status quo* is not without resonance in our Irish situation. I refer to two areas in particular. First, there is a predominantly middle-class ethos in church life in Ireland, north and south. So, despite the fine words of many documents, including the recent pastoral from the Roman Catholic bishops in Ireland on unemployment, the poor do not get a sense that the churches mean business here and that they strive might and main to rally their members to the call for a more just society. Where, for example, is the call to middle-class Christians to seek imaginatively and energetically for alternative ways of organizing society, perhaps introducing within business culture the notion of a social audit to replace the more conventional exclusively financial one, and all as a response to the call of the gospel within a divided Ireland to-day?[38] Secondly, while the Churches themselves are divided, and show little urgency about healing the divisions, they offer poor witness to an island in desperate need of just reconciliation.

Conclusion

If we have indicated ample scope for considerations of justice within the Christian notion of reconciliation, perhaps it is appropriate to end with a comment on the distinctive nature of reconciliation itself. Because the 'niggle' on the Christian side might be that too much talk of justice camouflages the wonder that is reconciliation.

And it is wonderful that one can be asked to consider and love everyone as a brother or sister, a fellow human being, and put this before other considerations like distance, enmity and so on. This is a challenge to see otherness, conflict and diversity not simply as threat but as potentially part of a process involving the enhancement of the richness of the world and of my own self-identity.[39] The gospel call is for relationship with all, and when relationships break down, for reconciliation. Despite all we have said about the need for such relationships to be built on a basic equality this gospel stress on gratuitous love comes as a shock to the system – even when we oursleves are the grateful beneficiaries of forgiveness and the offer of reconciliation, perhaps we find ourselves most often in the role of the Elder Brother in the story of the Prodigal, somewhat resentful and full of calculations of worth and justice which would do credit to Shylock. This calculus of worth is not what is primary to who we are – our foundation is being willed into existence out of love by the God of love, and our worth comes from this primary gratuity. And if in our broken world we need to observe a just order to our relationships, then we must know too that this justice is ordered towards love and its cost is paid for by the suffering love of God who invites us to share in this divine project.

NOTES

1. See G. O'Hanlon, Northern Ireland – Realisable Dreams, *Studies*, 81, (1992), 175–6 (171–9).
2. For a very good treatment of this issue see An Interchurch Group on Faith and Politics, *Burying our Dead: Political Funerals in Northern Ireland*, Belfast, 1992.
3. An Interchurch Group on Faith and Politics, *Remembering Our Past: 1690 and 1916*, Belfast, 1991.
4. See G. O'Hanlon, A Middle-class Church for a Working-class People?, *The Furrow*, 44, (1993), 3–11.
5. See also on this John O'Donnell, God's Justice and Mercy: What Can We Hope For? *Pacifica*, 5, (1992), 84–95; and Donald W. Shriver Jn, A Struggle for Justice and Reconciliation: Forgiveness in the Politics of the American Black Civil Rights Movement, 1955–68, *Studies*, 78, (1989), 136 (136–150).
6. For a clear presentation of three basic conceptual models of relationship (manipulative, contractual and fellowship) leading to different theories of atonement and reconciliation, see V. Brümmer, Atonement and Reconciliation, *Religious Studies*, 28, (1992), 435–452.
7. Mary Holland, *Irish Times*, Thursday, Sept. 10th, 1992.
8. See *I. Times*, Saturday Dec 19th, 1992.
9. See *Burying our Dead. op. cit.*
10. See Gabriel Daly, Forgiveness and Community, in *Reconciling Memories*, ed. by Alan Falconer, Dublin, Columba, 1989, 99–115.
11. See G. O'Collins, *Interpreting Jesus*, London, Chapman, 1983, ch 3.
12. See J. O'Donnell, *art cit*, 91–93.
13. See J.B. Metz, Suffering from God: Theology as Theodicy. *Pacifica*, 5, (1992), 274–287.

14. For this (and what follows about Anselm), see G. O'Hanlon, *The Immutability of God in the Theology of Hans Urs von Balthasar*, Cambridge, CUP, 1990.
15. See J. O'Donnell, *art cit*, 88–93.
16. See D. Nicholls, Trinity and Conflict, *Theology*, xcvi, 19–27.
17. See *Studies*, 78, (1989), Editorial on Towards a Healing of Memories, 125–126.
18. See, for example, Joanna Trollope, *The Rector's Wife*, London, Black Swan, 1991, 127 where the central character Anna, wife and mother, muses in growing if sad awareness: 'Why was it that she was made to feel that her claims had no validity, that her existence was only permitted by everyone as long as it remained relative? How did people, Anna cried to herself, how did people get to be primary people – the ones who made others relative? And why, if you picked up a different burden, was it then assumed that you loved your burden and would gladly carry it for ever and ever . . .'.
19. I am indebted to Cathy Molloy, *Christian Marriage – Theology and Lived Reality*. Unpublished STL dissertation, Milltown Institute, Dublin, 1992, 88–92 for a very perceptive and stimulating treatment of this whole area.
20. See H. Willmer, The Politics of Forgiveness – A New Dynamic, *The Furrow*, 30, 1979, 207–218; Geiko Müller-Fahrenlolz. On Shame and Hurt in the Life of Nations – A German Perspective. *Studies*, 78, 1989, 127–135 in which he outlines the position of Hanna Arrendt on the need to accept forgiveness as a political reality; D. Shriver, *art cit*, passim; E. McDonagh, *The Gracing of Society*, Dublin, Gill and Macmillan, 1989; A. Nolan, *Jesus Before Christianity*, London, Darton, Longman and Todd, 1977. Also the writings of other Liberation theologians and the social encyclicals of John-Paul II.
21. G. Daly. *art cit*, 110–115.
22. See G. O'Hanlon, May Christians Hope for a Better World? *Irish Theological Quarterly*, 54, 1988, 175–189.
23. Mary Holland. *I. Times*, Thursday, Sept. 10, 1992.
24. See Geiko Müller-Fahrenholz. *art cit.*
25. See Shriver. *op cit*, 136, 148, 138.
26. See H. Willmer. *art cit*, 214–215.
27. See P. Riordan, S.J., The Plausibility of Arguments from the Common Good, *Milltown Studies*, 28, 1991, 78–101.
28. M. Santer, The Reconciliation of Memories, in *Reconciling Memories*, 128–132.
29. G. Daly, *art cit*, 103, quoting Helmut Peukert.
30. See H. Willmer, *art cit*, 207–218; G. Daly, *art cit*, 101–103.
31. See A. Falconer, *Reconciling Memories*, Introduction (1–7) and The Reconciling Power of Forgiveness (84–98).
32. G. Daly, *art cit*, 106.
33. See J. Liechty, Testing the Depth of Catholic/Protestant Enmity (52–67) and F. Wright, Reconciling the Histories. Protestant and Catholic in Northern Ireland (68–83), in *Reconciling Memories*.
34. See R. Kearney, Myth and the Critique of Tradition, in *Reconciling Memories*, 8–24.
35. See *Remembering Our Past*, passim.
36. See G. O'Hanlon, Realisable Dreams, *art cit.*
37. See F. E. Powell, interviewed by Ann Cahill, in the *Irish Times*, Sept. 8th, 1992 on the occasion of the publication of his book *The Politics of Irish Social Policy 1600–1990*, New York, Edwin Mellen Press, 1992; G. O'Hanlon, A Middle-Class Church, *art cit.*

38. See G. O'Hanlon, A Middle-Class Church, *art cit*; P. Vardy, Business Morality: People and Profits, *The Way*, 32, 1992, 301–311.
39. See M. Bond, Reconciliation – An Ecumenical Paradigm, in *Reconciling Memories* (116–127) for an interesting philosophical development of this.

A RESPONSE

Rupert Hoare

Father Gerry's paper is rich in content and covers much ground with great care and precision. It deserves to be read attentively at least twice. I found myself writing 'agreed' down the margin of most pages, and where I had questioned something on first reading, I found on second reading that he had handled it elsewhere in his paper. So I hope the discussion will focus on his paper, rather than on this response.

I agree with him that there can be no true reconciliation between human beings without the struggle to restore justice between them, and that such just reconciliation is a process (page 53), which will only be complete at the end of time (pages 53, 54). Reconciliation, whether between God and human beings or between individuals or groups of people has to be realised again and again, though for Christians the fundamental act of reconciliation has surely been accomplished in the Incarnation. This is why we must ourselves be a reconciled people committed ourselves to the work of reconciliation.

So we can test claims of reconciliation by assessing the justice or otherwise of the reconciled relationship. But this is where problems can begin, because different groups of people work with different concepts of justice. Furthermore, the very word is, I believe, taboo in certain Protestant circles in Northern Ireland, because they believe it has been taken over by the nationalist cause. Father Gerry, in his paper, speaks of it as a 'basic equality' between human beings (pages 57, 62). The simplest paradigm he presumably has in mind is the relationship of two adults. As a particular instance he refers to marriage (pages 57, 58). He could also refer to different adult groups, collectively.

There are also other relationships which even after reconciliation display a just inequality in certain respects. For instance, parent and child, teacher and pupil, or small nation and large nation (for instance, Estonia and Russia, to take an example comfortably removed from these islands!). In these instances power is not equally distributed on both sides (as on page 52 of Father Gerry's paper). Here the language of equality perhaps needs to be supplemented by that which speaks of according infinite respect one to another, especially by the more powerful to the less. Such respect is primarily respect for the freedom of the other. To speak of infinite respect, I believe, allows us to affirm diversity within a justly reconciled relationship. It also implies a high status for justice, as for instance held by Kant. As mutual infinite respect justice is never left behind, as I thought Father Gerry might be implying when he spoke of 'transcending justice in reconciliation' (page 60).

Just reconciliation involves establishing the truth. Father Gerry refers to this when speaking of the need to be ready for conflict, for instance, in marriage. This can be painful, and will also , as he says, take time. It is particularly painful in unequal relations such as those between adult and child, for example, where sexual abuse has taken place. There is likely to be much resistance, showing itself as silence, a silence which hides irrational guilt and paradoxi-cal feelings of loyalty to the abuser. In such a situation, the need for healing of the abused, including his or her liberation from the effects of the abuse, the emergence of the truth, and the removal of the abuser from any position of power where abuse could take place again, have to precede reconciliation. Here reconciliation may be a distant goal, – and yet one which is likely to be very important to the abused, and indeed, to the penitent abuser.

In such situations to talk of reconciliation now can be prema-ture, or even counter-productive, because it may hinder the emer-gence of the truth, upon which alone hangs the possibility of just reconciliation. In a similar context Father Gerry refers to the Kairos Document (page 49). I am reminded of a conference in Cambridge in 1989, in which South African theologians met some British colleagues. One black South African spoke of the docility which afflicted so many of his race in South Africa, a docility which was reinforced by the pervasiveness of the church's use of the language of reconciliation. A mood or 'mindset' of docile submis-sion to subordinate status within South African society was a major affliction of the black community. In such situations what is needed first of all is what Walter Brueggemann in his book *Hope in History* (John Knox Press 1987) calls the articulation of pain and the espousal of Old Testament experience of Lament. When once the injustice of a situation has been recognised by those within it, and the pain that has been taken for granted 'owned' and expressed, the first step has been taken in the creation of something new, for which vision and imagination are then the necessary ingredients, as Father Gerry states on page 18. In South Africa, or in respect of the civil rights movement in the United States for example (page 62), reconciliation can only take place after the basic injustices have been overcome. The theologians we met from South Africa were adamant that that meant the return to the Africans of their land; any penitence on the part of the whites that did not involve that was illusory.

Here the language of 'basic equality' is essential. But the question which Father Gerry addresses in relation to Ireland (and I would of course want to add Britain too) is whether that 'basic equality' includes the redistribution of wealth. He asserts it does (page 64). I agree: the creation of a more or less permanent 'underclass' excluded from the mainstream of the life of society through poverty runs completely counter to any claim to be a reconciled society. And in South Africa, if and when apartheid is abolished, as also in Britain and the United States, such poverty is in practice associated very largely with the black and Asian communities. Economic and racial oppression go hand in hand. Reconciliation involves the overcoming of both.

There still remains the question how far economic 'equality' is feasible, or desirable, and at what point reconciliation can disregard economic imbalance and inequality. To my mind, the argument here is about the extent of the imbalance, both financially and in terms of actual power. But here we do come up against another and seemingly opposed understanding of justice, namely that of the New Right.

Here justice is held to consist in the right to hold on to what one has oneself earned, and to pass it on to one's children. Just relations are seen first in terms of commitment to one's parents, ancestors, children and grandchildren, rather than to one's peers, with whom equality is neither feasible nor necessary. Reconciliation will look very different on such an understanding of justice. But there are truths here which those of us who argue for Father Gerry's 'basic equality' must listen to – and somehow hold in tension with our own. Current political debate is about just such compromises, – which are themselves legitimate in a reconciled society, just so long as both justice and reconciliation do not lose their ultimate focus as truths which will come into their own definitively only at the end of time, – in the purposes of God.

One might also add that there are other sorts of loyalties, as well. For instance that of the bereaved towards a murdered relative, which some would argue does not allow the bereaved to pronounce the forgiveness of the murderer. The initiative for such forgiveness, and therefore reconciliation, has to remain with God alone, in so far as it does not issue from the penitence of the murderer (a subject Father Gerry refers to on page 53).

Finally, neither of us has dealt specifically with reconciliation between separated Christian bodies. Maybe we have felt justice belonged to the political spheres. But if justice involves truth, then religious division cannot be excluded. And here we must recognise the partiality of our own vision (I Cor. 13. verse 12). In the complexities of division that afflict us in Europe, where religious, economic, constitutional, social and racial factors are all bound up together, and where we each see injustice from our own position, we have to look *forward* to the reconciled justice, which God is offering us, and with that vision of *what is to come* in our minds, seek to address the divisions of the past and the present.

ECUMENISM AND RECONCILIATION

Geoffrey Wainwright

A Topical Prologue

If, within a human space inhabited by people for whom religion counts, one group considers another idolatrous and is itself in turn regarded as apostate by the other (or vice versa), then you have a recipe for trouble. It might be Bosnia. The Muslims will view Orthodox Christians as close to idolaters because belief in a trinitarian God is an affront to Allah. Orthodox Christians may see Muslims as apostate because they have followed the later prophet Mohammed whereas the incarnation of the divine Word in Jesus Christ was unsurpassable. Now change the geography and locate the human space within Christendom, in a place where Catholics and Protestants live cheek by jowl. In Protestant eyes, the Catholics may have apostasised from the Biblical faith and, by their 'breaden God' and their 'worship of Mary', be committing idolatry. In Catholic eyes, the Protestants may have quit the true Church and turned, let us say, to a God so transcendent of the incarnate realities of the sacraments and the saints that he passes over into deism and no longer even attracts worship, though still allowing his adepts to do very nicely for themselves. In such a case, you have a recipe for 'the Troubles'.

Perhaps my description would be caricatural if applied to Northern Ireland. But in attempting as a sympathetic outsider to address the Irish situation, I want to recognize that the conflict is at least in part theological, or even dogmatic. As a theologian, I ask what part Christians in my profession or vocation can play in the process of reconciliation. This is not, or course, to deny that social, economic, political and cultural factors have a role in the problem and its solution, for we still live in earthly history. But I wish to be explicitly ecclesiological in my approach, and to attempt a dogmatic analysis of the situation and propose dogmatic hints towards a process of healing, grounding what I have to say in the Christian liturgy or the life of worship. Any useful work that theologians may accomplish in the area of reconciliation will need to percolate into the preaching and teaching of the churches and the everyday conversation of Christians.

Introduction: The Example of an Ancient Rite

An eighth or ninth-century Irish Penitential, preserved at the monastery of St. Gallen in Switzerland, instructs the minister regarding the questions he is to put to a person seeking admission to the process of penance. He is to ask:

> Do you believe in the Father and the Son and the Holy Spirit?
> Do you believe that these three persons, whom we have spoken of as Father and Son and Holy Spirit, are three, and that God is one?
> Do you believe that in the day of judgement you are to rise in the flesh in which you now stand and are to receive either good or ill according to what you have done?
> Are you willing to forgive those who have sinned against you, since the Lord has said, If you do not remit to men their sins, neither will your heavenly Father forgive you your sins?

A person who answers affirmatively will be admitted to penance and later, on Maundy Thursday, sacramentally 'reconciled' to God and to the Church, and therefore to the communion of both.[1]

My suggestion is that this early medieval form can, with necessary adaptations, supply both a theological understanding and a practical model for the reconciliation of divided Christians and their communities to one another and their common restoration to the favour of God which has at least been jeopardized if not forfeited by their divisions. First, as the approach of the penitent presupposes, the desire for reconciliation must be present. Then, as the questions concerning the Holy Trinity and the last judgement indicate, there must be an awareness of God and the history of sin and redemption. (An adjacent penitential requires that the minister 'hold forth the word of salvation and give the penitent an explanation: how the devil through his pride fell from the angelic dignity and afterward through envy drove man out of

paradise, and how Christ accordingly for human salvation came
into the world through the virgin's womb and by his resurrection
both conquered the devil and redeemed the world from sin and
afterward gave the apostles the grace of baptism by which he
should deliver man from his sin, . . . and how in the end of the
age he shall come to judge the living and the dead and to render
to every man according to his work.'[2]) In fact, the penitential
interrogations, with their '*Credis?*' and the expected response
'*Credo*', recall baptism and the faith it signifies – which are the basis
of, and summons to, the life of communion in the body of Christ.
When divisions among believers nevertheless occur and disrupt
the body of Christ, there must be a willingness on all sides – for
faults rarely if ever reside with a single party – to forgive (as the '*Vis
dimittere?*' requires of the individual penitent) and to
be forgiven. Mutual reconciliation then allows the parties to come
before God with an open face and be embraced by God's peace,
the threat of divine judgement removed, the promise of
divine communion finally enjoyed, and witness borne afresh to
the gospel of grace.

Correspondingly, this chapter will have the following sequence
and structure. First, the history of salvation and the preaching of
the gospel will be seen in terms of reconciliation. Second, baptism
and the faith it signifies will be viewed as inclusion in that history
and response to that proclamation – and *ipso facto* the constitution
of membership in a new community. Third, the sad and grave fact
of divisions among that community will be shown to require repentance by admission of fault, sorrow for sin, and resolution to
amend; and the possibilities will be opened up for forgiveness and
healing, with a view to the restoration of peace and communion. A
conclusion will return to the witness made to a gospel of reconciliation whose credibility has been impaired by obstinate divisions.
The concrete cases and arguments will largely be presented on the
explicit or implicit assumption of a Catholic/Protestant polarity,
since this bipolar perception predominates in Ireland, although
there are of course nuances – and differences! – to be recognized
between the Church of Ireland (with its historic links to the
Church of England), the Presbyterian Church of Ireland (with its
historic links to the Church of Scotland), and the Methodist
Church in Ireland (with its Wesleyan origins and tradition). The
Orthodox Churches, so important in world ecumenism, will scarcely
be mentioned.

I.   The Divine Act and Message of Reconciliation

In the canonical Scriptures common to Catholics and Protestants, an apostle equally beloved of Protestants and Catholics describes the atoning work of Christ in this way:

> If while we were at enmity with God we were reconciled to God by the death of his Son, much more, now that we are reconciled, shall we be saved by his life. Not only so, but we rejoice in God through our Lord Jesus Christ, through whom we have now received our reconciliation.

Thus writes St. Paul in Romans 5:10f.; and in 2 Corinthians 5:18 – 6:1, he enlarges upon the apostolic ministry and message of reconciliation that derives from God's reconciling act in Christ:

> God . . . through Christ reconciled us to himself and gave us the ministry of reconciliation; that is, in Christ God was reconciling the world to himself, not counting their trespasses against them, and entrusting to us the message of reconciliation. So we are ambassadors for Christ, God making his appeal through us. We beseech you on behalf of Christ, be reconciled to God. For our sake he made him to be sin who knew no sin, so that in him we might become the righteousness of God. Working together with him, then, we entreat you not to accept the grace of God in vain.

The initiative of the reconciliation is God's, and its scope is as wide as the world. In Ephesians 2:11–21, the apostle declares that in Christ, who 'is our peace', a common reconciliation to God has been effected for both Jew and Gentile, 'those who were far off' and 'those who were near', which *ipso facto* 'breaks down the dividing wall of hostility' *between them* also. Clearly, the history of reconciliation to God entails reconciliation among the beneficiaries of God's grace. The message of divine reconciliation requires that its witnesses live at peace with one another: such is the connexion implicit in Romans 15 between the apostle's summoning of the Church to unity and his evangelistic and missionary endeavours in the world. Division among Christians is bound to impair, if not nullify, their testimony to the gospel.

Basic to the entire Christian faith, the atoning work of Christ and its consequences for believers are well recalled in the First

Eucharistic Prayer for Reconciliation of the current Roman Catholic
Missal, at the point of the anamnesis-oblation-epiclesis:

> We do this in memory of Jesus Christ,
> our Passover and our lasting peace.
> We celebrate his death and resurrection
> and look for the coming of that day
> when he will return to give us the fullness of joy.
> Therefore we offer you, God ever faithful and true,
> the sacrifice which restores man to your friendship.
> Father,
> look with love
> on those you have called
> to share in the one sacrifice of Christ.
> By the power of your Holy Spirit
> make them one body,
> healed of all division.[3]

Acceptance of reconciliation to God sets one in a community
where reconciliation among the members is the norm.

II.   The Community of Faith and Baptism

In the same context of 2 Corinthians previously cited, St. Paul
declares that 'if any one is in Christ, he is a new creation; the old
has passed away, behold, the new has come' (2 Cor. 5:17). By the
grace of God, one enters Christ by faith, of which baptism is the
sacrament. In Christ, the baptized believer can sing with Charles
Wesley:

> My God is reconciled,
> His pardoning voice I hear;
> He owns me for his child,
> I can no longer fear;
> With confidence I now draw nigh,
> And Father, Abba, Father! cry.[4]

To become a child of the heavenly Father is to acquire other
Christians as brothers and sisters. Ecumenically, the question arises
of the extent of the family.

On the Roman Catholic side, the Second Vatican Council declared that, even in separation, people 'who believe in Christ and have been properly baptized are put in some, though imperfect, communion with the Catholic Church', and 'the separated churches and communities are by no means deprived of significance and importance in the mystery of salvation' (Decree on Ecumenism, *Unitatis Redintegratio*, 3). The modern ecumenical movement has driven almost all Christian communities, whatever their fundamental ecclesiology, to recognize, and offer some account of, the existence of Christians beyond their own boundaries – whether it be along the lines of the 'traces of the Church' (*vestigia Ecclesiae*) still detected by Calvin in the Roman church (*Institutes* IV.2.11f.), the 'branch theory' of some Anglicans (as in Lancelot Andrewes' 'Eastern, Western, British' or William Palmer's 'Greek, Latin, Anglican'), or the 'all true believers' of John Wesley.[5] Baptism and faith have figured among the evidences that allow for recognition, though regrettably not always in such a conjoint formulation as that of *Unitatis Redintegratio*.

Yet problems remain with regard to baptism and faith as elements in mutual recognition among Christian communities. Take, for example, the responses of the Irish churches to the Lima text of the World Council of Churches (=WCC) on *Baptism, Eucharist and Ministry* (=BEM), and particularly its baptismal section.[6] The Methodist Church in Ireland notes an insufficient distinction 'between a sign and that which it signifies'. The Presbyterian Church in Ireland asserts 'an indirect identity between grace and baptism', so that 'baptism does not as such effectuate salvation' but is its – by no means 'automatic' – sign. The (Anglican) Church of Ireland finds in the Lima text a 'balanced and comprehensive' theology of baptism but regrets that the document is not clearer that the sacraments are '*effective* signs'. The Roman Catholic response finds that the Lima text 'has many affinities, both of style and of content, with the way the faith of the Church about baptism is stated in the Second Vatican Council and in the *Liturgy of Christian Initiation* promulgated by Pope Paul VI'; the gifts which Lima says baptism 'signifies and effects' are endorsed, and yet 'despite many important points made about the meaning of baptism, there seems to be lack of clarity on the full effect of baptism'. The Irish Presbyterians appear to regret the absence of the word 'sacrament', while the Roman Catholic response, acknowledging that that word 'because of its complex history needs a great deal of explanation in interchurch conversations', finds that Lima affirms 'the principal features of baptism that the word sacrament has served to express'. The Irish Presbyterians suspect Lima of affirming 'baptismal regeneration which we do not and cannot accept'; the Church of Ireland notes, apparently with regret, that 'Anglicans will find little reference to baptism as the sacrament of regeneration'. The Church of Ireland finds Lima 'a very positive document, admirable in its comprehensiveness, its honesty of approach, and its economy of style. As an effort in reconciliation, it deserves our serious consideration. It does not attempt to cover over differences, nor is it superficial in searching for areas of agreement.' On the other hand, the Presbyterian Church in Ireland, while finding in the Lima section on baptism 'more evidence of Biblical and Reformed emphasis' than in the sections on eucharist and ministry, detects much that is 'obscure', 'unfamiliar', 'unclear' and 'ambiguous' and judges that 'the Report in its main thrust presents us with a model and conception of the Christian faith with which we find it difficult if not impossible to identify. Briefly, it gives priority to the "Catholic" over the "Protestant" view, to historical continuity and tradition over the witness of Scripture, to the sacraments over the Word, to a view of the Church centred more on rites than on proclamation and witness.'

Nevertheless, the Presbyterian Church in Ireland affirms what Lima says under the heading 'Towards Mutual recognition of Baptism': 'Churches are increasingly recognizing one another's baptism as the one baptism into Christ ... Mutual recognition of baptism is acknowledged as an important sign and means of expressing the baptismal unity given in Christ. Wherever possible, mutual recognition should be expressed explicitly by the churches.'

The current promise and tension regarding mutual recognition is expressed in the comment of the Methodist Church in Ireland on the baptismal section of BEM: 'The statement is to be welcomed as a means to greater understanding among the members of the WCC. And the inclusion within the commission of theologians of the Roman Catholic and other churches which do not belong to the WCC is both welcome and important, since it holds open the possibility of a coming together into one body of brethren at present separated.' What measure of doctrinal agreement ('greater understanding') is necessary? And what else is needed for integration of/into (the) 'one body'? Paragraph 6 of BEM, and its internal commentary, are crucial:

Through baptism, Christians are brought into union with Christ, with each other and with the Church of every time and place. Our common baptism, which unites us to Christ in faith, is thus a basic bond of unity . . . When baptismal unity is realized in one holy, catholic, apostolic Church, a genuine Christian witness can be made to the healing and reconciling love of God. Therefore, our one baptism into Christ constitutes a call to the churches to overcome their divisions and visibly manifest their fellowship.

Commentary: The inability of the churches mutually to recognize their various practices of baptism as sharing in the one baptism, and their actual dividedness in spite of mutual baptismal recognition, have given dramatic visibility to the broken witness of the Church . . . The need to recover baptismal unity is at the heart of the ecumenical task . . .

Clearly, baptism cannot be abstracted from its dogmatic and ecclesiological context. That is why baptism and *faith* must be considered concomitantly as factors in the reconciliation of Christian communities and the restoration of churchly unity.

In his open *Letter to a Roman Catholic,* written from Dublin in 1749, John Wesley made a plea for mutual affection and help, even though (as he would say in the more broadly addressed contemporaneous sermon on *Catholic Spirit*) differences in serious theological opinion, mode of worship, and church government 'may prevent an entire external union'.[7] In setting out the basis for what he proposes to the Roman Catholic, Wesley says first: 'I think you deserve the tenderest regard I can show, were it only because the same God hath raised you and me from the dust of the earth and has made us both capable of loving and enjoying him to eternity; were it only because the Son of God has bought you and me with his own blood.' And then Wesley continues with a 'how much more', based on a large measure of *common faith.* He expounds what 'a true Protestant' believes in the form of an expansion upon the Nicene-Constantinopolitan creed. Taking up the Wesleyan precedent, the current Joint Commission between the Roman Catholic Church and the World Methodist Council, in its 1991 Singapore Report on *The Apostolic Tradition,* calls this creed, which is 'used by both Catholics and Methodists in their liturgy and teaching', 'a comprehensive and authoritative statement of Christian faith', which 'constrains us to take very seriously the degree of communion that Catholics and Methodists already share'.[8] On the multilateral ecumenical scene, the WCC Faith and Order study 'Towards the Common Expression of the Apostolic Faith Today' took the same creed as its 'theological basis and methodological tool', working – by way of an exposition of its historical origin, its scriptural ground, and its contemporary relevance – towards an ecumenical recognition, explication and confession of this classic summary of Christian belief.[9]

Would a solemn reaffirmation of the ancient ecumenical creed constitute sufficient dogmatic agreement for the restoration of full unity? Apparently not, given the kind of response made by the Vatican in 1991 to the 1982 'Final Report' of the Anglican-Roman Catholic International Commission.[10] Yet the real nub may finally prove itself to be, not so much the doctrine (say) of the eucharist or even of the Trinity, but rather ecclesiology – the doctrine of the Church and the concrete claims and perceptions of ecclesial identity.[11]

Summing up the present section of this chapter, we may conclude that some kind of mutual recognition of baptism and some measure of agreement in the faith is *necessary* to reconciliation, and that some kind of mutual recognition of baptism and some measure of agreement in the faith make reconciliation *possible*. Can we now envisage a process that would in fact, perhaps by stages, *realize* reconciliation – starting from the basis of the kind(s) of mutual recognition of baptism and the measure(s) of agreement in the faith that have persisted or been attained, and moving towards the fuller communion that properly belongs to the Church as the body of Christ?

III.   A Process of Reconciliation

Here I would like to suggest a process that moves from division through repentance and reconciliation to eventual communion. Maximizing whatever recognition of baptism and agreement in faith exist, let us contemplate a penitential procedure that should lead to peace and joy.

First, it is essential to register the gravity of the sin of division. Since dominical authority attaches to it, it may suffice to evoke the saying of Jesus at Matthew 5:23f., which has traditionally been employed to authorize and require an 'exchange of peace' before participation in the eucharist:

If you are offering your gift at the altar, and there remember that your brother has something against you, leave your gift there before the altar and go; first be reconciled to your brother, and then come and offer your gift.[12]

In so far as baptism and faith have established brotherhood and sisterhood between Christians and their communities, there is a clear warning that offending parties who have not sought reconciliation after a division in the family approach God only at the risk of rejection. Disunity among Christians is thoroughly castigated in the apostolic writings, by St. Paul especially. In fact, it gives the lie to their baptisms (1 Cor.1:10–17); it turns the Lord's supper into their own supper and brings the offenders under divine judgement (1 Cor. 11:17–34). This disunity can only be overcome by drawing again on the one Spirit by whom they were baptized into Christ (1 Cor 12:12f.) and by whom they confess Christ as Lord (1 Cor. 12:3).

But who is the offending party? A hint may perhaps be found in the text of St. James, which Catholics have seen as scriptural and apostolic support for a sacrament of penance (and healing): 'Confess your sins to one another, and pray for one another, that you may be healed' (Jas. 5:16). Certainly, hindsight usually reveals that the fault in any division – even though truth may have been at stake in a matter of doctrinal conflict – did not reside on one side alone. Even though one side rather than the other may somehow be 'proved right' in a matter of faith, the responsibility for the disruption will usually have been complex – and shared. Mutuality in confession of sin may therefore be appropriate between divided Christians and their communities.

In the case of an individual Christian coming to confession, penance involves – after recognition of the gravity of sin – the admission of fault, contrition (or sorrow for the offence), and resolution to amend. Modern ecumenical history displays some striking examples of this by communities vis-à-vis divisions among them, and even of the mutual asking of forgiveness. The 'sacramental' implications of such cases have not been fully appreciated, nor the full consequences drawn for reconciliation and the eventual restoration of communion.

Note the words addressed by Pope Paul VI, at the opening of the second session of Vatican II on 29 September 1963, to the observers 'from the Christian denominations separated from the Catholic Church':

If we are in any way to blame for this separation, we humbly beg God's forgiveness. And we ask our brothers' pardon for any injuries they feel they have sustained from us. For our part we willingly forgive whatever injuries the Catholic Church has suffered, and forget the grief she has endured as a result of the long years of dissension and separation. May the heavenly Father deign to honour our prayers and grant us true brotherly peace.[13]

In their 'common declaration' of 7 December 1965, Pope Paul VI and Ecumenical Patriarch Athenagoros I expressed 'regret for historical errors':

They regret the offensive words, the reproaches without foundation and the reprehensible gestures which on both sides marked or accompanied the sad events of that period [i.e. 1054] . . . They deplore the troublesome precedents and the later events which, under the influence of various factors, among them lack of understanding and mutual hostility led to the effective rupture of ecclesiastical communion.[14]

In his visit to the land of Luther in 1980, Pope John Paul II said of the history of division:

'We will not pass judgement on one another' (Rom. 14:13). But let us mutually confess our guilt. With respect to the grace of unity also, it is a fact that 'all have sinned' (Rom. 3:23). We must recognize and acknowledge that fact in all seriousness and draw the appropriate conclusions . . . If we do not try to avoid the facts, we will realise that human failings are to blame for the harmful division of Christians, and that our own refusals have time and again hindered the steps that are possible and necessary to unity.[15]

What is being looked for here includes what was called, in an Irish School of Ecumenics study, the 'reconciliation of memories',[16] an idea taken up in the dialogue between the Roman Catholic Church and the World Alliance of Reformed Churches.[17] There is also an implicit recognition of the divine judgement under which as Christians we presently stand on account of our persistence in division. At its gravest, schism dismembers the body of Christ. Even on a more moderate view, divisions inflict wounds on the body. At the very least, Christian disunity is a sickness of the body, and even chronic illnesses can be life-threatening. The mood is well caught by the moving prayer from the troubled England of the seventeeth century which has found its way into several subsequent editions and versions of the Book of Common Prayer:

> O God the Father of our Lord Jesus Christ, our only Saviour, the Prince of Peace: Give us grace to lay to heart the great dangers we are in by our unhappy divisions; take away all hatred and prejudice, and whatever else may hinder us from godly union and concord; that, as there is but one Body and one Spirit, one hope of our calling, one Lord, one Faith, one Baptism, one God and Father of us all, so we may be all of one heart and of one soul, united in one holy bond of truth and peace, of faith and charity, and may with one mind and one mouth glorify thee; through Jesus Christ our Lord.[18]

Repentance and reconciliation look finally to the future, where the amendment of life may take place.

A first step in the future may be the solemn exchange of peace. Dating from the 'holy kiss' encouraged by St. Paul as a greeting (Rom. 16:16; 1 Cor. 16:20; 2 Cor. 13:12; 1 Thess. 5:26; cf. 1 Peter 5:14), Christian communities have included in their assemblies, under several forms and with various accompanying formulations, a gesture that liturgiologists call 'the peace'. In a recent study of *The Ritual Kiss in Early Christian Worship*, L. Edward Phillips identifies several themes that could be interesting if we were envisaging an exchange of peace on the part of Christian leaders and members as a regular feature, or a special stage, in a process of reconciliation among divided ecclesial bodies.[19] Phillips places the kiss in the context of the Pauline and Johannine notion of the Church as a community of persons who both 'share and communicate' the indwelling Spirit given by Christ, the Holy Spirit ('holy breath'). In line with this, the kiss is seen by patristic writers as both 'a demonstration of union already present' and 'a means of union': Cyril of Jerusalem, for instance, says that the kiss 'joins souls together in search of complete forgiveness from one another', it is 'a sign of the fusion of souls, and of the expulsion of all resentment for wrongs', it is 'a reconciliation'.[20] The kiss is not only given by the bishop to the newly baptized, who then share for the first time in the congre-

gational kiss (thus in the so-called *Apostolic Tradition of Hippolytus*);
it is also given by the bishop at the reconciliation of penitents (so St.
Cyprian of Carthage, for whom the kiss of peace indeed prefigures
'the embrace and kiss of the Lord [*complexum et osculum Domini*]' in
heaven).[21] According to the Byzantine liturgy of St. Chrysostom, the
exchange of peace is a summons to 'love one another in order that
we may with one heart and mind confess the Father, Son and Holy
Spirit, consubstantial and undivided Trinity' – a confession which
is then immediately enacted in the recitation of the Nicene-
Constantinopolitan Creed before the anaphora or great eucharistic
prayer proper; but Phillips suggests, on the basis of geographically
scattered hints, that the greeting at the kiss of peace may originally
have constituted the opening exchange of the dialogue introducing the anaphora itself[22] – and the anaphora is the supreme
doxological confession of the Holy Trinity. Taking into consideration the associated themes of the Holy Spirit, baptism, reconciliation, unanimous confession of faith and praise of God, and the
anticipation of the consummation, it would appear that there is
room for the imaginative and productive use of the 'kiss' or
exchange of peace by historically divided Christian communities on
their way from mutual recognition of baptism to the joyful restoration of full eucharistic communion.

Conclusion: Witness in the World

The Joint Commission between the Roman Catholic Church and
the World Methodist Council envisages its dialogue as working
towards the goal of 'full communion in faith, mission, and sacramental life'.[23] Deepening mutual recognition of baptism and increasing agreement in the faith as a prelude to eventual eucharistic
communion can allow already for some cooperation in mission.
The progress of reconciliation can itself help to render more
credible the witness made to the gospel, for Jesus prayed 'that they
may all be one, that *the world may believe that thou hast sent me*' (John
17:21).

The Irish Church and churches have historically played a prominent part in the spread of the gospel, from the early evangeliza-
tion of Britain and continental Europe to the worldwide modern
missionary movement. In modern times, India was a choice spot
for their contribution; and so it may be appropriate to receive
back from there a testimony from the Church of South India,

which in 1947 brought together the fruit of labours on the part of missionary societies belonging to separated churches in the home countries (Anglican, Congregational, Methodist, Presbyterian). Here, then, is a prayer from the 'Order of Service for the Inauguration of Church union in South India'. *Mutatis mutandis*, it might be prayed in Ireland:

Almighty and everlasting God, who alone art the author of unity, peace and concord, we thank Thee for the Churches in this our land and for Thy grace in choosing us to be members in Thy Church. We bless Thee for our fellowship, and for our rich inheritance. We praise Thee for Thy messengers from other lands who have brought the gospel of Thy kingdom to this land, and for those who have faithfully proclaimed it to succeeding generations, and for all who have prayed and laboured for the union of Churches, especially in South India. Thou hast heard the prayers of Thy people and blessed the labours of Thy servants, and hast brought us to this day for the glory of Thy name. In obedience to Thy will and led by Thy Spirit, as we accept one another as fellow members and fellow ministers, do Thou strengthen the bonds between us and unite us and make us one body, Thyself, O Christ, being its head. Make us all of one heart and of one soul, united in one holy bond of truth and peace, of faith and charity. Grant that this Church may ever be zealous in commending Thy glorious gospel to the millions in this land, that India may find in Thee the goal of all her seeking and the fulfilment of her noblest aspirations. Hasten the time, O God, when throughout the world there shall be one flock, one shepherd, and in the name of Jesus every knee shall bow, and every tongue confess that Jesus Christ is Lord. Amen.

A Personal Epilogue

An earlier Yorkshireman, the Carolingian Alcuin, wrote to the Christians in Ireland on the obligation to preach the orthodox faith, on the Lord's command to love one another, and on the fruitfulness of confession and penance while this life lasts.[24] If I have dared to do the same in the cause of reconciliation, it is only because my own British Methodist Church is implicated in the sin of ecclesial division, and because the need for Christian unity, and the ecumenical search for it, are worldwide.

I have here deliberately treated the theme of 'Reconciliation: Irish and Ecumenical' in confessional and ecclesiastical terms. This does not imply that one can ignore social, cultural, psychological, economic and political differences and conflicts – what were, at an earlier stage in the modern ecumenical movement, exaggeratedly called '*non*-theological factors'. My thesis, however, is that faith, sacraments and ecclesiology engage human life at a more fundamental and decisive level than the social, cultural, psychological, economic and political. They set us directly *coram Deo*. The divine revelation and redemption told in the canonical Christian story provides a framework in which penultimate differences can be discussed; and, as progress is made in reconciliation in matters of faith, sacraments and Church, there emerges a hope for the resolution of those other conflicts in a gospel light. In other words, my bet is that water, bread and wine are more potent symbols than sashes, berets and flags. Hands lifted in prayer or laid on heads in forgiveness and healing are closer to reality than hands that plant bombs or squeeze triggers. The kiss of peace is more significant than a political pact, for which, however, it may lay the ground. If these things are not the case, then ultimately we are all losers.

NOTES

1 Latin in F. E. Warren, *The Liturgy and Ritual of the Celtic Church*, Oxford, Clarendon Press, 1881, p. 151f.

2 From the Poenitentiale Sangallense simplex, Latin in Herm. Jos. Schmitz, *Die Bussbücher und das kanonische Bussverfahren – nach handschriftlichen Quellen dargestellt*, original publication Düsseldorf, Schwann, 1898; reprint Graz, Akademische Druck- und Verlagsanstalt, 1958, p. 340; cf. pp. 177, 345. English translation from John T. McNeill and Helena M. Gamer, *Medieval Handbooks of Penance: A Translation of the Principal 'Libri Poenitentiales' and Selections from Related Documents*, New York, Columbia University Press, 1938, p. 280f.

3 *Glenstal Bible Missal*, London, Collins, 1983, p. 1593.

4 From the 'Hymns and Sacred Poems' of 1742 (*The Poetical Works of John and Charles Wesley* ed. by G. Osborn, volume 2, London, Wesleyan-Methodist Conference Office, 1869, p. 323f.). The hymn 'Arise, my soul, arise', number 368 in *The Methodist Hymn Book* (London, 1933), has regrettably been altered in *Hymns and Psalms: A Methodist and Ecumenical Hymn Book* (London, Methodist Publishing House, 1983), hymn number 217.

5 For Wesley, see Geoffrey Wainwright, *The Ecumenical Moment: Crisis and Opportunity for the Church*, Grand Rapids (Michigan), Eerdmans, 1983, pp. 207–9.

6 *Baptism, Eucharist and Ministry*, Faith and Order Paper No. 111, Geneva,

World Council of Churches, 1982. The official responses of the churches are gathered in *Churches Respond to BEM* ed. by Max Thurian, six volumes, Geneva, WCC, 1986–88. The Church of Ireland response is found in volume 1, pp. 61–69, the Methodist Church in Ireland in volume 2, pp. 230–235, the Presbyterian Church in Ireland in volume 3, pp 206–221, the worldwide Roman Catholic Church in volume 6, pp. 1–40.

7 See *John Wesley's Letter to a Roman Catholic* ed. by Michael Hurley, London, Chapman, and Belfast, Epworth House, 1968. Sermon 39, 'Catholic Spirit', is found in the Bicentennial Edition of *The Works of John Wesley*, volume 2 ed. by Albert C. Outler, Nashville, Abingdon, 1985, pp. 81–95.

8 Joint Commission between the Roman Catholic Church and the World Methodist Council, *The Apostolic Tradition*, Lake Junaluska (North Carolina), World Methodist Council, 1991.

9 See *Confessing One Faith: Towards an Ecumenical Explication of the Apostolic Faith as Expressed in the Nicene-Constantinopolitan Creed (381)*, Faith and Order Paper No. 140, Geneva, World Council of Churches, 1987; revised as *Confessing the One Faith: An Ecumenical Explication of the Apostolic Faith as it is Confessed in the Nicene-Constantinopolitan Creed (381)*, Faith and Order Paper No. 153, Geneva, WCC, 1991.

10 Text in *Origins* 21 (1991-92), pp. 441ff.

11 It was above all an *ecclesiological* insufficiency that the Roman Catholic response found in BEM (see Geoffrey Wainwright, 'The Roman Catholic Response to *Baptism, Eucharist and Ministry*: The Ecclesiological Dimension' in *A Promise of Presence: Studies in Honor of David N. Power, O.M.I.* ed. by Michael Downey and Richard Fragomeni, Washington, D.C., The Pastoral Press, 1992, pp. 187–206). The international bilateral dialogues turned to the theme of the Church in the 1980s – especially where the Roman Catholic Church was one of the partners, as with the Orthodox (*The Mystery of the Church*, 1982), the Methodists (*Towards a Statement on the Church*, 1986; *The Apostolic Tradition*, 1991), the Anglicans (*Salvation and the Church*, 1986; *The Church as Communion*, 1991), and the Reformed (*Towards a Common Understanding of the Church*, 1991).

12 Didache 14:1f. reads: 'On the Lord's day of the Lord, come together, break bread, and give thanks, having first confessed your transgressions, that your sacrifice may be pure. But let none who has a quarrel with his companion join with you until they have been reconciled, that your sacrifice may not be defiled' (cf. *Apostolic Consitutions* II.57.16 and VIII.12.2). In Eastern churches, the 'peace' occurs before the eucharistic anaphora; and the following patristic writers appeal to Matt. 5:23f. in that connexion: Irenaeus, *Adversus Haereses* IV.18.1; Cyril of Jerusalem, *Mystagogical Catecheses* V.3f.; John Chrysostom, *Baptismal Instruction* XI (Papadopoulos-Kerameus 3), 32–34 (see Paul W. Harkins, *St. John Chrysostom: Baptismal Instructions*, Ancient Christian Writers volume 31, Westminster (Maryland), Newman Press,1963, p. 171f.; Theodore of Mopsuestia, *Catechetical Homily* 15 = *Baptismal Homily* 4, 40 (see Edward Yarnold, *The Awe-Inspiring Rites of Initiation: Baptismal Homilies of the Fourth Century*, Slough, St. Paul Publications, 1972, p.234); Narsai, *Homily* 17 (R. H. Connolly, *The Liturgical Homilies of Narsai*, Cambridge, The University Press, 1909, p. 9). According to St. Augustine (*Sermon* 227; PL 38, 1099–1101), in early fifth-century North Africa the *pax* occurred just before communion, perhaps having been attracted to that position by the petition in the Lord's Prayer said at that point ('Forgive us our trespasses, as we forgive them that

trespass against us'); cf. perhaps already Tertullian, who also cites Matthew 5:23f. (*de oratione* 11; PL 1, 1269–70). This eventually became the Roman order: eucharistic prayer, Lord's prayer, (Agnus Dei), peace, communion.

13 English translation from *Council Speeches of Vatican II* ed. by Y. Congar, H. Küng, D. O'Hanlon, Glen Rock (New Jersey), Paulist Press, 1964, p. 146f.

14 French text in *Acta Apostolicae Sedis* 58 (1966), p. 20f.

15 German in *Papst Johannes Paulus in Deutschland* (Verlautbarungen des Apostolischen Stuhls 25), Bonn, 1980, pp. 80 and 86.

16 *Reconciling Memories* ed. by Alan D. Falconer, Dublin, The Columba Press, 1988.

17 *Towards a Common Understanding of the Church: Reformed/Roman Catholic International Dialogue: Second Phase, 1984–1990*, Geneva, World Alliance of Reformed Churches, 1991.

18 This 'prayer for unity' was included in the 1878 and 1926 versions of the Book of Common Prayer of the Church of Ireland (in the latter it was indeed promoted to first place among the 'prayers and thanksgivings [upon several occasions]'). Regrettably, no real equivalent is found in the Irish *Alternative Prayer Book* of 1984.

19 L. Edward Phillips, *The Ritual Kiss in Early Christian Worship* (Ph.D. dissertation, University of Notre Dame), Ann Arbor (Michigan), University Microfilms International, 1992.

20 Cyril of Jerusalem, *Mystagogical Catecheses* V.3 (see Edward Yarnold, *The Awe-Inspiring Rites of Initiation*, as in note 12, p.88f.); cf. Phillips, pp. 239f., 263f.

21 See Phillips, pp. 99–110, with reference to *Apostolic Tradition*, 18 and 21; and p. 131f., with reference to Cyprian, *Epistles* 6, 37, and 55.

22 See Phillips, pp. 196–212.

23 As in note 11: *Towards a Statement on the Church* (1986), §20; *The Apostolic Tradition* (1991), §94.

24 Alcuin, *Epistula* 225 (Ad fratres qui in Hibernia insula per diversa loca Deo deservire videntur), PL 100, 500–503; cf. Stephen Allott, *Alcuin of York*, York, William Sessions, 1974, pp. 45–47. Alcuin himself, who 'had shriving and being shriven very much at heart', was influential in the spread of the Irish practice of frequent penance in England and on the European continent (see Gerald Ellard, *Master Alcuin, Liturgist*, Chicago, Loyola University Press, 1956, pp. 207–209).

A RESPONSE

Thomas Corbett

Dr Wainwright's illuminating paper has shown how the atoning work of Christ has reconciled us to God and that 'acceptance of reconciliation to God sets one in a community where reconciliation among members is the norm'.[1] Christians through faith and baptism are entrusted with a mission of reconciliation which has made a great impact on recent world history by the development of closer ties and deeper mutual understanding between many christian churches and by the impetus it gave to christians to share the Gospel of grace and reconciliation with the troubled world of the end of the twentieth century. Dr Wainwright has noted, for example, the renewing interest in the Lima report among the churches but correctly adds that 'the real nub (of the process of reconciliation) may finally prove itself to be, not so much the doctrine (say) of the eucharist or even of the Trinity, but rather ecclesiology—the doctrine of the church and the concrete claims and perceptions of ecclesial identity'.[2]

A terrifying aspect of human history has been the capacity of human beings to wrangle and fight, to promote fear and hatred of the other, to wage war and to kill. The Irish capacity for 'splitting' has many counterparts in all societies and unfortunately the christian churches have not been exempted from this human condition. St. Paul's letters are clear testimony that from the beginning christians were unable to avoid strife and division. Because faith is both a gift of God and the free response of a human being it is never lived in isolation from the concrete historical, social, cultural and economic environments in which it is received and exercised. Religious differences then often express and are compounded by other factors and as here in Ireland political, social and economic divisions are superimposed on them. But, without being unduly pessimistic, from the beginning it was so!

Protestant and British, Catholic and Irish – these shibboleths have on the one hand endangered the christian vision by serious contraction and on the other have diminished the contribution one or other could make or felt free to make to the welfare and development of the wider community. The grace of the gospel was imprisoned by the fear of the Protestant community that 'ecumenism' would lead to a loss of their Britishness. On the other hand the experience of Catholics as unwelcome in their own country and not involved in the development of the governmental structures that ruled their lives made them look to their church for community rather than for a seemingly unproductive 'ecumenism'. Nobody was about to surrender!

In this context, then, Dr. Wainwright has again noted very accurately, that while ecclesiology may be the nub, it is impossible to exclude 'non-theological' factors when one seeks a complete understanding of the experience of a divided faith in the Irish situation. One may be, indeed as a christian believer in the risen Lord, one has to be convinced that 'hands lifted up in prayer or laid on heads in forgiveness are closer to reality than hands that plant bombs and squeeze triggers.'[3] but I think one truly lives the powerlessness of the cross when one faces the churches' failure, as Cardinal O'Fiaich noted, 'to secure the overall objective of a just and lasting peace. Perhaps we should have realized that the power of the churches to provide solutions in this field is strictly limited'.[4]

The churches in Ireland have had considerable success, I am sure, in the eyes of God, who, through their ministry, has seen the Gospel preached, grace and sacrament accepted, and human lives ennobled. The churches in the country, as we are glad to acknowledge, have been faithful servants of their own people and have been recognized by the majority as such. The churches, however, are also called to serve their Lord, not only by their faithfulness to their own but in their wholehearted commitment to the Kingdom he died to further and to the Spirit which he sent on rising from the dead. Jesus came not just to bring souls to justification and heaven but to refashion creation, to draw all things to himself. 'The Spirit of the Lord is upon me'. That spirit sent Jesus into the desert to fight the demons of power, pride and greed not just for each of us but for all of us.

And how might the churches continue the battle in the modern desert of frustrated human hopes? Dr. Wainwright mentioned the special contribution made to India by the Irish churches. In return I would like to let Indian insight help us. In a recent book *Responding to Communalism:The Task of Religions and Theology* edited by S. Arokiasamy, S. J.,[5] there is an extensive analysis of communalism which the writers perceive as a growing evil in the subcontinent. Competing segments of the population are identified by their religious affiliation and communalism is described as follows: 'A group becomes communal when they feel that because they belong to the same religion, they have the same economic, social and political interests . . . which must be defended as such.'[6] The very essence of communalism is 'a sharp divide between communities each pulling apart from the others and feeling superior, inferior, aggrieved, hostile to each other.'[7]

The contributors point to the dangers of communalism: the threat of religious belief being manipulated for merely party political purposes rather than serving to bring people to worship and the obedience of faith and to promoting justice, truth and love for all. There is the added danger that religious faith may surrender its trust in the goodness and power of God and be thereby reduced to self-reliance and seeking security in some thing less than God. Of course in the dramatic tension humans experience between trust in God and relying on oneself or the group we must ask at all times what we discern as Godlike and where the Gospel directs us.

Here the contrasting communities of response identified by Rosemary Haughton in her book *The Transformation of Man*[8] may be helpful. Her 'transformed community', exemplified by the radical Protestants of the 17th century who could not live under the Stuarts, was devout and resistant (and sometimes self-righteous) while her 'community of formation', exemplified by the Benedictines, was obedient and humble as they waited for grace (even if sometimes a little tepid and conformist). The contrast between an 'ecclesiology of the elect' and an 'ecclesiology of the being redeemed' is in question here. What we are asked today is to refocus our vision to see that God is calling us to accept his spirit which renews creation rather than just relive memories that keep us separate in our own needs and fears.

The Indian theologians are confronting the increasing communalism with the sometimes agonised recollection of the 'exclusivist' claims that christianity made in the past and are asking for an understanding which is more welcoming and universal. They call for a shift in evangelisation so that 'the main aim will be rather that as many people as possible live a selfless life of love and service for the well-being, freedom and happiness of their fellowmen and thus be encountered by the living God.'[9]

They ask us as followers of Christ to recognize the great differences and human failings which separate us but at the same time to be at least open to the possibility of receiving God's blessings of reconciliation in dialogue and hope. In Ireland we must try to take further steps to make all christians on the island more aware of the full demands of service of the Kingdom of God (and not of any other kingdom), so that segments of christians are not distant from each other and from the full responsibility of baptismal life. We must give recognition to the human rootedness of faith but also to the power of grace. Most of all we must attempt more critically and consciously to measure our real goals and achievements as christian churches by the standards of the Lord, who died and rose for all, not for any particular group.[10] Religion and politics are intimately related through their intersection in the concrete life of humanity but the transcendent element must reach beyond the interests and needs of any one church or group to serve the call and grace of God in a world rendered graceless by violence, greed and fear.

The historian may rightly ask if christians are speaking a new language granted the persecutions and harassments of the past. History is a sad witness that christian love and grace have had many faces and many frowns. To be truly universal in one's love and truly accepting of the other without fear is not achieved without welcoming God's love into life. And if our human failings and our refusals hinder greater unity (the words are Pope John Paul's) we are asked to believe that 'where sin abounded grace did more abound.' The idolatries of nation and party as well as the fears of threatened humans are redeemable; bread and wine can become more powerful if we work together at being christian people as both Catholics and Protestants. If this is not true and lived as truth then we are truly in deeper trouble than we think. And others may provide the salvation that we could not.

NOTES

1 Above p. 76.
2 Above p. 80.
3 Above p. 86.
4 McEvoy, J., Ecumenism in Northern Ireland, *The Month*, 17 (1984), p. 229.
5 Published by Gujarat Sahitya Prakash, Anand, 1992.

6 Arokiasamy, *op. cit.*, p. 120.
7 Arokiasamy, *op. cit.*, p. 109.
8 As mentioned by Gabriel Daly in Alan Falconer (ed), *Reconciling Memories* Dublin, Columba Press, 1988, pp. 110–112.
9 Arokiasamy, *op. cit.*, p. 296.
10 See E. McDonagh, *The Furrow* 1979, pp 19–30 and John Thompson in *The Irish Theological Quarterly*, 1992, pp. 264–75.

ECOLOGY AND RECONCILIATION

Céline Mangan

Introduction

There is a passage in the Book of Hosea in the Bible which speaks
of the interaction between God, the world and human beings:

> Hear the word of the Lord, O people of Israel;
> For the Lord has a controversy with the inhabitants of the land.
> There is no faithfulness or kindness, and no knowledge of God
>   in the land;
> There is swearing, lying, killing, stealing and committing
>   adultery;
> They break all bounds and murder follows murder.
> Therefore the land mourns, and all who dwell in it languish,
> And also the beasts of the field, and the birds of the air;
> And even the fish of the sea are taken away (Hos 4:1–3).

It would seem to me that we have a blueprint in this passage for a
consideration of reconciliation in relation to ecology. In the past
we have tended to interpret the Bible, and religion in general, as
dealing largely with how things are between God and human
beings but I think what a passage like this brings out is that when
human beings are 'out of sync' with God and with one another the
relationship with the earth is also soured. In this paper I would like
to spend some time with these three elements: **God, human beings
and the world** to see something of what needs to be done to make
reconciliation with the earth possible.

Because our past understanding of religion has tended to contain only two of these elements, God and us, we have understood
the biblical call to justice as a call to be just towards other people,
especially the poor and the marginalised. It is increasingly clear,
however, that justice also includes responsibility for the environ-

ment as a part of justice for the poor: 'There is no way we can attend to the needs of people who are poor, marginalised, and oppressed unless we attend at the same time to the "poor" of endangered species, strip-mined hills, eroded croplands, polluted rivers, acidified lakes and gutted mountains.' [1]

On the other hand, God can be left out of the picture[2] and the problem seen as one between the earth and us. The way human beings have related to the world in recent centuries, in particular in the West, has, in general, been one of domination and exploitation. There is even a problem about how we relate to the world from an ecological viewpoint. Most of what Governments especially see as ecological initiatives are undertaken solely from the point of view of the self-interest of human beings: 'If we don't watch it,' they say, 'we will create an environment in which human beings can no longer live.' This is very true but we are not the only species in the world. We need a much deeper approach to reconciliation with the environment than that; we need to see ourselves as part of the whole, not separate from or over against the rest of the world but firmly within the world community of all that is.[3]

While the politicians continue to engage in crisis management, it is up to dedicated people of all persuasions to work out and model more creative and global answers about the relationship between all three elements I mentioned earlier: **human beings, the world *and* God**. The important word here is 'relationship' because it is increasingly being realized that inter-relatedness at all levels is at the heart of the Universe.[4] It is possible to see a whole network of relationships between these three elements, God, human beings and the world, and I propose to take some aspect of each of them in turn and see what it calls us to in the area of reconciliation:

I   Human beings to the world
       Human beings to God
       Human beings to other human beings;

II   God to the world
       God to human beings
       God to God;

III   The world to the world
       The world to human beings
       The world to God.

I Human Beings to the World

Thomas Berry, one of the first to alert religious people to what their theology has done to the earth, says that 'we must return again to a sense of the earth as nurturer of the human, as primary revelation of the divine, as educator, healer, ruler, as primary commercial enterprise, as primary norm of all human values and activities.'[5] The way the Bible has been interpreted down the centuries has unfortunately led us to have a very exploitative attitude to the world. A misreading of Genesis 1, the first account of creation in the Bible, has contributed to the malaise. In the beautiful story of God's creation of the world and all within it in seven days (Gen 1:–2:4a) we have tended to see the creation of the human on the sixth day as the apex of creation, thus giving humankind dominion and power over everything else. But a re-reading of Genesis in the light of the milieu in which it was written shows clearly that the movement of creation is circular in form. The overall structure is that of a six day working week with God resting on the seventh day. On the six workdays, the creation of the sun and moon on day 4 answers that of light on day 1; the birds of the air and the fish of the sea on day 5 people the firmament and the sea created on day 2; the animals and humans on day six people the earth created on day 3. Human beings play a part within the circle of creation rather than being the primary reason for the creation of the remainder. To quote Berry again and looking at the world from a scientific account of creation this time: 'The entire earth community is infolded in the compassionate curve whereby the universe bends inwardly in a manner suffi- ciently closed to hold all things together and yet remains suffi- ciently open so that compassion does not confine, but fosters, the creative process.'[6]

The words which have caused most difficulty from the first creation account of Genesis are the words 'dominion' and 'sub- due': 'And God said . . . "Be fruitful and multiply, and fill the earth and *subdue* it; and have *dominion* over the fish of the sea . . ."' (Gen 1:28, italics mine). The word *radah* which is translated as 'domin- ion' was part of the technical language of kingship (e.g. 1 Kgs 5:4; Ps 72:8; Isa 14:6) as ideally exercised (Isa 11:3–5): 'This means, in modern terms, a rational, sensible, humane, intelligent and thoughtful ordering of God's ordered world . . . a challenge to responsibility and the duty to make right prevail.'[7] The other word, *kabas*, can be translated as 'subjugate' but it is also to be interpreted as the ideal behaviour of the king in Israel: to shepherd, to have a care for his flock.[8] Truth generally has a hard time catching up with falsehood, therefore I think we must try to continually inculcate the understanding of the Genesis account of creation as one of human beings shepherding and caring for the earth rather than as dominating and exploiting it, if we are to come anywhere near a reconciliation between ourselves and the earth. We need also to supplement the Genesis account with other creation accounts which clearly show that the earth shepherds and cares for us as well as we for it.

Human Beings to God

The kind of assumptions we have about God are important for the way we live out our lives on the earth. As I was growing up the God I learnt about was largely a transcendent God, outside of the world, a God who would save me out of sin and darkness. The only reconciliation possible with such a God was to do all the right things commanded to ensure one went to Heaven and not to Hell after death. The past few decades have challenged these assumptions, especially in the Catholic Church since Vatican II, and we have learnt to relate to a God who is also immanent within the world. The Bible and Christian tradition have given us a God who is both transcendent and immanent but cultures down the centuries have tended to stress one or other exclusively. It suited us, especially, to put God outside the earth because we could then do what we liked with it. What is new in very recent times is the realization that our idea of God is strongly coloured by the kind of world in which we live: 'Why do we have such a wonderful idea of God? Because we live in such a gorgeous world . . . If we lived on the moon, for example, our sense of the divine would reflect the lunar landscape.'[9]

If we still relate to God merely in terms of saving our own souls we limit the possibility of reconciliation with the earth because our eyes will be blinkered to the situation of the world around us. We will be caught into systems which are increasingly causing the ruin and devastation of our planet. What we need to do, then, as human beings at this particular moment of history, is to expand our narrow understanding of a personal, saving God into that of an universal God. It is interesting in the Bible that whenever the

people of Israel limited their understanding of God, God burst
out of those bonds. This is what happened in the time of the
prophet Jeremiah, for example, when the people used the fact of
having the Temple in their midst as an insurance policy against
the intervention of God in their lives (see Jer 7). The Exile to
Babylon followed and they were left without Temple, king, land
and even God. But out of that debacle came a new and deeper
understanding of God, a God who was not their own personal
property but the God of the whole world.

Our times demand of us such a universalizing of our understanding of God. We need a new return from Exile out of our
narrow, personalistic spirituality to one which is now universal, not
only as regards people, but towards the earth as well. I would
recommend the book *Befriending the Earth*, as spelling out the new
asceticism that is needed for such a spirituality.[10]

Human Beings to Human Beings

I will not spend much time in this area as it is something that other
papers at this conference will deal with in depth. Present world
events leave us in no doubt of the difficulties involved in reconciliation between one group of people and another. Those of you
engaged in this difficult aspect of reconciliation, especially here in
Northern Ireland, know the crucifixion of it. For what is the cross
after all but the extension of arms, one to the warring party on the
right and the other to the left where the person in the middle ends
up torn apart as Jesus himself was: 'For he is our peace who has
made us both one, and has broken down the dividing wall of
hostility' (Eph 2:14).

II God to the World

The recurrent phrase in the first account of creation in Genesis,
'and God saw that it was good' (see Gen 1:4, 10, 12 . . .), refers
above all to God's delight in creation (see Ps 65:8; Prov 8:30–31)
but many of us today have a problem with the phrase. When we
look around the world we see that there is much that we would not
term good in the natural sphere: volcanoes, earthquakes, deserts,
crops ruined by locusts. How can we call such a world 'good'? I
think the problem is that we take 'good' to mean 'absolute good'

or 'perfect'. The world in which we live is not perfect but it is a world that is 'good enough' to sustain life.[11] To date our planet is the only world we know of in which the necessary conditions occur for the creation of human life: 'Conscious human beings have sprung from the original fireball. They are the elaboration of the potential already contained in the great primordial blaze of energy.'[12]

One of the legacies left by the interpretation of the world as absolutely good is the belief in the expectation of endless progress. Ours is a society that unconsciously desires the bigger, the better, the brighter, the whiter; we are caught into a treadmill of endless expectation in which suffering and death have no place. But this is not the real world, the world 'good enough to sustain human life'. Theories of psychology and personal development over the past few years have taught us how to acknowledge the shadow, the dark side of life, as part of our personalities but we must also accept the dark side of the earth, the shadow potential of cosmic suffering, into our understanding of the world. Death is part of life and the energy of those who have gone before us is part of the world energy which is available in our one planet. We are now breathing the same air that was breathed by those who have gone before us.[13] The Red Indians of North America had a great sense of the continuing relationship of the dead to the earth. The famous Chief Seattle, for example, who in 1854 had to deal with the attempt of the white men to buy Indian land, had this to say: 'Every part of this earth is sacred to my people . . . The white man's dead forget the country of their birth while they go to walk among the stars. Our dead never forget the beautiful earth, for it is the Mother of the red man.'[14]

God to Human Beings

A new look at the second account of creation in Genesis (Gen 2:4b–25) which stresses more the creation of human beings, still reveals a close interdependence of all the component parts of the world. The life of the human creature[15] is taken from the earth; so also is that of the plants and the animals. The human is asked 'to till' the earth and 'to keep' it, words which in their original meanings meant to give loving care and attention to something. The relationship as in Genesis I, is again one of caring steward-ship: 'A theological view of the human person within creation can only be a theology of inter-relatedness.'[16] This loving care of the earth as the original intention of the Creator for human beings was not to last and the remaining chapters of the primordial history in Genesis 1–11 show that the alienation of human beings from God meant alienation from the earth as well: alienation from the animals in the story of Genesis 3,[17] blood spilled calling out from the earth (Gen 4:10–11), the whole earth destroyed because of the sinfulness of human beings (Gen 6–8).

The pattern has repeated itself over and over in the history of the world. Those of us coming from European traditions, for example, have to beat our breasts at the rape of the New World by the adventurers from our side of the Atlantic, not to mention the wholesale despoliation of the African continent as witnessed most recently in the famine of Somalia. Maybe something practical we could do is to call repeatedly wherever we have influence for the total remission of the national debts of all Third World countries as some measure of reparation for the wrongs done in the past.

God to God

As we saw in an earlier section, a call to reconciliation is a call to ask ourselves what kind of a God we believe in. We can only think of God out of the language and thought patterns of our own culture and so the understanding of God we get in the Bible is hide-bound by the culture and ethos of the times in which it was written.[18] Modern liberation theologies and feminism have sought to go behind the patriarchy of the Bible to discover other ways of speaking about God which are not alienating.[19]

I think our own Celtic spirituality has much to offer us here. For example the Celts had an idea of undifferentiated *neart* (meaning 'power', 'strength' or 'energy') which was thought to pour itself out as the energies of the Sea, the rivers, the land. When Christianity came to Ireland this *neart* was quickly used as an understanding of who Jesus was as Word of God. The Word (*dabhar*) of God in the Prophets of the Bible meant much more than the spoken word – it connoted the power of God active in creation and salvation. The New Testament in speaking of Jesus as the Word of God points out that he is the new place where the energy of God is to be found in the world.[20]

The special revelation of God in Christ is central for Christians. John's Gospel speaks, in an analogous way, of the coming of Jesus, the Word of God, as a new creation. The 'In the beginning was the Word . . .' (Jn 1:1) takes up the *Bereshit* of Gen 1:1 and the events of Jesus' life in the Gospel are portrayed as happening within the framework of the seven days of creation: 'John brings me before the wonder of creation, a creation that Teilhard de Chardin began to understand when he wrote: "By means of all created things the divine assails us, penetrates us and molds us. We imagined it as distant and inaccessible, whereas we live steeped in its burning layers."'[21] The Epistles celebrate Christ at the heart of the cosmic processes (see Col 1:13–20; Eph 1:3–14) and show that his death and resurrection are not just for human beings but for the whole Earth (see Rom 8:18–23).[22] The implications of Jesus as the new creation have not yet been fully worked out in practice, for the simple reason that very soon after New Testament times the encounter of Christianity with Greek thought patterns set in motion the whole train of dualistic interpretation of the Bible which has led in recent centuries to such an exploitative attitude to the earth.[23]

III World to the World

Looking recently at an abandoned mineshaft which had gouged out the side of a hill on a mountainside, I was struck by the sight of two little meadows at the bottom of the hill which had escaped the devastation. Though seemingly abandoned by their owners because there was no easy access to them, they were bravely putting out sweet flowers and grasses each year at the very edge of the mine. As I asked myself whether there was any possibility of reconciliation between these two extremes, my eyes were arrested by clumps of furze and heather gradually overtaking the barrenness of the hillside though also encroaching on the meadows. Nature will always be trying to heal itself but it is extremely difficult to replace what is lost. But at least we should be making efforts to do so. A friend of mine home from South Africa told about a programme in the Cape Flats to try and cultivate the sand that is the only soil there: the people dig what they call grave pits, throw in refuse and more sand, then refuse again, allow it to ferment and in no time at all they are growing vegetables and flowers.

The desert and desertification can be reversed but slowly. It would be much better not to let the land go to waste in the first place. This is what the biblical notion of 'jubilee' calls us to: to allow the land to recover its strength after a period of harvesting (see Exod 23:10).[24] This recalls the resting of God on the seventh day of creation. Maybe we here in Ireland could consider the recent EC directive of 'set-aside' in a positive sense as a kind of jubilee for the land and our contribution to the mending of the earth? For it is not enough for us in the First World to preach to the poorer countries about the need to rest the land as often they have no choice: 'The issues of poverty, environment and development are intrinsically linked, forming a vicious circle. Poor people have no choice but to degrade their environment as, in order to survive, they over-exploit their natural resource base and, in so doing, deny future generations a protective environment.'[25]

But the over-exploitation which the poorer countries are doing to survive is nothing to what we in the West are perpetrating on a global scale. We in Ireland fear the recent round of GATT negotiations because of their implications for the Common Agricultural Policy of the EC, but we should also be worried about the presuppositions they carry with them and what that has to say to the environment. To quote *Care of the Earth* again: 'Since GATT is an instrument of macro-economics the agreement needs to take on board the environmental critique of the industrial and commercial policies which have been pursued, especially in northern countries, in recent decades. While these policies have brought higher living standards and more consumer goods to the minority of the world's population ... they have caused widespread and often irreversible damage to every ecosystem on the planet.'[26] And the environmental group, 'Earthwatch' has gone so far as to say that GATT is likely to 'herald the beginning of an environmental dark age.'[27]

The World and Humans Beings

Visiting my own native Kerry recently I was struck by the thought that my generation and culture are only a passing phase on the face of the landscape. The beautiful mountains, lakes and rivers were there before me; they will be there when my generation has passed on – or at least I hope they will. Our times are critical, I believe, as we have it within our power to slow down the irreversible pollution that is occurring daily in all our areas. At the World Women's Forum in Dublin last July an Indian economist, Dr. Devaki Jain, suggested that we change our way of speaking of world civilizations from *First-Second-Third World* into *waste-generating, waste-avoiding, waste-rejecting and waste-minimizing* societies. We need to learn to live more lightly on the land and many of us are aware now of some initial steps we could all take: reduce consumption, avoid disposable products, recycle products, avoid overpackaged products, avoid plastic bags, favour locally produced products, favour products made from recycled materials, favour natural coloured paper products over bleached products, favour small company products over multinational ones, avoid products which adversely affect the Third World.

Our biggest sin in relation to the world is what could be called 'fragmentation': we see the world out there in so many bits and pieces: mountains, rivers, this plant, this person, rather than as one flowing whole with its own interiority: 'What needs to be gauged in any environment is the types of intervention it can absorb and to what degree. One consequence of this, is the importance of learning to live within one's own locality, and not importing a life style with a set of demands that jeopardize one's local environment.'[28]

Ultimately, however, we should not get into the trap of thinking of an ecological reconciliation with nature in terms of moral obligation, binding us to the minimum of what we can get away with so as not to bring the world crashing down around our heads. Let us see instead the world around us, *inviting* us to identify with it 'in an orientation of steadfast (as opposed to fair-weather) friendliness. Steadfast friendliness manifests itself in terms of a clear and steady expression of positive interest, liking, warmth, goodwill, and trust; a steady predisposition to help or support; and, in the context of these attributes, a willingness to be firm and to criticize constructively where appropriate.'[29] As the Californian poet Robinson Jeffers says: 'This whole (Universe) is in all its parts so beautiful . . . that I am compelled to love it.'[30]

The World and God

A friend of mine uses the word 'wholth' for the kind of holiness we need today. It is a word that has reconciliation built into it, containing as it does 'healing', 'hale', 'health', 'hail', 'whole' and 'holy', all of which come from the same root. Our spirituality today should be one that is inclusive: 'We have to learn again to listen to our bodies, and to the Earth, and to see ourselves as companions with other creatures on a fragile planet.'[31] In this we will be imitating the world itself which is governed by the three principles of *bonding, interiority* and *differentiation*. These principles are also the essence of the traditional understanding of contemplation but we need to expand our concept of the God we contemplate 'out there' to include the context of the beautiful world to which we are heir. I think it is no accident that scientists today are often speaking the language of the mystics.[32] Maybe it is only when we too open our eyes to the wonders of God's relationship to our world that we will learn to be a people of reconciliation in relation to it at this time now.

Conclusion

What small steps can we take in the relationships we have outlined so that reconciliation can take place in this important area in our time? Those suggested in this paper would include:

(a) changing our sense of human beings as having the right to 'dominate' the world in the way Genesis 1 used to be understood; rather seeing ourselves as part of the global circle;

(b) considering the world as a 'good enough' place to support human life but fragile and needing our all-out cooperation if it is not to explode in our face;

(c) changing our image of God from one that is transcendent, outside the world to a more immanent image, involved with us, in the world;

(d) above all changing our image of ourselves to becoming people at the cutting edge of reconciliation with the world;

(e) becoming more aware of our local environment and answering the demands this will make on us: *think global; act local* has become the catchword of all environmental groups;

(f) on the political front, lobbying Governments to invite us to amend Constitutions to include protection of the environment as a basic right for the Earth: to put 'natural security' above 'national security'.[33]

NOTES

1 'Care of the Earth', Briefing of the Conference of Religious of Ireland for the Rio de Janeiro Earth Summit, Dublin: 1992, p. 4.

2 For example a recent book (P.W. Atkins, *Creation Revisited*, Oxford and New York: W.H. Freeman and Co., 1992) would see no reason for positing a creative God as being responsible for our Universe.

3 See W. Fox, *Towards a Transpersonal Ecology*, (Boston and London: Shambhala, 1990) for a discussion of the different kinds of approaches to ecology.

4 See F. Capra and D. Stindl-Rast, with T. Matus, *Belonging to the Universe*, London: Penguin, 1992.

5 T. Berry, 'Classical American Spirituality and the American Experience,' *Riverdale Papers VII*, Riverdale Center for Religious Research, New York, p. 13.

6 T. Berry, *The Dream of the Earth* San Francisco: Sierra Book Club, 1988, p. 20. See M. Dowd, *The Meaning of Life in the 1990's*, Ohio: Living Earth Christian Fellowship, 1990, pp. 29ff. D. Carroll, *Towards a Story of the Earth* (Dublin: Dominican Publications, 1986) spells out the key theological insights of the first account of creation (pp.25–27).

7 B.Vawter, *On Genesis A New Reading*, New York: Doubleday, 1977, p.59.

8 See T. F. Dailey, 'Creation and Ecology' *Irish Theological Quarterly* (1992) 5; S. McDonagh, *The Greening of the Church* pp. 120–121; A. Ganoczy, 'Ecological Perspectives in the Christian Doctrine of Creation' *Concilium* (1991) 45.

9 T. Berry, with T. Clarke, *Befriending the Earth A Theology of Reconciliation Between Humans and the Earth*, Mystic, Connecticut: Twenty-Third Publications, 1991, p. 9. See M. Fox, *Original Blessing*, New Mexico: Bear & Co., 1983, pp. 117ff.

10 T. Berry with T. Clarke, op. cit. pp. 40–55.

11 See S. McDonagh, *op. cit.* pp. 112ff for an understanding of the kind of world biblical people experienced and how this influenced the way in which they spoke of creation.

12 D. Edwards, *Creation, Humanity, Community. Building a New Theology*, Gill and Macmillian, 1992, pp. 38; See T. Berry, T. Clarke, *op. cit.* pp. 13–15.

13 M. T. McGillis, Lecture Notes, Termonfeckin, July 1992.

14 Chief Seattle, 'You must teach your children' in *The Earth Speaks*, van Matre, S. & Weiler, B., Warrenville: The Institute for Earth Education, 1983.

15 *ha'adam* (2:5ff) can be understood as the undifferentiated human being which in the episode of the rib (2:21–24) is then differentiated into male and female: see P. Trible, *God and the Rhetoric of Sexuality*, Philadelphia: Fortress, 1978, pp. 72–143.

16 D. Edwards, *op. cit.* p. 48.

17 The story of the sin of the man and woman in Genesis 3 has usually been called the 'Fall' story, but there are many Fall stories in Genesis 1–11: Cain and Abel; the Flood, the Tower of Babel, all are outlines of the sinfulness of human beings.

18 A recent book (R.B. Coote and M.P. Coote, *Power, Politics, and the Making of the Bible: An Introduction*, Minneapolis: Fortress, 1990) speaks of the Bible as an artifact of history. See McDonagh, op. cit., pp. 109–111.

19 See, for example, S. McFague, *Models of God Theology for an Ecological Nuclear Age*, London: SCM, 1987.

20 See J. Plevnik, *Word and Spirit*, Willowdale, Ontario: Regis College Press, 1975, pp. 113–149.

21 D. McGann, *The Gospel of John Through a Jungian Perspective*, London: Collins, 1988, p. 12. See M. E. Boismard, A. Lamoille, *L'Evangile de Jean*, Paris: Cerf, pp. 71–79.

22 See B. Byrne, *Inheriting the Earth: The Pauline Basis for a Spirituality for our Time*, Homebush, NSW: St. Paul, 1990.

23 For a good outline of the historical development involved see D. Carroll, *op.
    cit.* pp. 29–35; see also D. Senior, 'The Earth Story: Where does the Bible Fit
    in?' in A. Lonergan, C. Richards, *Thomas Berry and the New Cosmology*, Mystic,
    Connecticut: Fortress, 1987, pp. 41–50.
24 See J. Moltmann, 'Reconciliation with Nature', *Pacifica* 5 (1992) pp. 311–313.
25 *Care of the Earth*, p. 5.
26 *ibid.* p. 11.
27 See report in the *Irish Times*, February 8, 1993.
28 See B. Connor, 'Where can "The Integrity of Creation" be found?' *Grace and
    Truth* 1991/1992 92–107.
29 Fox, *op. cit.* p. 256.
30 Quoted in Fox, *op. cit.*, p. 256.
31 D. Edwards, *op. cit.* p. 50.
32 See F. Capra, *op. cit.*, pp. 135–139; Fox, *op. cit.* pp. 249–268.
33 See Moltmann, *op. cit.*, p. 310.

A RESPONSE

Julian G. Greenwood

In Ireland we are fortunate to be blessed with some of the most beautiful landscapes of the world, including the wonderfully moist oakwoodlands of Killarney in Kerry, the Gentian-strewn limestone pavements of the Burren in Clare, the romantic, rolling uplands of Donegal and the Giant's Causeway of the north Antrim coast. Any one of these places, or indeed any other place, could be used to illustrate how life on earth works, for that, in essence, is what we mean by ecology: the way that life on earth works. I shall, however, consider how life on earth works by considering my wood – a woodland near the heart of Belfast.

In my wood, I can see the ebb and flow of a multitude of living things throughout the seasons and across time. Each spring, my wood produces fresh green leaves which nourish the countless hoards of aphids that, in turn, provide for the blue tits which periodically satisfy the needs of sparrowhawks. There are many such food chains that interweave and interact in my wood: food flows *through* life. Faeces from fox and finch alike accumulate on the woodland floor throughout the year, where, in autumn, falling, yellowing leaves deepen the duff, sending damp smells between the naked boughs: food flows *from* life. An autumn foray shows fungi glistening in the paling light as they return nourishment to the soil so that the sap-rise of the following spring may regrow leaves once more: food returns *to* life. This is the constant recycling of food for life as nutrients are used over and over again. The community of trees which are my wood; its shrubs, mosses, birds, mammals, spiders, insects, worms and fungi are all required to maintain the great cycle of life, through time and season.

The cycles of life in my wood are powered by tremendous nuclear reactions – sunshine. The sun's energy is gathered by the green foliage where by mind-boggling steps of biochemistry in photosynthesis, sugars are formed. These sugars provide the en-

ergy for the animals that feed upon the leaves, and for the carni-
vores that in turn feed upon them. At each stage however energy is
lost just to keep the animals moving – a fact which explains why we
have so few foxes and so many rabbits. All the sun's energy is
ultimately lost and, unlike nutrients, cannot be used again.

This little glimpse of my wood indicates how life on earth works,
though some would say that this is shallow ecological thinking. We
can, however, develop deep ecological thinking and as Aldo
Leopold did, we can 'think like a mountain'[1]. Like him, I can think
like a wood. I feel the moods of my wood as it remembers the
family of wolves that denned up in cold winters past. My wood
remembers the mesolithic family that cleared a south-facing slope,
fed upon crayfish in the stream, collected the fruits of the forest
and lived as a natural part of the wood, as natural as butterfly or
badger. After that family's departure, saplings sprang up in the
abandoned clearing, deer browsed the lower leaves and robins
welcomed each day in song. My wood remembers, too, the north
winds that brought choking sulphurous fumes from the smoking
chimneys of Falls, Divis and Shankill. When I am in my wood I
think like a wood, I am part of the wood, I am the wood. This is
deep ecology: a truly ecocentric view of the world. As Fritjof Capra
says, 'Shallow ecology sees human beings as above or outside
nature, whereas deep ecology sees human beings as a particular
strand, one of many strands, in the web of life'[2]. Indeed Capra
maintains that 'ecological awareness and ecological consciousness
goes far beyond science, and at the deepest level it joins with
religious awareness and religious experience'[3].

15 000 years ago, humankind existed in the web of life occupy-
ing as much of the globe as is presently occupied, although the
human population probably did not exceed one million individuals. Agriculture began at about that time and, for the first time,
humans had the potential to produce more food than was required and this allowed the human population to grow. Agriculture, together with the technosphere in recent centuries, allowed
the population of the planet to push past five billion in 1987.

The costs to the planet of such an increase in human population are clear for all to see. While 'acid rain', 'global warming',
'ozone holes' are words that trip easily off our tongues, their
meanings and implications are often poorly understood. We humans grub out hedges, infill farm ponds, and build houses on
good agricultural land. We no longer think like a mountain. We

have lost our ecocentric view of the world and have become anthropocentric chauvinists [4, 5]. We have, at the most, a shallow ecological view as we forever dip into the cornucopian horn of plenty[6]. We should remember the wisdom of the American Indian, Chief Seattle, who warned of such folly 'Whatsoever befalls the earth befalls the sons of man. Man did not weave the web of life; he is merely a strand in it. Whatever he does to the web, he does to himself'[7].

Are we then today in danger of following the patterns set by previous civilisations? We have mirrored the rise of the Egyptian, Syrian, Hellenic and other civilisations[8]. These civilisations responded to challenges and grew, but eventually lost their flexibility for change, so that the civilisations began to disintegrate. Will our western civilisation also disintegrate? If we want the answer to be 'no', we need to maintain our flexibility so that we become once more part of the web of life, to think like a forest, to think like a mountain. If we don't change, then western civilisation will be surely doomed. Our earlier flexibility allowed us to tap into the enormous fossil fuel supplies, to the extent that, today, we use eight billion tons (oil equivalent) of energy per year, about three-quarters of which comes from fossil fuels[9]. Fossil fuels are non-renewable; one day they will be exhausted. The peak of use will be around the turn of the millennium; after that it's all downhill. At current rates of use, the world's reserves of oil, gas and coal will last another 43, 58, and 238 years respectively[10]. This does not take into consideration our ever increasing energy demands, nor the demands of developing and under-developed countries, as they, too, scramble aboard the energy band-wagon. The energy situation for western civilisation is nearing criticality.

As far as western civilisation is concerned, the early warnings of inflexibility are becoming clearer: not only do we have species extinction and habitat loss occurring at a rate never ever seen before, we now confront civil unrest and urban decay. In the face of all this humankind must make rational decisions about the future, enter once again the web of life and become part of a new solar age. Each year, the living systems on this planet produce one hundred and seventy billion tons of new plant material[11]. And that represents only a fraction of the energy that reaches this planet from the sun! Once the decision has been taken to enter the solar age and tap into this energy supply, we shall come to recognise that we are part of the web of life and that we must adhere to the objectives of the World Conservation Strategy[12] and its successors[13]. In thinking like a forest, we will maintain ecological processes and life-support systems, we will preserve genetic diversity, and we will use species and ecosystems in a sustainable way. As Céline Mangan has said 'we will care for the earth rather than dominate it.' We will no longer be anthropocentric; through reconciliation we will become ecocentric. We will all think like a mountain. We will all think like a wood. We will learn to walk lightly on the earth.

NOTES

1 Leopold, A. *A Sand County Almanac*, Oxford, OUP, 1949, p.129–133.
2 Capra, F. *Belonging to the Universe*, London, Penguin, 1992, p.97–98.
3 Capra, *Belonging*, p.70
4 Devall, B. *Simple in Means, Rich in Ends*, Salt Lake City, Peregrine Smith, 1988, p.184.
5 Devall, B. & G. Sessions. *Deep Ecology*, Salt Lake City, Peregrine Smith, 1985, p.243.
6 van Matre, S. *Earth Education. A New Beginning*, Warrenville, The Institute for Earth Education, 1990, p.34–41.
7 Chief Seattle. 'You must teach your children' in *The Earth Speaks*, van Matre, S. & B. Weiler, Warrenville, The Institute for Earth Education, 1983, p.122.
8 Capra, F. *The Turning Point*, London, Fontana, 1982, p.8.
9 Simpson, S. *The Times Guide to the Environment*, London, Times Books, 1990, ch.7.
10 Ebrahimi, A., G. Elliot, & J. Taylor. 'Towards an Energy Policy', *RSPB Conserv. Rev.*, 1992 p.12–17.
11 Begon, M., J.L. Harper, & C.R. Townsend, *Ecology*, Oxford, Blackwell Scientific, 1986, p.631.
12 IUCN/UNEP/WWF, *World Conservation Strategy*, Gland, Switzerland, 1980.
13 IUCN/UNEP/WWF, *Caring for the Earth. A Strategy for Sustainable Living*, Gland, Switzerland, 1991.

POLITICS AND RECONCILIATION*

Duncan B. Forrester

A Christian understanding of reconciliation is primarily in the indicative mood. It rests on something that has happened, something that has been achieved, accomplished, done. The situation has been changed; something objective has happened, which has made everything different. And this reconciliation is more than a change of mind or a call for alteration of behaviour, although it is of course good if behaviour and thought respond to the realities of the situation. Furthermore, this reconciliation that has been achieved does not belong in a 'religious' world, nor is it something affecting only that artificial intellectual construct the isolated individual. 'God was in Christ reconciling the *world* (i.e. the cosmos) to himself', we read, and it is only in this broad cosmic context that 'he has reconciled us to himself through Christ' (II Cor. 5. 18–19). The passage, of course, goes on to speak of 'the ministry of reconciliation' and 'the message of reconciliation' which have been entrusted to us. The objective change, in other words, calls for a response: we cannot be detached and impassive in face of it. We have to do something about it. We have to spread the message and minister the reconciliation in which we participate. Reconciliation has been achieved; it is already there, even if not recognised; we are called to point to, to declare what has been done, and adapt ourselves to this gracious reality. Similar points are made powerfully in Ephesians 2 in a passage which deals unambiguously with the relations between communities: on the cross Christ has in fact broken down 'the barrier of enmity' and annulled the law, the two paradigmatic signs of division, suspicion and hostility. He has thus

---

*I am indebted to Professor Ted Weber of Emory University and various participants in the Reconciliation in Religion and Society Conference, held by the Irish School of Ecumenics and the University of Ulster, in May 1993, for comments on the draft of this paper.

reconciled Jew and Gentile in one new humanity, so making peace. Accordingly there is good news of peace and reconciliation to proclaim: a gospel rather than a law, a declaration that something decisive for good has happened rather than a call to action or an ethical demand. The indicative is prior to the imperative. We are dealing with facts rather than values.

I want to make these points as strongly as possible right at the beginning because of the pervasive assumption in the modern world that the Church is primarily concerned with values, with ethics, with good behaviour, with the 'moral fabric of society', and that the Gospel is a narrative way of communicating ideals and moral education to the masses, not an account of things that have happened, events rather than fairy stories with edifying lessons attached. And I also want to affirm that the gospel belongs in the public realm where it engages with issues of communities and nations as well as the individual heart, and the matters that are commonly labelled 'religion'. Remember that in Matthew 25 it is the *nations* that are called to account.

Such assumptions do not, of course, dispose of imperatives and calls to action; they simply place them in their proper light, as responses to a gracious context, the recognition of the deeper realities of life, allying oneself with God's just and loving purposes, rather than desperate attempts to transform a hostile reality into love and fellowship. This gracious context generates confidence, generosity, pertinacity and hope and provides an alternative to a narrow realism which is circumscribed by the hostilities and suspicions of the moment. *Christian* ethics is a response to the God of justice and love who has in Christ reconciled the cosmos to himself and has already overcome the hostilities and suspicions of today.

There remains the widespread assumption that reconciliation and forgiveness belong in some religious sphere and are relevant in face-to-face relationships, but do not belong in politics. Traditionally, this position has sometimes been grounded in theories of the two kingdoms: reconciliation, grace and forgiveness belong in the spiritual sphere, while the temporal sphere operates on quite other principles. In modern days similar conclusions flow from the assumption that theological language is simply the in-house converse of the Church and can have no validity in the public realm. It is not too hard to show that this leads to a massive impoverishment of public political discourse, as well as a drastic narrowing and domestication of theological language. It is easy to pooh-pooh two kingdoms theory by citing extreme expressions of it, which appear to set politics free from any theological constraint, such as Luther's declaration that 'the hand that wields this sword and slays with it is then no more man's hand but God's, who hangs, tortures, beheads, slays and fights'[1], or his savage call: 'Quick, head off, away with it, in order that the earth does not become full with the ungodly'[2]. And such quotations could be parallelled with examples of a no less alarmingly distorted individualistic understanding of the Christian faith.

But for all that, it is still necessary to affirm that there are two different spheres, that the Church is not the state, and must not try to act as such, and that the state must not attempt to operate as a Church. Even theological documents as politically challenging as the Barmen Declaration (1934) are careful to draw limits and define functions. The central attack on the Nazi regime here is that it refused to recognize its boundaries, it usurped the task of the Church, and it made exaggerated claims for itself. For Barth the alternative was not politicisation, the Church striving to take over the task of the state, but rather that the Church should do its own task more faithfully.[3]

But it is clear that there are reciprocal responsibilities between the Church and the political realm. For Barth, the Church is responsible for what happens within politics because this is closely related to the Gospel of the Kingdom. And the gospel provides some knowledge of the context, the significance and the purpose of political activity and offers a language – particularly the discourse of reconciliation, forgiveness and justice – without which politics becomes distorted and malign.

So the Church and theology in their responsibility to God for the political sphere have to offer an account of reality, a language which is adequate to the intractable problems of politics, and a call to respond creatively to the reconciliation which has been achieved in Christ.

Within this frame I wish to discuss three aspects of the relation of reconciliation and politics – politics as safeguarding space for reconciliation; reconciliation as a *telos* or goal for political activity; and politics as an agent of reconciliation.

1. Politics as Safeguarding Space for Reconciliation

Here we are considering politics in traditional terms as a 'dyke against sin', a function which may appear initially somewhat negative but which is in fact very important if positive processes are to develop properly. We have to recognize that there are in existence powerful inner and outer forces which divide, disrupt and nourish hostility and suspicion, forces, that is, which are opposed to reconciliation and erode any kind of authentic community. Particularly in ways of thought influenced by Augustine a major function of politics has been seen as restraining, limiting, excluding these destructive, sinful forces. They must be confined and disciplined if reconciliation and community are to be experienced as contemporary public realities in a still sinful world. This dyke against sin is not like the old Berlin Wall, keeping people apart and making fellowship impossible. It is not even like the so-called Peace Wall in Belfast which has the function of stopping people attacking and threatening one another, and thus provides a fragile and partial security – although that in some circumstances is a good which should not be underestimated.

The image of politics as a dyke against sin has to do not with creating and enforcing frontiers which keep people apart, recreating, that is, the dividing walls of hostility which Christ has destroyed. It is not boundary maintenance as much as the creation of space within which reconciliation may take place and community emerge.

Boundaries, of course, need to be defended, and the space within provided with a degree of order. This is the police function of politics: politics should provide the sort of environment in which people can function normally, without fear or uncertainty. Politicians in this model have a vocation as creators of community, not leaders of the pack, or referees regulating a ritualised political game which has become in Alasdair MacIntyre's phrase, 'civil war carried on by other means'. The politician sees the role as acting on behalf of the community in the broadest sense rather than taking sides in group conflicts. The task is to bring people together rather than keep them apart, in a context where they dare to speak the truth and relate to one another with confidence. The referee model of politics is not to be despised – channelled, limited and ritualized conflict is better than anarchy. Fouls must be recognized and dealt with if conflict is not to become intolerably destructive. *Ius in bello* is better than no *ius* at all! But there are, of course, massive problems when police and security forces are perceived, rightly or wrongly, as taking sides.

The space that is protected by dykes and policed by politics provides an alternative arena for working through conflicts and seeking their resolution through talk, and bargaining, and sharing. This space is neutral ground; it is not the territory of either party or group in which others are interlopers. It is space for non-political methods to be used. Here in this context, what the sociologists call intermediate institutions which cut across class and interest groups flourish and help people to understand and relate to one another. In schools, and trade unions, clubs and churches civil society is given substance, misapprehensions are gradually broken down and friendships are created. Such institutions, of course, may be recruited into tribal politics, in whole or part, and become cadres in conflict, or organs of one or other ghetto in the city. But their true function is to be agents of reconciliation and community building in the space that politics provides. This is why integrated education is so important. When the children of the two communities are educated apart from one another misunderstandings and suspicions inevitably arise and the community building function of education is compromised.

This is also space for the Church to *be* the Church, to work for the healing of relationships, to announce that reconciliation has been achieved, and to show that it works. But the Church as a visible institution, a network of congregations belonging to various denominations, is frequently hijacked by warring parties, so that the divided Church proclaiming a gospel of reconciliation reflects and reinforces the divisions of the warring parties and thereby denies the reconciliation it preaches. When I returned to Scotland in the late seventies I found a Baptismal Certificate in common use in the Church of Scotland. At its top there was a symbol which could be seen in two ways. It was simultaneously a dove descending and a thistle, and both were unambiguously tartan ! What a vivid reminder of the dangers of confusing membership in the Body of Christ with membership in an ethnic community ! Similarly, for example, Enda McDonagh has pointed out how the understanding of baptism is commonly distorted in Northern Ireland:

Baptism in a particular Church, Protestant or Catholic, expresses integration into a particular historical community of Christians with its own cultural and political traditions which set it apart from and against another community of Christians. Affiliation to the Unionist or Nationalist community is the other side of the baptism event in Northern Ireland, which is in opposition to and sometimes in deadly conflict with integration into the Body of Christ.[4]

This is in danger, McDonagh suggests, of rendering baptism futile. The easy solution in a way would be to stop baptising. But that would be to lose 'the challenge and empowerment' which baptism offers Christians in these hard days in Northern Ireland. Thus he suggests that both branches of the Christian Church should be fully represented in every baptism as a sign of the true Church and a symbol of reconciliation.

Only if the Church takes with profound seriousness the damage done by its own divisions and the urgent need to show that in the Church – at every level – reconciliation is a recognized and recognizable reality can the Church faithfully point to reconciliation in the space that politics provides.

2. Reconciliation as the Goal of Politics

Two schools in contemporary thought are particularly vehement in suggesting that politics has no goal, no *telos* beyond itself; they see politics as a self-contained game which has no need to justify itself in relation to some external standard. Politics, according to many proponents of political realism, is about the rational pursuit of the national interest. There is no *telos* beyond this national interest, and since there are many nations there are many interests in tension with one another. Politics thus becomes the business of balancing and channelling conflicting interests. Out of this process, if the protagonists are reasonably restrained and sensible, a rather tenuous kind of order emerges in which a good proportion of interests find at least partial satisfaction and the scales provide a tolerable degree of stability as a kind of by-product of the pursuit of national interest. This stability is on the whole an accidental benefit rather than a conscious goal of policy.

The second type of theory which rejects the notion that political activity should be orientated towards a goal or *telos* explicitly rejects the possibility or desirability of goals such as the 'common good' or 'social justice'. Modern societies, the argument runs, are large and complex, and individuals and groups have very diverse understandings of the good. The state should recognize this and acknowledge that no arbitrator is possible between these divergent notions of the good. Thus the state, according to Bruce Ackerman and others, must be morally neutral and see its role as simply enabling individuals and groups to pursue their interests with the minimum of interference, in the expectation that through the benign impersonal operations of an 'invisible hand' some general benefit may emerge. Northern Ireland might be seen as a standing refutation of this process.

But in this imbroglio of differing and often conflicting goods no such thing as a common good can be found, and indeed the attempt to establish a common good for a complex modern society inevitably leads to totalitarian tyranny, or so the argument runs. In what Hayek calls 'teleocratic societies' freedom is eroded and dictatorship is the only way to sustain a common good. Society, to this way of thinking, should be like an hotel – a set of facilities available to guests to enable them to pursue their diverse purposes with as little interference and as few rules as possible. It is not at all like a family or a sports team, closely integrated and held together by a common destiny and a network of shared commonalities.

The majority Christian tradition has, of course, strongly stressed community and the common good. The Aristotelian/Thomist tradition sees the human being as a social and political animal whose individual good cannot be separated from the common good, and whose destiny transcends the political and the worldly. Here politics can only be understood in the light of the *telos*, which is to do with reconciliation and the restoration of community.

Politics, then, is directed to something beyond itself. If it is not understood within such a transcendent frame it becomes warped and destructive. To give a specific instance: if just war thinking is detached from two fundamental theological convictions – that violence is sinful and evil, and that the aim is reconciliation and the restoration of fellowship – it quickly is transformed from being a way of limiting damage into being a justification, even sometimes a glorification, of violence and destruction.

Presenting reconciliation as the *telos* of politics is by no means to reject or question what I said earlier about reconciliation as something that has happened, something that has been achieved. Indeed it is integral to Christian belief that the fellowship which has been established by Christ is also the end, the goal. But when we speak of reconciliation, as Christians we see it as a gift, a promise and a hope on the basis of the reconciliation which has already been achieved. The future indicative is grounded in the past indicative.

Thus we should understand reconciliation as a central dimension of the Christian hope. We hope for the fulness of the *telos* which God will give us as a gift. People in situations of long-drawn-out conflict are frequently condemned to despair, deprived of hope. They begin to assume that hostility and conflict are perennial aspects of their situation, that there is no escape. Without hope we are imprisoned in the present. Christian hope is the seeking of a city, not one that we design but one whose architect and builder is God. The seeking of the city is the proper function of politics, although attempts to *construct* the heavenly city are projects doomed to frustration. What we can and must strive for is the kind of partial anticipations of that city which give people its flavour and help to sustain hope and the constant seeking of the city. And that is also the Christian vocation of the politician.

3. Politics as an Agent of Reconciliation

There is much conflict in life, and conflict can sometimes be productive. But when adversarialism is accepted as a fundamental principle it becomes profoundly destructive. In medicine, for example, it has been argued that when the model of care and healing is replaced by an emphasis on struggle between the physician and the ailment or tumour, a struggle in which 'defeat' must never be acknowledged, and secondly, when patient and doctor regularly see themselves as potential antagonists in court, the situation and the relationships are fundamentally adulterated.

So it is in politics if conflict is accorded finality. Then the politician becomes simply the leader of the pack, pursuing with the minimum of restraint the interests of the group represented. Adversarial politics exacerbates the existing tensions and divisions in society, and politics becomes defensive – or offensive, depending on one's point of view – rather than creative, looking forward to a broader sense of community, and attempting to move towards that community. Augustine argued that 'political authority exists to resolve at least some of the tensions in human society . . . (It) serves to remedy the conflict, tension and disorder of society'.[5] Only if this can be recovered as a central dimension of the vocation of politics can we reaffirm a broader and more Christian understanding of community, and overcome the heresy that politics is a war to be won through total victory and unconditional surrender. Politicians are not generals, or leaders of the pack, or shop stewards; they have a broader vocation as pastors, creators of community, mediators, healers – somewhat like the shepherd-kings of the Bible.

This does not mean plastering over the cracks, disguising real conflicts of interest, suggesting that sordid settlements imposed by the powerful are in fact *shalom*. There has been and continues to be too much of this. The fruits are there for all to see in the former Yugoslavia today – and closer to home as well ! Conflicts need to be recognized and worked through with integrity. Martin Luther King and other leaders in the American Civil Rights Movement or Gandhi in India show both how difficult and how costly it is to struggle to right wrongs, heal antagonisms and overcome deep-seated conflicts of interest, and simultaneously create a broader and more authentic sense of community.

The Kairos Document from South Africa raises a series of very important caveats about glib or hasty or simplistic appeals for reconciliation, in effect for seeking instant reconciliation which is simply crying, 'Peace, peace where there is no peace'. Its criticisms of what it calls 'church theology' are fair; and it makes a number of important points about reconciliation. The passage is so important that it deserves to be cited at length:

> 'Church Theology' takes 'reconciliation' as the key to problem resolution. It talks about the need for reconciliation between white and black, or between all South Africans. 'Church Theology' often describes the Christian stance in the following way: 'We must be fair. We must listen to both sides of the story. If the two sides can only meet to talk and negotiate they will sort out their differences and misunderstandings, and the conflict will be resolved'. On the face of it this may sound very Christian. But is it ?
>
> The fallacy here is that 'reconciliation' has been made into an absolute principle that must be applied in all cases of conflict or dissension. But not all cases of conflict are the same. We can imagine a private quarrel between two people or two groups whose differences are based upon misunderstandings. In such cases it would be appropriate to talk and negotiate to sort out the misunderstandings and to reconcile the two sides. But there are other conflicts where one side is a fully armed and violent oppressor while the other side is defenceless and oppressed. There are conflicts that can only be described as the struggle

between justice and injustice, good and evil, God and the devil. To speak of reconciling these two is not only a mistaken application of the Christian idea of reconciliation, it is a total betrayal of all that Christian faith has ever meant . . .

In our situation in South Africa today it would be totally unChristian to plead for reconciliation and peace before the present injustices have been removed. Any such plea plays into the hands of the oppressor by trying to persuade those of us who are oppressed to accept our oppression and to become reconciled to the intolerable crimes that are committed against us. That is not Christian reconciliation, it is sin. It is asking us to become accomplices in our own oppression, to become servants of the devil. No reconciliation is possible in South Africa without justice.

What this means in practice is that no reconciliation, no forgiveness and no negotiations are possible **without repentance** . . .

There is nothing that we want more than true reconciliation and genuine peace – the peace that God wants and not the peace the world wants (Jn 14:27). The peace that God wants is based upon truth, repentance, justice and love. The peace that the world offers us is a unity that compromises the truth, covers over injustice and oppression and is totally motivated by selfishness.[6]

This passage, I think, has important things to say to us, even if we feel we read it in a very different context where the rights and wrongs are much less clear and where serious Christians are much more divided about the way forward. First, we must attend to the assertion that most deep conflicts have their roots in situations of injustice which must be remedied and put right if reconciliation is to be actualised. We must also recognise that concepts of justice become weapons in social conflict, with their meaning warped to serve the interests of groups. It seems to me that as Christians we should be suspicious of any understanding of justice with which we can be entirely comfortable. F. Hayek's account of justice, for example, at no point is calculated to disturb the wealthy and the powerful. A Christian understanding of justice seems to me to be profoundly disturbing, because it calls for more than fairness, for a move to generosity. This is particularly relevant in situations where the entail of history cannot be undone, where it is impossible for past injuries to be cured or full restitution made. In such situations healing depends on the generosity of the victims. Secondly, there is the need for repentance if forgiveness and reconciliation are to be realised. It is very hard for collectivities to repent, and there are few instances of this happening. But without repentance the way forward is closed. 'A politics of forgiveness . . . might be the ultimate realism, the recognition of the inevitable imperfection of society.'[7] And repentance and forgiveness are the only real way to reconciliation. Thirdly, premature or wrongly timed attempts at reconciliation are worse than useless as James Cone emphasises.[8] Real deep-seated conflicts have to be analysed, worked through and there must be genuine repentance. Evils and obstacles must be named, unmasked, and repented of. This all takes time. And only after these matters have been worked through is reconciliation on the agenda. Haddon Willmer puts the point well:

> Forgiveness in politics cannot be an easy-going acceptance of what is, a whitewashing tolerance. It has to be a practicable policy in which what is wrong is reckoned with, but forgivingly rather than punitively. Forgiveness is not reconciliation on any terms but takes form in the agreement to work together a political system which expresses the will to forgive, is sustained by forgiveness and encourages and enables men to enter into it. 'Forgiveness' in politics must be a quality of events, institutions, processes and participants.[9]

And finally *The Kairos Document* reminds us that Christian politicians must endeavour seriously to read the signs of the times, to analyse their situation objectively in order to glimpse what God is doing and saying through it. They must rise above group interests which distort and confuse.

Finally, a word about the politics of hope and the necessity of hope for any politics worth the name – a theme reiterated in *The Kairos Document* and also, I believe, one of the most urgent responsibilities of Christianity in the public realm today. Is it possible that in societies which have lost their grip on social hope the Christian faith, in all its obvious frailty and weakness, may stand as more than an empty husk of unfulfilled expectations and a bastion of group interests? Can Christian faith give shape to hope and sustain hope even here – the kind of hope that strengthens and comforts the weak and vulnerable, that disturbs the comfortable, and rouses the complacent? For this is the kind of hope which makes reconciliation and community possible. And without it we are doomed to continuing internecine strife and suspicion.

NOTES

1 Martin Luther. 'Whether Soldiers too can be Saved', *Martin Luther's Works*, Philadelphia Edition, Vol. 5, p.36

2 Cited in David Garland, *Punishment and Modern Society*, Clarendon 1991, p. 227

3 See Eberhard Jungel, *Christ, Justice and Peace: Toward a Theology of the State in dialogue with the Barmen Declaration*. Edinburgh, T. & T. Clark, 1992. This includes a translation of the Barmen Declaration by Douglas S. Bax

4 Enda McDonagh, *Between Chaos and New Creation*. Dublin, Gill & Macmillan, 1986, p. 85

5 Peter D. Bathory, *Political Theory as Public Confession: The Social and Political Thought of St. Augustine of Hippo*. New Brunswick, Transaction Books, 1981, p.160

6 Charles Villa-Vicencio, ed., *Between Christ and Caesar: Classical and Contemporary Texts on Church and State*. Cape Town, David Philip, 1986, pp.256–7

7 Peter Hinchcliff, *Holiness and Politics*, London, Darton, Longman & Todd, 1980, p.190

8 James Cone, *God of the Oppressed*, New York, Seaburg, 1975, pp 243–4

9 Haddon Willmer, 'Forgiveness and Politics', *Crucible*, July/Sept. 1979, pp. 103–4

A RESPONSE

Terence O'Keeffe

Duncan Forrester's thoughtful paper raises the important question of the relationship between religion, reconciliation and politics. There is a religious notion of reconciliation, often seen as opposed to more pragmatic political notions. It is frequently seen as a process which is psychological, subjective or spiritual, even though such a process is thought of as leading to an end state which is actual, real and temporal – the state of being reconciled. It has a positive connotation: reconciliation of sides in a conflict is to be sought and valued, and few would wish to be thought of as opposing or obstructing reconciliation.

There is a danger in this positive connotation. It can be suspected of serving a purely ideological function. By ideology I mean those ideas in society which function to conceal or cover over contradictions and conflicts and thus, whether used deliberately or indeliberately, create a false and illusory resolution of those conflicts. Terms like reconciliation, harmony, community and the like can all too easily serve the ideological function of suggesting a premature bridging of differences while leaving the issues of conflict unresolved.

By reconciliation I therefore do not mean the purely psychological overcoming of bitterness and hatred, nor a premature and illusory surmounting of division and conflict. I mean the processes of understanding and accommodation of differing objectives, viewpoints and actions, through negotiation, compromise and agreement, such that a reconciliation of difference is reached. If we think in terms of the political realm, this will inevitably involve the participants in tolerance, concession and, eventually, pluralism.

I therefore like Duncan Forrester's notion of politics creating a *space* for reconciliation – politics in his words as 'restraining, limiting, excluding (these) destructive forces'. I think the problem arises when politics itself is based on such forces. Thus, in

conflicts where *religious* differences provide one of the most powerful focuses for conflict – and Northern Ireland is by no means
unique in this respect – two things happen. Politics finds it extremely hard to work to create such a reconciling space; and
reconciliation itself tends to become more ideologically suspect as
it spiritualises and psychologises itself.

Part of the difficulty is that the relationship of religion to politics, and therefore of reconciliation to politics, is ambiguous.
Duncan Forrester mentions in this connection the protest of Karl
Barth against the Nazi regime. Let me dwell on this example for a
moment for it is instructive. Germany in the early 1930's offered at
least three models for the relationship of religion to the political
realm. The question at issue was the relationship between human
and divine in the sphere of the political. Three theologians typi-
fied constrasting positions. Karl Barth sought to separate them,
Emmanuel Hirsch confused them and Paul Tillich attempted to
distinguish them. The Barthian position was a protest at the en-
croachment of the political into the religious sphere. As Forrester
says, the central criticism is that the political regime is seeking
to usurp the task of the Church. This, in the face of a demonic
regime like Nazism, can be thought of simply as 'patrolling
the boundaries' and defending group, in this case ecclesiastical,
interest.

Another theologian, Emmanuel Hirsch, went in the opposite
direction. For him, Nazism represented the advent of the true
destiny of Germany. It represented a *Kairos*, a 'right time' for the
German people and so was a sacred task. Hirsch represents the
sacralisation of the political, the elevation of finite political reality
to unconditional status. Hirsch's theology of politics was openly
ethnic-centred. For him, the ethnic state creates absolute bonds
and obligations. Using the neo-Lutheran concept of an Order of
Creation established by God, he argued that 'what is to be built is
not the Kingdom of God but the Kingdom (*Reich*) of the Germans
established in humble adoration of the Lord of History'.[1]

Paul Tillich, from whom Hirsch borrows the notion of the
Kairos, comes to consider the relation of politics to religion originally from the same standpoint – all three theologians begin as
religious socialists. Tillich wants to avoid the depoliticisation of
religion represented by Barth and the sacralisation of politics
espoused by Hirsch. He sought to show how religion impacts on
the political sphere while still preserving the autonomy of the

secular. Tillich was critical of Hirsch's first declaration of this thesis and wrote an open letter to him, to which Hirsch replied.[2] Tillich's warning against the too comfortable separation of religion and politics, or the confusion of the two in Hirsch's vision, is a timely attempt to balance the autonomy of the political and the prophetic role of criticism of the political order by religion.[3]

It is a highly ambiguous task to seek the relation of politics to religion. Many of our theologians in Ireland have been content to establish boundaries and to preserve for the churches their own sphere of influence. Many more have allowed themselves to be tempted into giving a religious blessing to political arrangements. They allowed themselves, to use Forrester's words, to be 'recruited into tribal politics, in whole or in part, and become cadres in conflict or organs of one or other ghetto'.

Let me return to the concept of reconciliation and to another theme enunciated by Forrester. I instanced the danger of an ideological use of terms like reconciliation as a cover for the continuation of the elements of conflict. Indeed, the concept of reconciliation is sometimes thought of as something which can distract from the real struggle. Thus the *Kairos Document* warns:

> There can be no doubt that our Christian faith commits us to work for *true* reconciliation and *genuine* peace. But as so many people, including Christians, have pointed out there can be no true reconciliation and no genuine peace without *justice*. Any form of peace and reconciliation that allows the sin of injustice and oppression to continue is a *false* peace and a *counterfeit* reconciliation.[4]

This is an important warning. It is the same warning against ideologically tainted reconciliation and against a 'spiritualisation' of the notion of reconciliation. Many will see this warning as licensing them to postpone reconciliation until justice and freedom have been achieved. This is however a false dichotomy and choice. The end state of being reconciled will certainly not be achieved without those values being embraced and installed in society. But reconciliation can be the process also – a political process in a divided society which involves understanding, accommodation, negotiation, compromise and tolerance. We should also seek to build into this reconciling political process the more specifically religious themes of repentance for past wrongdoing and forgiveness of the other. In a society such as ours, where religious fervour has been added to the conflict cocktail, the churches have a particular obligation to underscore this religious dimension of the work of reconciliation.

NOTES

1 E. Hirsch *Christian Freedom and Political Obligation* (1935)
2 See the excellent account of the Tillich-Hirsch exchange in the article by Walter Bense in *Tillich Studies 1975*, edited John J Carey, Chicago 1975, pp. 39–50.
3 The Tillich open letters to Hirsch were in *Theologische Blatter*, vol. 13 (1934), and vol. 14 (1935).
4 *The Kairos Document* (C11R/BCC, 1986) p. 9.

EVANGELICALISM AND RECONCILIATION

Dennis Cooke

The labelling of groups or parties within the Christian Church can be a misleading and sometimes offensive exercise. There is always the possibility of making inaccurate assumptions concerning others, of including those who prefer to be excluded and of excluding those who regard themselves as within the group. This is particularly true in relation to Evangelicalism in that the term is clearly related to the 'good news' or 'the Gospel' of Jesus Christ. As such it could be argued that all Christians from the beginning of the Church and throughout its history have been 'evangelicals', believing and witnessing to the Gospel of Jesus Christ. It is with this qualification and reservation in mind that we approach the subject of Evangelicalism and examine it according to its most commonly accepted historical usage, namely, as a popular Protestant movement beginning in the 1730's and, though subject to considerable changes and variations, continuing to the present day.

David Bebbington has identified four characteristics as the special marks of Evangelicalism over this period: '*conversionism,* the belief that lives need to be changed; *activism,* the expression of the gospel in effort; *biblicism,* a particular regard for the Bible; and what may be called *crucicentrism,* a stress on the sacrifice of Christ on the cross. Together they form a quadrilateral of priorities that is the basis of Evangelicalism.'[1] Continental pietism of the late seventeenth century is thought to have contributed to the eighteenth century Evangelical Revival in Britain and parts of North America which resulted in the rise of Methodism and created a new spiritual stimulus within the churches arising from the Reformation. It developed therefore within Protestantism, had much in common with earlier Protestant traditions, and has been regarded ever since as a movement within the Protestant churches. However, as we shall see later, this Protestant monopoly of Evangelicalism has ended with the formation in the last decade of this century of an Evangelical Catholic movement within the Roman Catholic Church.

Consideration of 'Evangelicalism and Reconciliation' places the Evangelical movement under careful scrutiny and analysis in relation to one of the central emphases of the Gospel. If reconciliation is understoood as the establishment of new and improved relationships of trust and love between persons or groups previously estranged which has its origin and motivating force in the reconciling work of God in Christ, then the question must be asked regarding the success or failure of Evangelicalism in promoting these aims. In such a vast area of enquiry this study will give particular attention to the role of Evangelicalism in Ireland while not forgetting the wider Evangelical movement to which it belongs. Of specific interest therefore will be the attitude of Evangelicalism to the whole question of Protestant-Catholic relationships in Ireland.

John Wesley: A Legacy of Anti-Catholicism

John Wesley, the founder of Methodism, and undoubtedly the dominant figure within Evangelicalism during the eighteenth century, undertook twenty-one preaching tours in Ireland during the period 1747–1789. Scholars have differed in their assessment of Wesley's attitude to Protestant-Catholic relationships in Ireland. Some, while acknowledging his identification with the anti-Catholic spirit of his age, have preferred to highlight his irenical writings, and credited him with anticipating approaches and perspectives similar to those followed in the ecumenical movement.[2] On the other hand, David Hempton, while conceding that he was no bigot, has suggested that 'Wesley's anti-Catholicism was one of his profound and enduring legacies to the Wesleyan connexion, and the connexion's vigorous anti-Catholicism – in which it genuinely reflected its following – was a most important determinant of Wesleyan political attitudes during the nineteenth century'[3]

Hempton's reference to Wesley's anti-Catholic legacy appears to summarise more accurately the consequences of his general approach to Catholicism although a case can be argued that the years 1749–1750 represent a brief and quite unusual departure from his otherwise consistent anti-Catholicism. His publication, *A Word to a Protestant*[4], written at the time of the 1745 Jacobite Rising in Scotland and England, set the tone for much of his later writing on Catholicism. He warned against seven errors established and legalised by the Council of Trent: 'their doctrine of seven sacraments; of transubstantiation; of communion in one kind only; of purgatory; and praying for the dead therein; of veneration of relics; and of indulgences, or pardons granted by the Pope, and to be bought for money'. These errors, he suggested, 'defile the purity of Christianity' but three other doctrines in his opinion were much more destructive of true Christianity: 'these grand Popish doctrines of merit, idolatry, and persecution, by destroying both faith, and the love of God and of our neighbour, tend to banish true Christianity out of the world'.

A more conciliatory approach is evident four years later in his *Letter to a Roman Catholic*[5], written in July, 1749, during his third visit to Ireland. Serious rioting involving threats and injury to Methodist members and property in Cork during the months of May and June, possibly the most serious instance of opposition which the Methodist movement had to face in Britain or Ireland during the eighteenth century, made Wesley fearful for the prospects of his mission to Ireland and undoubtedly prompted the writing of this letter. While not acknowledging the Nicene Creed as his source, he uses its basic structure to remind his readers that Protestants and Catholics have the fundamentals of the faith in common. He also identifies areas of Christian practice which both have in common: worshipping God in spirit and in truth; an emphasis on Christian service; love for one's neighbour, whether they be friend or enemy; the absence of malice, hatred or avarice; and the need for sobriety, temperance and charity. He refers to these common areas of faith and practice as 'true primitive Christianity' and suggests that differences of opinion in other matters should not prevent them from encouraging each other to love and good works: 'let us resolve, First, not to hurt one another; to do nothing unkind or unfriendly to each other . . . Secondly, God being our helper, to speak nothing harsh or unkind of each other . . . Thirdly, to harbour no unkind thought, no unfriendly temper towards each other . . . Fourthly, to help each other in whatever we are agreed leads to the kingdom'. Finally, of particular significance is his comment: 'My dear friend, consider, I am not persuading you to leave or change your religion'. It is a letter which is generous in spirit, friendly, sensitive to the feelings of Catholics, and hopeful that in the future Protestants and Catholics can support each other in every possible manner. Two sermons published in 1750, *Catholic Spirit*[6] and *A Caution against Bigotry*[7] express and reflect the same generosity of spirit.

Wesley's change of outlook within a very short space of time is nothing short of remarkable. By 1752 he had altered his position and published *A Short Method of converting all the Roman Catholics in the Kingdom of Ireland*[8]. It would appear that despite his conciliatory letter of 1749 earlier thoughts of converting Catholics had never entirely left his mind. Wesley now considered it important to prepare what in retrospect might be described as 'Information Packs': *The Advantage of the Members of the Church of England over those of the Church of Rome*[9], 1753, and *A Roman Catechism, with a reply thereto*[10], 1756. He was now publicly declaring that a conversionist policy towards Catholics was part of his missionary strategy in Ireland. While Wesley always regarded the Roman Catholic Church as within the universal Church[11], as the Reformers in the sixteenth century had also maintained, he clearly viewed it as an illiberal organisation and one that was responsible for distorting the Christian message.

It is around this period that Wesley seems to have developed a mistrust and suspicion of Catholics in relation to their political loyalties. An entry in his Journal, 3 June 1758, suggests that he now became aware of an intense hostility experienced by Catholics in their attitudes to Protestants: 'I preached at Minulla, a village four miles from Castlebar. I was surprised to find how little the Irish Papists are changed in an hundred years. Most of them retain the same bitterness, yea, and thirst for blood, as ever; and would as freely now cut the throats of all the Protestants, as they did in the last century'.[12]

This mistrust of Catholics surfaced in his reaction to Savile's Relief Act, 1778, which had passed easily through both houses of the Westminister Parliament, and was designed to alter legislation which had previously excluded Roman Catholics from serving in the armed forces. According to the new Act, military recruits were now required simply to take an oath of fidelity to the Crown. However, the apparent lack of opposition in Parliament may not have reflected the feeling in the country. Successful resistance to the introduction of the measure in Scotland in 1779 encouraged Lord George Gordon to form a Protestant Association to voice opposition in England. Wesley became indirectly involved in the controversy when he published in 1779 *Popery Calmly Considered*[13], basically a repeat of earlier publications, and wrote in defence of the Protestant Association to the *Public Advertiser*[14] on 21 January 1780. For Wesley the nub of the problem lay in the uncertainty surrounding the loyalty and trustworthiness of Catholics when taking the oath of allegiance to the Crown: 'Nothing can be more plain, than that the members of that Church can give no reasonable security to any Government of their allegiance or peaceable behaviour. Therefore they ought not to be tolerated by any Government, Protestant, Mahometan, or Pagan'.

It is surprising that the usually well-informed Wesley did not realise the weakness in his main argument. He had suggested that the maxim 'no faith is to be kept with heretics' established and practised at the Council of Constance, 1414–1417, when it failed to keep the assurance of safe conduct given by Emperor Sigismund to John Huss, was indeed 'a fixed maxim of the Church of Rome'. If Wesley was intent on delving back into history, the Council of Constance was not the best example to select as it represents the period when the power of Conciliarism was at its height and that of the papacy at its lowest, as is evident in the conciliar decrees of *Sacrosancta*, 1415, and *Frequens*, 1417, which affirmed that popes were subject to the power and regular supervision of councils. Wesley's analysis did not go unchallenged. Father O'Leary, a Capuchin Friar in Dublin, in a series of published *Remarks* in the *Freeman's Journal*, questioned Wesley's interpretation of the Council, and, as was to be expected, elicited *Two Letters*[15] in reply.

Wesley had identified himself with the aims and objectives of the Protestant Association and must share some of the responsibility for the serious rioting in London which lasted for ten days after the presentation of a petition to Parliament on 2 June. However, two years later his *Disavowal of Persecuting Papists*[16] indicated that he was unrepentant for what he had written.

Similarities may be drawn between Wesley's dislike of Catholicism and his support for the abolition of slavery. In each he understood his mission as securing liberty for those held in bondage, one being spiritual and the other physical. However, he was conservative at heart and this may have prevented him from fully comprehending the grievances of the American colonists with whom he was initially sympathetic. It certainly limited any contribution which he might have made in the areas of education and prison reform, and, in relation to Ireland, it seriously restricted his understanding of the underlying political, social, economic and religious problems of the country. He believed that civil power derived from God and therefore did not question English rule in Ireland, regarding it instead as bestowing civilising influences on the population. The Methodist societies, whose membership had reached 14,000 by the time of his death in 1791, had been encouraged in a spirituality which expressed itself in a conversionist policy towards the majority of their fellow citizens. It was this legacy which they now had to interpret in the changing pattern of Irish society.

Anti-Catholicism and Entrenchment

A conversionist policy towards Roman Catholics became a more clearly defined tradition within Protestantism in Ireland during the nineteenth century even though it was not always actively and enthusiastically pursued. At the beginning of the century it was evident in the evangelistic work of the Irish Methodist Mission, founded 1799, particulary in the preaching of Gideon Ouseley, and also in the attitude of militant Evangelical Anglican bishops like Power le Poer Trench, Archbishop of Tuam, 1813–1839. Trench was unapologetic in his approach:

> We are proselytisers. We plead guilty to this terrific and unpardonable charge. Nay, if we were not proselytisers we could lay no claim to the name of Christians . . . Am I to be told that for fear of offending an unscriptural church I am to join in league with its priesthood to close the pure simple unnoted book of inspiration, to withold the Book of God from his condemned and perishing creatures?[17]

Dr. William Urwick's pamphlet entitled *A Brief Sketch of the Religious State of Ireland*[18], 1852, indicates the intensity of this interest in the conversion of Roman Catholics in the period immediately following the Great Famine, 1845–1849. In addition to providing statistics of membership, numbers of clergy and places of worship, for both Roman Catholics and Protestants in all four provinces of Ireland, and an extensive report on the success of missionary work among Roman Catholics, he lists the number of societies engaged in this work: General, 6; Church of Ireland, 13; Presbyterian, 2; Methodist (reflecting the schisms then existing),3; Congregationalists, 1; Baptists, 1; United Brethren, 1; Others, 1. One of the Anglican societies listed by Urwick, The Society for

Irish Church Missions to the Roman Catholics, whose founder and main inspiration was Alexander Dallas, rector of Wonston, Hampshire, is generally portrayed as the most aggressive of all these groups. Supported mainly by English Evangelicals, many of whom were in prominent positions in the Church of England, this and other societies inevitably drew strong condemnation from Cardinal Paul Cullen, the Roman Catholic Primate, who described their work as 'the disgraceful and unchristian system of proselytism which is reprobated by all liberal and generous people of whatever denomination'[19]. Historians have suggested that these missions to Roman Catholics were counter-productive for Evangelicalism[20]. While reports in the early 1850's indicate that they initially met with some success, numbers of conversions dwindled and the divisive effects of the campaign on the community eventually made them unpopular among Protestant clergy serving in these areas. In addition, it has been suggested that the crusade policy provided Cullen with the opportunity to re-organise the Irish Catholic Church along Ultramontanist lines.

Despite the fervency of the crusade policy, Evangelical leaders did accept the Roman Catholic Church as a Christian Church. Even Dallas acknowledged that members of the Church of England and Roman Catholics both agreed that Christ had founded a Church upon earth within which people would find salvation, and that both Churches appealed to the authority of Scripture[21]. A few years later at the time of the 1859 Revival in Ulster when the General Assembly of the Presbyterian Church in Ireland discussed the validity of baptism of Roman Catholics who had joined Presbyterianism, Henry Cooke, perhaps the leading Irish Evangelical of the nineteenth century, defended the traditional reformed view that the Roman Catholic Church is part of the visible church, though, like all churches, in need of reformation under the Word of God[22]. There had therefore developed a clear Evangelical tradition, evident in Wesley during the eighteenth century, which held in balance, on the one hand, the right to criticise in the Roman Catholic Church what they considered to be errors in Christian belief and deviations in Christian practice, with, on the other hand, an acknowledgement that it is a Christian Church.

The anti-Catholic emphasis of Evangelicalism influenced Protestant political opinion to a remarkable degree during the nineteenth and early twentieth century. Evangelicalism in Ireland had never sought or considered any degree of accommodation with the majority Roman Catholic population. Any attempts to find common cause with Roman Catholics, like the radical Protestants among the United Irishmen, were thought to have ended in failure, and indeed the events of the 1798 Rebellion had only served to underline in the Protestant mind their fears and suspicions regarding Catholic intentions in Ireland. In their organisation of mission societies Evangelicals had adopted an attitude of superiority to Roman Catholics and it was this attitude throughout the nineteenth century which made them vigilant in preserving Protestant rights and privileges. Any measure concerned with or related to Catholic rights was interpreted as one which would endanger Protestant privileges. With predictable consistency and almost complete unanimity Irish Evangelicals opposed Catholic Emancipation, 1829, O'Connell's Repeal movement in the 1840's, the increase of the Maynooth grant, 1845, Disestablishment of the Church of Ireland, 1869, and the various Home Rule measures introduced between 1886 and 1912. In taking this negative approach they were not always in step with Evangelical opinion in Britain, which was often divided in its attitude to Ireland.

The Home Rule issue, and the growing realisation that major political changes in Ireland were inevitable, contributed towards the formation of an Ulster Protestant ideology. If Protestant privileges could not be guaranteed on a national basis, then the alternative would be to preserve these rights within the North-East of the country where Protestants were in a majority. Hempton and Hill in their recent significant publication *Evangelical Protestantism in Ulster Society, 1740–1890*[3], have analysed the nature of the Evangelical contribution to the creation of this Ulster Protestant ideology:

> Ultimately, the most important contribution of evangelicalism to the Ulster Protestant ideology was the sheer vigour of its anti-Catholicism. The Roman Catholic Church in Ireland was regarded as all pervasive in influence, monolithic in scope, imperialist in intention, persecuting in its essential nature and impoverishing in its social effects. No state in which its representatives were in control could offer any credible safeguards for the rights of religious minorities. Faced with such a possibility Ulster Protestant theology had the capacity to adapt to new circumstances. The view that all Christian citizens had a sacred duty to support lawfully constituted authorities was capable

of being transformed into a sacred duty to resist religious tyranny[24].

The signing of the Solemn League and Covenant by representatives of the Protestant Churches at a public ceremony and rally at the City Hall, Belfast, on 18 September, 1912, firmly identified Protestantism with the Unionist cause. This continued to be the case with the formation of the Northern Ireland State in 1921, following the Government of Ireland Act, 1920. Evangelicals, with a few exceptions, had supported the redrawing of political boundaries in Ireland.

Changes in Evangelicalism

Considerable changes have occured in Evangelicalism in Ireland during the twentieth century. A variety of opinions and emphases have gradually evolved and made it into a much more complex and diverse movement. Three significant developments can be discerned: firstly, the growth from the 1950's onwards of an extreme anti-Catholic wing of Evangelicalism associated with the Revd. Dr. Ian Paisley and the Free Presbyterian Church of Ulster; secondly, the statement in 1988 of a group of Protestant Evangelicals repudiating earlier triumphalism and affirming their commitment to a ministry of reconciliation; thirdly, the formation in 1990 of a group of Evangelical Catholics within the Roman Catholic Church.

Steve Bruce in *God Save Ulster! The Religion and Politics of Paisleyism*[25] has referred to 'the conservative evangelical beliefs of men like Paisley'[26] and portrayed him as representing the Evangelical tradition in Ireland. Paisley, while emphasising his loyalty to historic Protestantism, has been hesitant to describe himself as an Evangelical as he believes that others have misused the term. Instead, he has preferred to identify himself with Fundamentalism, being a regular participant at the World Congress of Fundamentalists. Since Bebbington has accepted that 'Fundamentalism in any sense has been merely one feature among many, at some times and in some places, of Evangelical religion'[27], Paisley must be viewed as within Evangelicalism. However, his denial that the Roman Catholic Church is a Christian Church would suggest that he has adopted a new extreme position out of step with the sixteenth century Reformers, historic Protestantism, and the whole corpus of

Evangelical tradition[28]. One of his complaints against Protestant ministers is the fact that 'they are going about this country preaching Rome is a Christian Church'[29]. This anti-Catholic invective has permeated every aspect of life and worship in the Free Presbyterian Church, as is illustrated in their hymnal:

1. Our Fathers knew thee, Rome of old,
   And evil is thy fame;
   Thy fond embrace, the galling chain;
   Thy kiss, the blazing flame.
2. Thy blessing, fierce anathema;
   Thy honeyed words deceit;
   Thy worship, base idolatry;
   Thy sacrament, a cheat.
3. The Mystery of Wickedness,
   Right surely is thy name.
   The Harlot in the Bride's attire,
   As all thy ways proclaim.
7. Thy sentence dread is now pronounced,
   Soon shalt thou pass away.
   O soon shall earth have rest and peace –
   Good Lord, haste Thou that day[30].

Throughout his life Paisley has been very critical of the ecumenical movement. Outright condemnation of the World Council of Churches and various ecumenical leaders has been unrelenting. He has declared the Council to be 'the assembly of the ungodly' and 'this great ecumenical assembly of Baalism'[31]. Church leaders have been described at various times as 'a peddler of lies'[32], 'hypocrite', 'another vomit-eating dog'[33], and 'dupes of the Roman Catholic Church and dupes of the Jesuit order'[34]. This strident anti-ecumenism is a direct consequence of his anti-Catholicism as he sees no grounds for dialogue between Protestantism and the Roman Catholic Church: 'And there's no agreement between Protestantism and Popery, no agreement between the gospel of Jesus Christ and the trash of the Antichrist. Can't make them agree. And I'll not be taking half part with those who nailed my Saviour to the tree'[35]. Yet again his divergence from the Reformed tradition is evident as his position ignores the significance of the Colloquies of Hagenau, Worms and Regensberg, 1540–41, and the Colloquy of Poissy, 1561, when various Reformers met with representatives of the See of Rome in an attempt to find mutual understanding and even reconciliation[36].

Ian Paisley represents in a rather unique way the interweaving of Protestant and Unionist interests which was so evident at the beginning of the century. The Democratic Unionist Party, formed in 1971, has given full expression to his particular brand of Unionism, much of its energy and support coming from members of the Free Presbyterian Church[37]. It is the combination of these factors, both religious and political, which has introduced a new dimension into Ulster society.

A different approach to the understanding of Christianity and its application to society is evident in the 1988 statement, *For God and His Glory Alone*[38], issued by a group of Protestant Evangelicals. This is a conciliatory document written in a spirit of repentance and humility. They acknowledge that Evangelicals have been guilty of un-Christlike attitudes: bigotry, prejudice, hatred, arrogance, and triumphalism in the celebration of cultural and political traditions. They confess their insensitivity for the feelings of others in the community, 'we must accept our share of the blame for any way in which we have contributed to the alienation felt by many of the minority community in Northern Ireland'[39]. Believing that it is insufficient just to pray for peace they have resolved to be peacemakers, active in the ministry of reconciliation and involved in working for a just society. Most significant of all is their wish to dissociate Evangelicalism from exclusive identification with one particular culture or political ideal:

> As citizens of heaven, our primary loyalty is to the Lord Jesus Christ. All other loyalties are secondary and must be judged by the values and priorities of this one. It is idolatry to equate God with any one culture or political ideal. It is quite wrong to require allegiance to any of them as evidence of allegiance to Him . . . For too long Ulster Protestantism has passed without question as biblical Christianity when in many particulars, it owes as much to culture as it does to Scripture. Seldom is it admitted among us that one can be a true Evangelical and not a Unionist[40].

This new spirit of reconciliation shown by some Irish Evangelicals reflects the friendlier relationships between Evangelicals and Catholics in other parts of the world as indicated in *The Evangeli-*

cal-Roman Catholic Dialogue on Mission, 1977–1984: A Report[41]. As both Evangelicals and Catholics had been engaged separately on special studies on evangelism it was felt that dialogue would be appropriate and useful. Seven theological questions were debated: Revelation and Authority, The Nature of Mission, The Gospel of Salvation, Our Response in the Holy Spirit to the Gospel, The Church and the Gospel, The Gospel and Culture, and The Possibilities of Common Witness. The significance of the report, presented not as an agreed statement but rather as 'a faithful record of ideas shared'[42] is twofold. Firstly, it is important that dialogue has started. Rather than criticize from a distance and possibly misunderstand each other, they have met for fellowship and serious study. While they found many areas of agreement, they were prepared to discuss some of the controversial issues which have traditionally divided them, for example, the relation between Scripture and tradition, the role of the Church in the interpretation of Scripture, the effect of sin on human nature, the meaning of the Atonement, and the role of Mary in salvation. Secondly, it is significant because they have suggested areas in which Evangelicals and Catholics can share in common witness: Bible translation and publishing, use of the media, community service, social thought and action, dialogue, and common praise and prayer. Although the participants were aware that in some parts of the world Evangelicals and Catholics have felt able to make common witness in evangelism they thought that this was premature as substantial agreement on the nature of the Gospel still eluded them.

Protestant monopoly of Evangelicalism ended in 1990 with the formation of an Evangelical Catholic movement within the Roman Catholic Church in Ireland and with its official approval. In *What is an Evangelical Catholic?*[43] they trace its origins to the various Renewal Movements in the Catholic Church. They believe that they share a common ground of faith with Evangelicals in the various Protestant Churches and want to remove misunderstanding which Protestants have had about the Catholic Church. Many of their emphases are similar to those traditionally held within Evangelicalism: personal faith in Jesus Christ as the one Mediator between God and humankind, belief that salvation cannot be earned since it is the free gift of God, acceptance of the Scripture as the inspired authoritative Word of God, and belief in the eternal reality of heaven and hell. They underline that the Eucharist (Mass) is not a repetition of Christ's work on the Cross but accept that Roman Catholics may have been 'over-sacramentalised and under-evangelized'[44]. They have confidence that the work of the Holy Spirit in renewing the Church will eventually correct any un-Christian practices previously taken on by the Church.

The issue of reconciliation between Protestants and Catholics and between people of different political loyalties has revealed the wide diversity of opinion existing within Evangelicalism in Ireland. The ecumenical movement, with its encouragement of inter-confessional dialogue at international, national and local levels, has met with a variety of responses among Protestant Evangelicals. Some, with varying degrees of intensity, have opposed such dialogue while others have participated. The context in which Evangelicalism has existed over the past three centuries has been continually changing and this in part explains the changes within Evangelicalism. However, the formation of an Evangelical Catholic group within the Roman Catholic Church could prove to be the most radical development yet witnessed in Evangelicalism and lead to an acknowledgment that the terminology, so closely identified with the Gospel of Jesus Christ, was always inherently comprehensive and inclusive of all within the Christian Church.

NOTES

1 D. W. Bebbington *Evangelicalism in Modern Britain, A History from the 1730's to the 1980's,* London, Unwin Hyman, 1989, p.3.
2 See *John Wesley's Letter to a Roman Catholic,* ed Michael Hurley, Belfast, Geoffrey Chapman, 1968, and Frederick Jeffrey *Methodism and the Irish Problem,* Belfast, Epworth House, 1973.
3 David Hempton *Methodism and Politics in British Society, 1750–1850,* London, Hutchinson, 1984,pp.42–43.
4 *The Works of John Wesley,* Vol.XI, Grand Rapids, Michigan, Zondervan, reproduced from the authorized edition published by the Wesleyan Conference Office in London, England, in 1872, pp. 187–195.
5 *Works,* XI, pp. 80–86
6 *Works,* V, pp. 492–504
7 *Works,* V, pp. 478–492
8 *Works,* X, pp. 129–133
9 *Works,* X, pp. 133–140
10 *Works,* X, pp. 86–133
11 *Works,* VI, pp. 392–401
12 *Works,* II, p. 446
13 *Works,* X, pp. 140–158
14 *Works,* X, pp. 159–161
15 *Works,* X, pp. 162–173
16 *Works,* X, pp. 173–175

17 Quoted in Desmond Bowen, *The Protestant Crusade in Ireland, 1800–70*,
    Dublin, Gill and Macmillan, 1978,p.73.
18 William Urwick *A Brief Sketch of the Religious State of Ireland*, Dublin,John
    Robertson, 1852 in *Methodist Pamphlets,* Vol. XV bound at St. Patrick's
    Reformatory School, Upton, Co. Cork, but no date given.
19 Bowen, *Protestant,* p.267.
20 R.F.G. Holmes, *Our Irish Presbyterian Heritage,* Belfast, Presbyterian Church
    in Ireland, 1985, p.114 and Bowen, *Protestant,* p.312.
21   Bowen, *Protestant,* p.233.
22 Holmes, *Presbyterian,* p.123.
23 David Hempton and Myrtle Hill, *Evangelical Protestantism in Ulster Society
    1740–1890,* London and New York, Routledge, 1992.
24 Hempton and Hill, *Evangelical,* p.183.
25 Steve Bruce, *God Save Ulster! The Religion and Politics of Paisleyism,* Oxford,
    OUP, 1986.
26 Bruce, *God,* p.50.
27 Bebbington, *Evangelicalism,* p.276.
28 Ian R.K. Paisley, *Concise Guide to Bible Christianity and Romanism,* Belfast,
    1991, p.116.
29 I.R.K. Paisley, *This is my life,* Martyrs' Memorial Recordings, Belfast, Tape 3.
30 *Psalms, Paraphrases and Hymns,* Presbytery of the Free Presbyterian Church
    of Ulster, Belfast, 1989, No. 757.
31 Paisley, *This,* Tape 2.
32 Paisley, 'The Black Pope and his murdermen' in *Classic Sermon Tapes,*
    Martyrs' Memorial Recordings, Belfast.
33 Paisley, *This,* Tape 2.
34 Paisley, The Black Pope.
35 Paisley, *This,* Tape 4.
36 Basil Hall, 'The Colloquies between Catholics and Protestants, 1539–41,
    Studies in Church History, 7 (1971) p.243.
37 Clifford Smyth, *Ian Paisley, Voice of Protestant Ulster,* Edinburgh, Scottish
    Academic Press, 1987, p.51 confirms the author's own research.
38 *For God and His Glory Alone,* Holywood, Co. Down, 1988.
39 *For,* p.7
40 *For,* p.9
41 The Evangelical-Roman Catholic Dialogue on Mission, 1977–1984: A
    Report *International Bulletin of Missionary Research,* Vol.10, No.1.
42 ERCDOM, p.4.
43 *What is an Evangelical Catholic?* Dublin 1990
44 *What,* p.3.

A RESPONSE

Gemma Loughran

One of the underlying themes of Dr Cooke's paper is that Evangelicalism, since its origins in the 1730s until the last five years – with the 1988 statement *For God and His Glory* and the 1990 publication of *What is an Evangelical Catholic?* – and Roman Catholicism have been apparently mutually exclusive. Evangelicalism has been not only a Protestant monopoly but has been generally (although not universally) marked by a hostility towards Roman Catholicism. This hostility was rooted in genuine theological opposition to Roman Catholic teaching on matters such as the nature of salvation, transubstantiation, the sacraments and, while Evangelicals generally saw the Roman Catholic Church as a Christian Church, they were nonetheless committed on grounds of religious principle to the conversion of its members. In Ireland the theological opposition was overlaid by two other factors – experience of anti-Protestant bigotry by Catholics and a mistrust by Protestants of the political attitudes and aspirations of Catholics.

Paragraph 1 of the Introduction to *The Final Report* (London, 1982) of the Anglican/Roman Catholic International Commission could be read as a summary of this analysis: 'Our two communions have been separated for over 500 years. This separation, involving serious doctrinal differences, has been aggravated by theological polemics and mutual intolerance, which have reached into and affected many departments of life.'

There is an implicit recognition by ARCIC that the historical opposition between Roman Catholics and Protestants, including Evangelicals, was a sad reflection of that doctrinal siege mentality which led the differing religious groups to seek to protect the perceived purity of their own position by emphasising their distinctiveness in opposition to the errors or inadequacies of others. One of the most important developments in inter-faith relationships in the present century has been the attempt to overcome this siege mentality.

It was in response to the first three of the ARCIC documents that a group of Anglican Evangelicals wrote an Open Letter criticising 'bureaucratic pragmatism which seeks ecumenical success by superficiality, ambiguity and accommodation of opposed convictions' but nonetheless recognising with 'confidence that (deep doctrinal divisions) will yet be dispelled through God's blessing on appropriate argument . . . and serious, unhurried theological discussion.' (Beckwith R.T. et al *Across the Divide,* 1977)

And the tone of such argument and discussion should be nonjudgmental. Gabriel Marcel argued that the Lord's words 'judge not' were the key to the most profound metaphysics of the human person. Cardinal Daly has suggested that the words are the key to that growing together to full maturity in Christ which is the aim of all reconciliation in religion. Such reconciliation will demand a change of heart – a movement away from exculpating ourselves and apportioning blame to others towards the Pauline ideal of considering 'the other person to be better than yourself, so that nobody thinks of his own interests first, but everybody thinks of other people's interests instead' (*Phil* 2, 3–4). Dr Cooke's paper is an excellent example of this kind of approach.

'Over-sacramentalised and under-evangelised'

Dr Cooke quoted from the Evangelical Catholics the phrase that Catholics have been over-sacramentalised and under-evangelised. I read that phrase for the first time in the work of an Irish Jesuit priest, Michael Paul Gallagher, (Gallagher Michael Paul *Struggles of Faith,* Dublin 1990, p20) who has over the last 20 years drawn to the attention of Irish Catholics the phenomenon of atheism within. The following are some of Gallagher's conclusions, based on his experience of working with and befriending people who were baptised as Catholics.

> In many cases the young people who are rejecting Church practice may not be rejecting Christ at all, for the simple reason that they may never have experienced him as real or as the living Lord . . .
> Up to now much teaching and preaching seemed to assume that continuity of practice was possible and sufficient. It was never sufficient and in our new situation it may not be possible either unless rooted in some adult conversion . . . (*op. cit.*, p 14)

There seems to be a spiritual hunger that is not being answered through any adequate initiation into prayer either in
school or church . . . (*op. cit.*, p 21)

We are still emerging from a 'period of sacramental enthusi-
asm' which tended to think of grace as conveyed too exclusively
through sacramental worship; but 'experience of the Spirit' is
wider and more varied than the sacramental life.(*op. cit.*, p 63)

Gallagher is not alone in seeing as one of the most significant post-
Vatican II developments in the Catholic Church the rediscovery
of the Rite of the Christian Initiation of Adults (RCIA). It com-
prises four stages of pre-catechumenate; catechumenate; illumina-
tion; mystagogia. Gallagher describes RCIA as inviting the
catechumen forward through a careful evangelisation to the threshold of a new commitment . Stage 2 focuses on the basic realisation
that our God has 'loved us and sent His son to free us from our
sins'(1 Jn 4:10); Stage 3 enters into the cost of discipleship and
sees baptism as the sharing with Christ in his death and resurrection; Stage 4 fills out the life of the newly baptised (or newly
committed even if long baptised) 'faced with the injustices and
idolatries of what is normal for the world, s/he experiences the
need to belong to a community of critique and of compassion,
rooted in the Spirit and courageous in active service.' (Gallagher,
op. cit., p 65)

The detached observer could not but be struck by the evangelical flavour of the RCIA; indeed a striking feature of Roman Catholicism in the last 30 years has been the number of crucially
important developments which have been described using words
derived from *evangelium*, including Pope Paul VI's encyclical
Evangelii Nuntiandi, Pope John Paul's encyclical *Christifideles Laici*,
the dedication of the 1990s as the Decade of Evangelism. It was in
1966 that Karl Barth, after a visit to Rome where he felt the impact
of the Second Vatican Council, said that he arrived in Rome as a
stubborn Evangelical and left no less an Evangelical but happy to
describe himself as a Catholic Evangelical. The subsequent evangelical developments in the Roman Catholic Church should make
any Barthian today no less happy to describe himself in similar
terms.

Indeed, no convinced and committed Roman Catholic today
should be unhappy to be described as evangelical – understood to
mean called by God into a relationship of loving surrender to

Christ Crucified for our sins and Risen from the dead, and challenged to bring the Gospel into the world so that the Gospel will transform the secular.

The challenge of secularism

And it is above all before the challenge to transform the secular that all of us Christians must see that what we share is far more significant than what divides us. The thrust of secularism is manifold; its false gods may be material welfare, sex, power, hedonism. In Ireland its most sinister expression is in the idolatry of political goals – everything is justified in the name of republicanism or loyalism. The worship of these secular substitutes has been a stain on the history of this land; it has led over the last 24 years to the almost overwhelming tragedy of 3,053 people dead, including 2,123 civilians and 930 security force personnel and the placing of over 14,000 bombs with the consequent destruction of property.

Reconciliation between different shades within Christianity is essentially and primarily a divine imperative; in the context of Northern Ireland it is also an urgent human imperative.

GENDER AND RECONCILIATION

Flora Winfield

We are each of us affected by gender; this is the one division in humanity from which none of us is free. So is it possible to talk of this biological division being healed, in a reconciliation of our relationships? Each of us is affected by our division in gender – physically, emotionally, socially, psychologically, in our spirituality; each of us approaches the division from a unique perspective of involvement. Nothing saves us from this – not celibacy, not happy marriage, not separatism, and certainly not denying the reality of our dividedness, or our need for healing and freedom, in this one sphere of life which touches all others. One of the gifts of feminist theology to the discipline is the freedom to name and own the unique, authentic perspective of involvement in every approach to theological reflection. My own perspective of involvement in this issue of gender and reconciliation is that I am a woman, a Christian in the Anglican tradition, a feminist.

A part of the present context of the struggle for gender reconciliation for me is the debate on the ordination of women to the Priesthood in the Church of England. I cannot deny that this would have been a different paper if the Legislation had failed to gain a two-thirds majority in the General Synod on November 11th 1992. In particular, my own first response to the news of the result – 'This is the healing of every hurt' – has brought me to look at the origin and basis of the hurting and to understand and define it in a new way. The movement towards the ordination of women is itself set within the context of the development of female emancipation through this century, with wider availability of education, enfranchisement, entrance to professions and public life and a changing perception of the roles of both women and men in public life and in the home. Attempts to understand the nature of the division between women and men within the framework of Christian theology must not obscure the fact that this is not a debate which is the sole concern of the church, or the fact that, however important the theological enterprise, this is about human relationships, concrete and based in physical and often sexual reality. This discussion can be about who is on top, who cares for the children, who washes up and who changes the cat's litter tray or the extra smelly nappy. This discussion needs to remain in engagement with the experience of poverty and social and cultural deprivation which is the lot of many human beings, and certainly of many women. If this discussion is not rooted in the theology of people's lives and relationships, as well as in the groping after an understanding of Trinitarian divine activity, then it is not much of a discussion, or come to that not much of a theology.

The context is also in the framework of Christian history: women's ordination is an issue which highlights, or perhaps casts into shadow, the ancient issue of the relation of men and women to one another and to God. The question of whether or not it is theologically possible or ecclesiologically expedient to ordain women to the priesthood is not the issue itself; indeed ordaining women without facing the radical challenge of building a renewed, godly human community is a fruitless exercise: but it has been an opportunity to focus on the wider issue of a Christian anthropology, on how women and men are able to participate in the life of the church and the world, and on how we understand God in terms of gender definition, and religious language as an expression of provisional meaning.

In examining possibilities for reconciliation, we need to begin with an understanding of the sources and history of our division, to look at the primary text of the Jewish Christian tradition on our division – the story of life in the Garden of Eden, and departure from the garden for a life in the world of pain and labour.

The story offers an account of Original Sin as Original Division. Out of that Original Division has grown sin – a dualistic view of humanity and of creation, dominance, violence and rape, exploitation in economic and sexual relations, inequalities in health and education and employment. Where there has been sin, for reconciliation to take place there must be recognition of the wrongs done, repentance and forgiveness. For the sin of this division – sexism – has harmed not only women but men also, turning biological diversity from a wonder of co-operation in creation into a source of fear and revulsion. Sexism has harmed human community, and stunted its growth into godly human community. Sexism does not create a context for human flourishing. Reconciliation here is about relationships between human beings and with God, about a fundamental one-ness in the *oikumene*, God's world house. Reconciliation is not about fiddling around with the social structures of our inter-relationship until we get them right – 'Dreaming of systems so perfect that no one will need to be good'[1] – but about the groaning of the whole created order to come into unity, where the Original Division, perhaps generating all others, is between men and women and God.

The story of 'the Fall' can help us to define the fault lines in relationships with God and between human beings. Eden defines an experience of limitless intimacy in community. The Garden from which we are now excluded is the place where we freely encounter God and one another. The exercise of reconciliation in this context requires us to recognise our need of one another, our inability to move towards God without the gift of one another, and the imperative towards re-creation in mutuality which we experience in God's gifts of healing and freedom, an imperative which urges us on in the commitment to building and dwelling in the new garden of God's world household, the new creation.

In approaching the story, both patriarchal readings (women are responsible for the woes of mankind) and feminist readings (patriarchy is responsible for the oppression of women) can enable a flight from reality: our mutual responsibility, our shared suffering. In spite of 'demythologising', re-interpretation, a broader understanding in terms of 'existential estrangement', the story 'has projected a malignant image of the male-female relationship . . . continues to colour the functioning of the theological imagination in the Christian tradition . . . The myth undergirds destructive patterns in the fabric of our culture'[2] and has deeply affected civil law and social custom. It is simply not good enough to read into the story a glib universalisation; a myth about separation from God, an attempt to explain the human condition. The sexual politics of the story are as real now as when it was written. Firstly because we continue to be affected by the idea that the presence of evil, pain and labour in the world is due to the moral weakness of a woman. (This idea has had a profound effect on attempts at a Christian anthropology). And secondly because in trying to re-interpret we shy away from the real and important challenge of the story: that Original Division is gender based, that sexual oppression is therefore not a non-problem. This is a hurt which cannot be healed unless it is named as a hurt, and which has wounded us all.

We must admit, and engage in honest struggle with, the sexual politics of the story and the critique that they offer to our lives and experience, if it is to speak to us not only of gender and division but of the possibilty of gender reconciliation. Engagement with the story leads us to admit the importance of liberation from sexual oppression in the human struggle for healing and freedom. The achievement of what seems like wholeness and liberty has no value or meaning without such liberation. Sexism is not a unique and isolated phenomenon, but a strand in the web of oppression in which all kinds of division are linked; this web 'Challenges both individuals and churches to recognise their own complicity in oppressive structures, and to commit themselves to the struggle for freedom and justice in a global context.'[3] We cannot build our Household of Freedom on the sand of sexual oppression, but only on the rock of reconciliation.

The story must be read with reference to the bigness of God's purpose for the whole creation, which is the *oikos*, God's world household. This household is not that of the isolated nuclear family or single parent, cut off from an experience of broader human community (although it embraces these) but rather it is God's *oikonomia* or householding of the whole earth.[4] God's household is the place where freedom dwells; it is not identified solely with the church, but when the church 'becomes a place where the Household of Freedom is experienced, it also becomes a sign of God's Household'.[5] The vision has been described by Letty Russell: 'Household of Freedom is a metaphor for the glimpses of God's Household we catch from time to time in our own relationships. Household of Freedom is experienced as both a present and future reality where women and men glimpse the intention of God's Household as they share authority in community with one another.' Where men and women experience the *koinonia* of the Household of Freedom in their human community, they find a foretaste of the healing of God's creation.

The story of 'the Fall' marks and locates the original division of humanity as being between the norm, myself and my experience, and the other, you in your difference from me. From this division is born the dualistic dividing of creation; women from men, chaos from order, dark from light, physicality from intellect, the domestic sphere from the public domain. God has been divided unnaturally from creation, the spiritual from the material. The reconciliation of these dualisms must be underpinned with a richer theology of the *koinonia* of Humanity and Trinity, and a re-emphasis on the indwelling of the Holy Spirit throughout creation. Women and men have a role in the purposes of God for calling into one-ness the *oikumene*, the whole created order. The healing of this division is essential for every other kind of growing into one-ness/reconciliation. This healing also demands a renewing of our theological imagination and of our God-language. The words which we use about God and humankind shape our perception and understanding, as well as giving it expression. This renewal of our theological imagination focusses on the integration of our understandings of God as transcendent and immanent, bringing forth from the tradition and the experience of God's people a fund of rich, diverse ways of imaging and approaching God. The renewal seeks to re-integrate the religious experience of women and men with their experience of life in the human community.

So what are we striving to reconcile? We are trying to bring into unity and community actual physical human male and female beings, rather than a philosophical idea of 'the male' and 'the female'. And in striving to build Godly Human Community, the goal of all reconciliation, it is not only any longer this Original Division which divides humanity, but it is a division in which none of us can deny our immediate, constant life-long participation; no one is exempt from gender, or from engagement in this struggle. This is a vital, personal recognition: for only in reconciliation to your own nature can reconciliation with the other be formed. To recognise shared humanity in God's image, it is first necessary to recognise one's own humanity in God's image. 'Your body is a temple of the indwelling Holy Spirit' (I Cor.6:19); this is a primary text for our reconciliation with one another and with ourselves, a powerful statement about the holiness of the human.

This reconciliation to your own self and gender, and to there being many different and equally valid ways of being in that gender and expressing it – a womanly woman or a manly man – is an important aspect of a Christian anthropology which attempts to express a value for individual personhood which goes beyond defining people by gender stereotype. In our necessarily personal engagement in this debate we must accept the challenging and disrupting of comfortable ideas of what is normal, defined by the self; both women and men have suffered and are suffering from the distortions of a stereotyping gender division which is born of a dualistic understanding of humanity and of creation. Both women and men have been deprived of the chance to grow into the full stature of humanity to which God has called them. Biological gender is not the only or even the most significant way of differentiating humanity; if biological form and function is the focus, then attempts at reconciliation and the building of a new human community are limited by ideas of biological complementarity.

Complementarity as a basis for gender reconciliation is an idea which has a long pedigree in Christian anthropology. But behind a rhetoric of complementarity may lie: equal but not of equal value; equal but different; equal but separate; and beyond these the subordination of the lower to the higher in obedience, and the polarity of the active and the passive elements in life and in sexuality, of inner space and creative urge, with physical undertones of D.H.Lawrence's Sir Pestle and Lady Mortar. St Paul and Milton assert that Man is the Glory of God and woman the Glory of Man:

> 'For contemplation he and valour formed;
> For softness she and sweet attractive grace,
> He for God only, she for God in him:'[6]

However, underlying such statements is not the value they purport to express but a hatred/fear of the Other, the deviant different defined by the male self as the Norm, and also underlying them is an anthropology in which women are characterised as faulty, incomplete men. This idea has a long pedigree in the history of science and of attempts at a biological understanding of gender determination, from Adam's rib to the 'misbegotten male' theory of Aristotle and Aquinas to penis envy in Freud. But complementarity depends on agreed gender characteristics which are not only physical and biological, but also psychological and spiritual: women are caring, men are decision makers, and exceptions prove the rule. Complementarity as an approach to gender reconciliation and the building of community is the product of a Christian anthropology which understands men as having a fuller potential to reflect the divine image than women. It builds up and reinforces division and dualism; complementarity denies the possibility of renewed human community in *koinonia*. It is a denial that sexism is a problem. Our priority for the development of personhood in community leads us away from complementarity, which sets in a kind of biogically defined social concrete what women and men are allowed to be or to long to become, and which reinforces the artificial divide between the domestic world and the public domain as gender-defined spheres of influence. It is important to remain open to the continuing debate about nature/nurture influences in human development, but theological reflection on the 'special nature of women' seems to lead almost invariably to the conclusion that women are really rather less special than men. It is vital that sexism is named in church and in society as a sin, a distorting perversion of human relationship, a diminishing of the full possibility of human community. The cosy scenario of complementarity also leads to the creation of a Household of Faith in which there is no room for gay people, who become homeless, and to a narrowed understanding of human and divine inter-relationship.

In her novel '*The Handmaid's Tale*' (Virago London 1987) Margaret Atwood works with the idea of complementarity, taking it forward to a future state (which is perhaps more accurately described as a pseudo-theocratic phallocracy than a patriarchy). In this land of Gilead, women are domestic ornaments, domestic labour or wombs, entirely existent for the purposes of the ruling male. In this Brave New World, the roles played by individuals justify their continuing existence, and the roles are entirely biologically determined along gender lines; other kinds of differentiation within the human race are of far less significance. There is no question of deviating from the role prescribed. Along with many other important issues, about societal organisation and whether it is possible to define human beings solely by their gender, Atwood's novel raises a central question: What is SEX about? She examines both sex as an act and sex as a characteristic. Sex as act becomes in her creation not making love but coupling, by the deliberate removal of love, pleasure or relationship; these are the things which render sex a sin outside the controlling regulation of this nightmare state. Sex as an act has come to mean power and procreation. Relationships between men and women are seen only in terms of genital sexual activity, never in a broader context. But the novel is illuminated by personal longings for love, pleasure and relationship, which name the Other as fully participating in a shared humanity which transcends sex as a characteristic.

Un-regulated relationship has been named in Gilead as the most dangerous sin because through the vulnerabilities disclosed in relationship there exists the possibility of mutual recognition of the value and worth of the Other, of personal dignity in independence, of women and men in relationship not as master and servant, father and child, begetter and bearer, but as adult, human equals, living in mutuality. It is significant that the first thing that women lose is their control of their own money in their own bank accounts, and that in this perverted Household of Faith, all reading is forbidden to women and the Bible is kept locked away as a dangerous document of liberation, to be read only by the male head of the household. But the most important thing of which women are deprived in Gilead is their individual human-ness, and the possibility of dreaming of change, development and growth in their lives. The Handmaids are women deprived of identity and individuality, women valuable only for their biological function; but for the Wives and the Commanders also this absolute definition and restriction to certain gender roles has meant a narrowing of their field of inter-relation. The development of separate spheres of influence in Gilead is the end of human community. Building godly human community is the goal of our reconciliation, but it is built with the stones of specific human relating.

Atwood's picture of sex as an act without love, pleasure or relationship, within a society where sex as a characteristic is totally determining, is a powerful and extreme case but a pertinent one for our reflection. For if sexual expression, of whatever kind, is made in the context of a mutual honouring that each partner is fully a human person, then each partner can grow in honouring and being honoured into the full stature and expression of their own humanity. Recognition of the Other brings the understanding that the community is less than complete without the Other, and the challenge to the self as norm that the Other represents.

This value for the physical, the individual, the particular in community, the local within the universe, is a part of the consequence of approaching the question of gender and reconciliation from the perspective of a whole creation made by God, and seen by him to be good. This views human beings, male and female, as made in God's image; and the Incarnation, the word made flesh, as God come among and in us. There are connections here with the vision of Peter at Joppa, with the growing realisation in early Christianity that 'God was in Christ reconciling the world to himself' (2 Cor.5:19). Through the Incarnation 'matter has itself become at least potentially sacred, the vehicle of the divine. The very stuff of creation is revelatory and is to be celebrated . . . God has made all things clean.'[7] God's good creation, and humanity within it, is blessed and claimed in the Incarnation, which breaks down every barrier and gives to all things the potential to be made new. This renewal in God's world Household represents what Monica Furlong has called a 'Harrowing of Hell', to bring again into the realm of grace many parts of humanity and of creation which have been previously consigned to the pit – sex, chaos, dark, intuition, feeling. All this is possible not only because God was and is among us, but because of the way of his coming – a once for all affirmation that 'Matter is sacramental, instinct with the divine, and when used aright is the vehicle of the divine presence.'[8]

Just as complementarity is a distortion of community, so the cult of false perfection in human beings denies and distorts the glory of full human stature in all. It creates an anthropology which is based in distorted fantasy. This cult is widely promoted in aspects of western popular culture which are widely available – pornography (mainly targeted at men) romantic fiction and magazines (mainly targeted at women) and advertising (targeted at everyone). The images which are presented of both men and women are images of false perfection – physical perfection, sexual performance, total success in every arena of life. Such images create unrealistic fantasy expectations for both women and men, and reinforce their captivity in stereotypes of what are 'normal' or even desirable male or female charactistics and behaviour, for example domination and submission. The cult of false perfection limits the scope of what men and women may long for in themselves and in one another, and it denies the true wonder of looking into the mirror and seeing the potential for God's image and likeness, looking into the faces and bodies of those around you and seeing it there also.

If complementarity and false perfection present visions for human aspiration which are distorted and misleading, what could a genuine Christian anthropology look like? Anthropology attempts an understanding of human beings as individuals and in relationship with one another and with the world. A Christian anthropology attempts that understanding in terms of divine activity in the act of creation and in the promotion of godly human community. Human beings are characterised by diversity and creativity, and by a search for meaning and revelation in the universe. A Christian anthropology names and embraces humanity as good, godly within a good creation; it speaks of the groaning for coming into new creation of humanity and all that is made. This new creation of God's world Household is brought about through the Incarnation, the Word made flesh for the healing of every hurt and the renewing of human potential to grow into the full stature of humanity as individuals in relationship, and as communities of persons. The new community made possible in the Incarnation means that human beings do not relate to one another out of the isolation of their human experience, but in the possibility of community with and through the divine.

The Church has the potential to be a prophetic sign of how the Household of Freedom will be built and will stand, but the Household of Freedom cannot be built as a home only for those who already find their dwelling place in the churches. The Household of Freedom is an enterprise inspired by the generosity of God, in constantly renewing and fulfilling divine community with humanity, and constantly calling us to a vision of renewed community which embraces the whole *oikumene*. If the church has a vocation as an eschatological sign of God's reign, present and future, what does its present form signify about right gender relationships? In gender relationships as in many other fields the Church is not yet a well ordered household. In fact in this field some parts of the church might more properly be described as a house of ill repute, failing to proclaim the Gospel as good news for women and for men and for shared human flourishing. The churches are struggling with the question of gender and reconciliation at the moment, and the world may also be a prophetic witness to the church in the building of places for human flourishing, even of godly human flourishing. We must not deny the engagement of the Church and the world, as if sacred and secular were not in constant, developing and changing relationship, reflecting and influencing one another. For example, in my own context, church women involved in the Suffrage movement in the early years of this century then came back to look again at the place of women in the church, founding and leading the movement of women and men calling for women's ordination. This does not have to be identified as an 'illegitimate, worldly' influence on the church's life: the witness for healing and freedom can be in both directions. But the secular psycho-counselling model of healing and freedom as self-actualisation, autonomy, self-fulfillment, freedom from your self to be yourself is not a model for our striving towards gender reconciliation. Christianity worships God as a community of persons in unity, and Christianity is primarily about the building of communities of persons, in *koinonia*/partnership with God and with one another, and in that the community of the Household (which includes not only those now living in this world, but also the Communion of Saints). Eden is described as an historical incident, but paradise is not only in the past; the building and habitation of the Household of Freedom is for the present and the future also.

In the Household of Freedom paternalism, patriarchy, matriarchy and autonomy are replaced by the partnership of the interdependent members of the Household. 'Partnership is an authority of freedom that uses people's need for solidarity and care to empower them through a relationship of mutuality.'[9] We are called to ask the question, not 'What is a good, nice or pleasant pattern for relationship?' but rather 'What kind of relationship does God will for us?' There are clues for the manner of our relating in unity and diversity in the inter-relation of the Trinity, and in God becoming freely a partner with humanity. In Jesus, God reached out to restore human wholeness and community; this partnership offers:

> a new focus of relationship in Jesus Christ that sets us free for others. Partnership – *koinonia* – is a relationship of trust with God and others that comes to us as a gift of Christ's love ... *koinonia* is a word used frequently in the New Testament for sharing with someone in something, and it usually stresses a common bond in Jesus Christ that establishes mutual community.[10]

The World Council of Churches' study on the Community of Women and Men in the Church envisioned a renewed human community with the following characteristics:

- An inclusive community in which no individual or group would be excluded, oppressed, subjugated or exploited
- A community in which relationships would be characterised by love and mutuality
- A community of equals without domination, subordination, superiority or inferiority

- A community embracing and celebrating diversity and difference
- A community encouraging the full participation of all its members and the development of the gifts of each individual
- A community of women and men living together as equal partners.[11]

This kind of renewed human community reflects the life in relationship of the Trinity, enjoys a relationship of *koinonia* with God, and reaches out to share with the whole creation the healing and freedom which it has received. The vision of this Household is a glorious one, but the renewed community is itself made up of individually renewed human relationships. For this quality of life in human community to be established women and men need to speak to one another of the hurts which they have inflicted and received: 'Brothers, can you not hear the sighs too deep for words of women who suffer war, violence, poverty, exploitation, disparagement in a world so largely controlled by men? Sisters, can you not see how the lives of men have been trapped by the effects of their having power and a supposed superiority?'[12]

Partnership/*koinonia* is God's gift and calling to us, but we must also work to develop this partnership between men and women and God, which is the healing of every hurt. This development takes place in sharing responsibility, vulnerability, equality and trust in the task of builing the Household of Freedom. Partnerships 'are living relationships that share the already/not yet character of God's new Household'[13]. By definition, partnership involves growing interdependence in relationship to God, persons and creation. It is in the building of the Household that the relationships of human with human with God develop that enable the Household to be built. In living in community/companionship we are living an essential quality of our humanity. We need to find new paradigms of partnership within the life of the human community, which lead us to become together godly human community, dwelling in and building up God's Household of Freedom in our mutuality in honouring diversity and variety in unity.

This reconciliation of the Original Division will not and cannot be brought about until women and men, in personal relationships and in the structures of our societies, find the courage to stand once more naked in the garden and to recognise the Other in the self and the self in the Other and the indwelling Holy Spirit in all; the courage also to own their need for God's grace of mutuality and intimacy and for the gift of one another.

I end with a comment by the Jesuit, Philip Sheldrake:

Patriarchy ceases to be a theoretical issue and profound change starts only when we begin to listen not only to the voices of women but to our own inner voices, which speak to us of our damaged selves, the flawed nature of our relationships, and yet the possibility of a new freedom.[14]

NOTES

1 T.S.Eliot *Choruses from the Rock iv.* 1934.
2 Mary Daly *Beyond God the Father* The Women's Press London 1986, p45
3 Janet Crawford 'The continuing significance of the Community Study: Sheffield and beyond.' in *Beyond unity-in-tension: unity, renewal and the community of women and men* ed. by Thomas F. Best, WCC Publications 1988, p52.
4 Letty M. Russell *Household of Freedom – Authority in Feminist Theology* The Westminster Press, Philadelphia 1987, p26.
5 Russell, *Household of Freedom* p26
6 John Milton *Paradise Lost* bk iv, 1297.
7 Richard Holloway 'Introduction' in *Who needs Feminism? Men respond to Sexism in the Church* ed. by Richard Holloway , London SPCK 1991, p1.
8 Holloway *op. cit.*, p2
9 Russell, *Household of Freedom*, p92
10 Russell, *Household of Freedom*, p92
11 quoted by Janet Crawford *op. cit.*, p52
12 'Letter to the Churches' from the WCC International Consultation on 'The community of women and men in the church' Sheffield 1981 quoted by Constance F. Parvey 'The Community Study: its mixed meanings for the churches' in *Beyond unity-in-tension* ed. Thomas F. Best, WCC Publications 1988, p41.
13 Russell *Household of Freedom* p92
14 Philip Sheldrake, 'Spirituality and Sexism' in *Who needs Feminism?* ed. Richard Holloway , London SPCK 1991, p95.
Biblical quotations from the Revised English Bible, OUP/CUP 1989.

A RESPONSE

Pamela Stotter

Mary, Mary, quite contrary,
How does your garden grow?
With silver bells and cockle shells,
And pretty maids all in a row.[1]

I am a gardener – I do not feel 'contrary' when I am in the garden
– no, far from it! It gives me a feeling of well-being and of harmony
with the whole of the created world.

I do not wish to see extraneous garden ornaments there and
when I am in a garden with other women, our purpose in being
there is not to look decorative!

I am a gardener – how **does** my garden grow? It grows well when
I work in cooperation with living plants respecting the natural
processes of growth to achieve the vision I have for that garden; a
vision of a place of colour and form that will bring pleasure to
myself and others now and in the future beyond my own life-span.
And the garden works with me to produce fresh food for the
household to enjoy; roots and seeds, leaves and fruit. It is the place
where perhaps I feel most profoundly myself and in touch with the
'deep-down things' of God and God's creation.

I come from a family of gardeners – some have been profesional
horticulturalists but many, like me, are enthusiastic amateurs who
seem to be magnetised by gardens and plants and growing things!
Perhaps it is because of this that something within me resonates to
the notion of 'singing the land' which is, I am told, an important
concept in the culture of the Australian Aborigine people. Having
a strong sense of their bond with the earth, they realise that they
need to bring it to consciousness and celebrate it if it is to remain
an intrinsic part of their self-understanding. In spite of the prevailing rational philosophy of the Western world, there is within me
an intuition that there is the possibility of becoming more fully in

tune with God if we seek God in wholeness together as a people in relationship and in harmony with the created world. This is our land and we need to 'sing' it, we need to make the vision a reality and become a community of mutuality.

In view of this, I am fascinated by Flora Winfield's use of the garden of Eden imagery in her paper. In it, you will remember, she speaks of reconciliation between the genders being achieved when women and men find

> the courage to stand once more naked in the garden and to recognise at last the Other in the self and the self in the Other and the indwelling Holy Spirit in all; the courage also to own their need for God's grace of mutuality and intimacy.

The question I will attempt to address in this response is how we can move towards recapturing this 'experience of limit-less intimacy in community' with one another, both women and men, and with God and the whole *oikoumene* of the created world.

As a woman, and in common with members of other marginalised groups, I sometimes feel that I am like a visitor walking around a beautiful garden in a city square but I am prevented from full participation in both caring for that garden or even enjoying it to the full. There are railings between me and the garden; yes, there are gates but if I go in, I must only go where there are paths. It seems to me that the residents of the surrounding houses in the square consider that they own the land and they use the garden as their own and have full rights to go wherever they wish. They sometimes let us into the garden and may do so very courteously but they do so on their own terms. It is as though the garden of God's world which is given to all people has become owned by some and is a restricted area for others.

What are the railings and how can we take them down for one another? Perhaps I might suggest a few ideas which you may wish to take up in discussion.

Perhaps the primary task is to reflect upon our own gender identity in order to experience reconciliation within ourselves. This will enable us to appreciate and value our gender as completely as pos-sible. We need to discover the truth of it and not to assess it by the values which predominate in society and in the media. We can then value the gender of others and approach them with similar respect.

We need also to become aware of the conditioning to which both genders have been subject – we accept certain things and have certain attitudes as the norm and have never reflected upon them. There can be no blame attached to this but we need to alert one another to these facts and help one another to look at them and transform those which inhibit true mutuality.

Following on from this, it could be helpful to challenge the traditional association of women with nature (hence Mother Nature) and men with culture. Catherina Halkes, in her book *New Creation*,[2] suggests that men have been the shapers of culture and that culture carries many of the attitudes which divide people according to gender. She concludes that the transformation of culture is a necessary task for today if discrimination against women and minority groups is to be overcome.

Culture is also responsible for much gender stereotyping and it is a common way of diminishing a person – 'Women are always emotional'; 'Men are always so agressive' – so that their contribution is discounted or not heard. The refusal to stereotype people in this way would, I suggest, contribute to a move towards a model of human inter-relatedness instead of that of competitive interaction which is so prevalent and divisive.

In the Christian context, we are reminded of the prophetic calling of the Church to be a sign of God's Kingdom where true *koinonia* is to be found. How can the Christian Church fulfil that task of nurturing true partnership between God, women and men?

Both genders embody the divine, both are baptised into the Body of Christ, and Lavinia Byrne suggests that it is vital to acknowledge women's experience of knowing and loving God and of human relationships, not only as part of their faith development but also as a necessary contribution to the teaching and practice of our churches. In relation to this, inclusive language is important because language affects concepts and we need to be careful not only about excluding half of humanity but also of stereotyping God by using limited adjectives and verbs in our prayers. 'The imagery of creation must be fed into that of destruction'.[4] For example, building and fighting imagery are common but images of nurturing, hospitality, listening and gentle loving care should be equally used.

We need to realise more and more that there is no division between the sacred and the secular and that as the story of Jesus illustrates his mission to transform the cultural matrix, we must continue that mission proclaiming mutuality-in-relationship. This message affects all dimensions of reconciliation as it reveals very clearly that the fundamental meaning of divine creation is both relational and organic but it also contains a particularly strong challenge for human mutuality and ecological justice.

Mary Grey suggests that the Church needs to promote a 'Christology of Connection',[5] one which re-images Christ as empowering women, children and minority groups into the fulness of being and being himself empowered by the encounter. Jesus needs to be recognised as the one who expressed the vulnerability of God as he shared the fragility and ambiguity of life on earth. He is our model for making connections with others, for empowering the weak, for bringing the margins to the centre. This stands in contrast to another point made in Mary Grey's writings[6] that women must avoid being caught into a false theology of the Cross which projects upon them a role of enduring suffering and victimhood. Just as Christ empowers, so the Cross inspires us to protest against injustice and to be courageous in living out a prophetic witness to society today.

We need to realise that there are links between sexism, racism, classism, militarism, ageism, etc. If these are to be overcome, we need to seek a different framework for public life other than the logic of domination and control. Carol Gilligan speaks of an alternative 'ethic of care and responsibility'[7] which would make connections between the on-going oppressions and approach these problems at their common roots.

Related to the above, I do not believe that it is enough for women to seek merely inclusion into predominantly male institutions, whether it be the clerical state or any other. To do so carries the danger of being co-opted by a myth of society which is individualistic, exclusive of all but the privileged few, success-oriented and competitive. We can all think of examples of this in political and other public spheres. I have met some women who have gained or are seeking access to predominantly male domains who have saddened me – either because they have bought into the predominant attitudes of that institution or because they are submissive and grateful to their male colleagues for allowing them to have some small role to play in the institutional structures. Again, we must ask the question about inclusion and equal access – on whose terms? Women who are the pioneers in traditionally male strongholds have a tough task ahead but unless they are prepared to analyse the existing systems honestly in order to work for their transformation, they can make it harder for their sisters to take their rightful place in society.

Reconciliation usually involves forgiveness. In the area of reconciliation and gender, there has to be forgiveness for the unintentional and historical hurts as well as for the deliberate acts of exclusion and words of division and derision. Not only must we all be willing to receive forgiveness but we must also be prepared to show that we have been hurt. We can then, with God's help, be ready to forgive in a way which precludes rejecting the people who hurt us or acting unjustly or taking revenge – so says Una Kroll in her foreward to Brian Frost's book, *Women and Forgiveness*.[8] This book examines the outstanding forgiveness of two women, one of whom is the Irish woman, Una O'Higgins O'Malley, who is quoted as saying '. . . we need to strengthen and extend links of forgiveness, so that they embrace this whole island.'[9] Can we make this island a microcosm of God's garden where we can stand naked and open before God and each other and in touch with the deep down things of life? I suggest that the rags behind which we hide are the rags of unwillingness to forgive or be forgiven.

During this seminar, I trust that we are making some small steps towards true reconciliation as we begin to recognise the hurt and pain in others and ourselves and to acknowledge our need of God's loving tenderness as we reach out to touch and heal one another in God's name.

NOTES

1 Traditional nursery rhyme.
2 Catharina J.M.Halkes, *New Creation*, p.10ff
3 Lavinia Byrne, *Women Before God*, p.8, 9.
4 *Op. cit.* p.12
5 Mary Grey, *Christian Women in Public Life – Leaven for a New Culture?*, Position Paper B11, p.2
6 *Op.cit.* p.1
7 Carol Gilligan, *In a Different Voice?*
8 Brian Frost, *Women and Forgiveness*, p.5
9 *Op.cit.* p.16

OTHER RELIGIONS AND RECONCILIATION

RECONCILIATION IN ISLAM

Redmond Fitzmaurice

Introduction

Since the Iranian revolution (1979) Islam has had a bad press. The Salman Rushdie affair has reinforced the impression of Islam as typically harsh, aggressive and unforgiving. In my opinion, recent events have not so much formed a modern western view of Islam as reawakened old phobias.[1] From the rise of Islam in the seventh century, until the decline of the Ottoman empire in the eighteenth, Islam was experienced as the great threat to the Christian west. That fear, and the accompanying virulent anti-Muslim propaganda, has entered our common consciousness. A special effort is therefore demanded of Christians if they are to be open to what Islam has to say about itself.

Also when we speak about Islam we are not talking about a monolith. There are real differences in the way Muslims speak and act with regard to reconciliation and forgiveness in society. My own impression of the aftermath of the Iranian revolution – I was there at the time (1976–1980) – was of a spirit of revenge and a harsh clerical dictatorship which did not tolerate any divergence from its own ruthless programme, even by committed, pious Iranian Muslims who had risked a lot for the revolution. This fierce brand of radical Islam has surfaced prominently in parts of the Islamic world in the last twenty five years. It is very powerful and worrying, but I do not accept that it represents the majority of Muslims. Most of them, I believe, wish to lead their lives peacefully and freely and, if necessary, alongside others. There are modern interpretations of Islam which are tolerant and eirenic[2].

In order to get behind different expressions of Islam in our time I will confine myself to the Qur'an which is fundamental for all

Muslims. I hope to tap into what is the single most formative element in an Islamic understanding of forgiveness and reconciliation under the following headings:

1. Pardon and forgiveness with regard to God.
2. Forgiveness and reconciliation within the Muslim community
3. Relations with non-Muslims.

Allah a God of Mercy and Forgiveness

According to the Qur'an, one of the outstanding characteristics of God is that he is merciful. Every surah (chapter) of the Qur'an (except surah 9) begins with the invocation: *bismilahi al-Rahman al-Rahim* – 'In the name of God the Merciful the Compassionate'. The divine mercy is most outstandingly manifested in the guidance God has offered to all human beings by means of prophetic messengers among whom the Qur'an lists Moses and Jesus. The purpose of all divinely revealed scriptures – and, according to Muslims, especially of the last and most perfect (the Qur'an) which was revealed through Muhammad (570–632 AD) – is to proclaim the reality of the one true merciful God – Allah – and to make clear the 'straight path' of moral and legal righteousness along which all are called to walk securely in submission to God's will. The great sin, then, is to refuse to be a Muslim; to deny the unity of Allah or to multiply gods by attributing divinity to any other being besides Allah. To do this, or to deny the definitive prophethood of Muhammad is to place oneself outside the sphere of God's mercy and therefore outside the mercy, and possibility of reconciliation with the community. In this context we read in the Qur'an:

> Surely those who disbelieve, and bar from the way of God, have gone astray into far error. Surely the unbelievers, who have done evil, God would not forgive them neither guide them on any road but the road to Gehenna (hell), therein dwelling forever and ever; and that for God is an easy matter. (Surah 4:165–167)

Those who choose not to align themselves with the Muslim community as it 'struggles in the way of God' are excluded from the prayers of the community.

And pray thou never over any one of them when he is dead, nor stand over his grave; they disbelieved in God and His Messenger, and died while they were ungodly. (Surah 9:85)

To grasp the meaning of divine reconciliation and forgiveness in Islam one has to note the qualitative difference between the crime of unbelief and all other failures in obedience. Lesser sins will be forgiven if the individual approaches God in that attitude of repentance which is so well expressed in the concluding verses of the second surah of the Qur'an (Surah 2:286).

O Lord take us not to task if we forget, or make mistakes. Our Lord, charge us not with a load such as thou didst lay upon those before us. Our Lord, do thou not burden us beyond what we have the strength to bear. And pardon us, and forgive us, and have mercy on us; thou art our protector. And help us against the people of the unbelievers.

As long as one holds fast to the core profession of faith, sin in Islam is not seen as having anything like the profound consequences it has in Christianity. It is not a foiling of God's plan for humankind nor the breaking of an intimate covenantal relationship with God. Most sins are an individual failure in obedience which God can forgive or the individual can repair by an act of repentance *(tawbah)* and the Qur'an assures Muslims that God is *al-Tawwab* – 'ever ready to accept repentance' (cf. Surah 9:119).

Even though the story of Adam's and his wife's disobedience is found in the Qur'an[3], the Pauline idea[4] of an 'original sin' on the part of the 'one man', Adam, through which 'all men' became sinners is not found there. Adam is punished and banished from the garden, but because he is repentant he is forgiven, comes again under the divine guidance, and is made a source of guidance to the whole human race.

Adam disobeyed his Lord and so he erred. Thereafter his Lord chose him, and turned again unto him, and he guided him . . . but if there comes to you from me guidance, then whosoever follows my guidance shall not go astray, neither shall he be unprosperous. (Surah 20:119–122)

The concept of a saviour reconciling the human race to God, the heart of the Christian idea of reconciliation, is not found in Islam. Reconciliation simply does not have the significance for Muslims that it has for Christians. For Muslims, men and women do not come into the world as sinners – they come by nature submissive to God. It is individuals and communities who place themselves outside the divine mercy made present in Islam. Muslims do not have the Christian experience of the agony and the ecstasy of sin and redemption.[5]

Reconciliation Within The Muslim Community

From the time of the *Hijra* Islam has had a deep conviction that it is a divinely assembled *umma* (community) whose unifying bond is no longer blood or race (as in the old tribal society) but belief in the one God and acceptance of Muhammad as his Prophet. The Qur'an insists that the Muslim community is to be exemplary – one that manifests the will of God and remains an invitation to others to 'surrender' to God and become Muslims.

> You are the best community ever brought forth to men, bidding to honour and forbidding dishonour, and believing in God. Had the people of the book believed it were better for them. (Surah 3:10)

The Qur'an places great stress on the unity of the Muslim community whose mission is to restore the original unity of humankind when in Adam it submitted to God.[6] The unity of God was to be reflected in the unity of human beings: 'Mankind were only one nation, when they fell into variance' (Surah 10:20).

The term *Islam* itself contains a theology of a reconciled humanity. The word means 'surrender' and it comes from the same root as the Arabic word for peace – *salam*. Implied in the term *Islam*, and its active participle *muslim*, is the notion of peace through surrender. There will be peace and divine order in the world when all men and women submit to God as he has spoken through Muhammad and accept to order their lives according to the *shari'ah*. Islam recognizes that human beings cannot be compelled to become Muslims – that 'there is no compulsion in religion' (Surah 2:257). However, from the beginning Muslims have felt justified in using military force to establish the Islamic order – *the dar-al-salam* – 'the abode of peace' – so that Muslims may live securely in peace and so that those who are not yet Muslims may be able to see and admire a community that is truly living under divine guidance and so opt for it. Five times a day the muezzin summons Muslims not only to prayer (al-salat) but also to *al-falah* – to 'total wellbeing' i.e. to live securely within the righteous community of God. The implication is that others live in disorder and disunity in the *dar al-harb* – the abode of war'. So there is a deep Muslim conviction that a truly reconciled humanity, one that corresponds to the merciful will of God, can only be achieved within the obedience of Islam. Here would be a truly peaceful community where all classes could live in justice.

There is, however, in the context of reconciliation, one aspect of the Islamic law and order that startles western Christian readers when they read the Qur'an for the first time – the law of retaliation (*qissas*). Here there are echoes of the Bible e.g. 'eye for eye, tooth for tooth, the injury inflicted is the injury to be suffered' (*Leviticus* 24: 17–21). The Qur'an does not adopt Jesus' ideal of uncondi- tional forgiveness but it does soften the prescription of *Leviticus* by encouraging the injured party to settle for something less than that to which it is entitled by law.

> (In Torah) . . . we prescribed for them: 'A life for a life, an eye for an eye, a nose for a nose, an ear for an ear, a tooth for a tooth, and for wounds retaliation; but whosoever forgoes it as a freewill offering, that shall be for him an expiation. (Surah 5:49)

In an earlier surah we read.

> O believers, prescribed for you is retaliation, touching the slain (i.e. those who have been murdered): freeman for freeman, slave for slave, female for female. But if aught is pardoned a man by his brother, let the pursuing be honourable, and let the payment be with kindness. That is a lightening (concession) granted you by your Lord, and a mercy. (Surah 2:173)

In v.175 of that same surah we read: 'In retaliation there is life for you'. Retaliation was seen as essential to avoid even worse violence in societies where there was no central authority. Montgomery Watt points out that in Muhammad's time when a man accepted an alternative compensation, of say a hundred camels for the life of a man, conservative Arabs taunted him with being 'content with

milk instead of blood'.[7] The Qur'an in principle accepts the practice of retaliation but encourages Muslims to accept a blood-wit of
goods or money in place of an actual life. These ideals still affect
the moral responses of Muslims in cases of killing and serious
injury within the Muslim community. Even today, in some places
and situations, the sentence imposed by courts, and the carrying
out of that sentence, will depend on the attitude of the families
involved. At the same time it is a reminder that the idealism of the
Sermon on the Mount (which many Muslims consider to be unrealistic and in fact not observed by the vast majority of Christians) is
not part of the Muslim ethos in questions of forgiveness and
possible reconciliation.

Relations With Non-Muslims

In this section I will confine my remarks to what the Qur'an has to
say about those who are referred to as 'People of the Book' *(ahl al-
kitab)* – the collective term most frequently used for Jews and
Christians whom Muslims believe also received a 'book' – a written
revelation from God. There is in fact a range of attitudes. There is
the underlying expectation that those Jews and Christians who
have been truly faithful to the message they received from God
through Moses (i.e. *the tawrah*) and through Jesus (the *injil*) will be
in fundamental agreement with the Muslims regarding the absolute unity of God and the divine will for humankind.

> Dispute not with the People of the Book save in the fairer
> manner, except for those of them that do wrong; and say 'We
> believe in what has been sent down to us, and what has been
> sent down to you; our God and your God is One and to him we
> have surrendered'. (Surah 29:45)

However, when Muhammad and the first Muslims encountered
Jews and Christians their ideal expectations were not always realized. The Jewish tribes in Medina did not accept the prophethood
of Muhammad. Later they were accused by the Muslims of conspir-
ing with the pagan enemies of Islam. For this they were expelled and
the males of one tribe were massacred. So in some Medinan
revelations we find the Christians being favoured over the Jews.

> Thou wilt surely find the most hostile of men to the believers are

the Jews and the idolaters; and thou wilt find the nearest of them in love to the believers are those who say: 'We are Christians'; that is because some of them are priests and monks, and they wax not proud, and when they hear what has been sent down to the Messenger, thou seest their eyes overflow with tears because of the truth they recognize. (Surah 5:85)

At a still later stage, the Muslims began to hear that probably most Christians believed in a triune God and that they referred to Jesus as the 'Son of God'. Muslims saw this as *shirk* – the great sin of compromising the absolute unity (*tawhid*) of God, and of attributing divinity to what is not God. In one verse of the Qur'an it is implied that the Christian Trinity consists of Allah – Mary- Jesus[8]. So there is a call in the Qur'an to 'Say not three . . . God is only one God' (Surah 4:169), and an assertion 'It is not for God to take a son unto himself' (s.19:35). In the later revelations quite a harsh attitude is adopted with regard to Christians as well as Jews.

Fight those who believe not in God and the last day and do not forbid what God and His Messenger have forbidden – such men as practise not the religion of the truth, being of those who have been given the Book – until they pay the tribute (*jizya*) out of hand and have been humbled. (Surah 9:29)

Yet even in the middle of passages of harsh criticism of Jews and Christians there are redeeming passages such as the following:

Yet they are not all alike; some of the People of the Book are a nation upstanding, that recite God's signs in the watches of the night, bowing themselves, believing in God and in the last day, bidding to honour and forbidding dishonour, vying with one another in good works; those are of the righteous. (Surah 3:110)

So with regard to non-Muslims, Jews and Christians in particular, but not confined to them, there is a range of religious attitudes that Muslims may adopt both positive and negative. My own impression is that the majority of ordinary Muslims have serious doubts about the possibility of salvation for non-Muslims because they are seen as having chosen to reject the true word of God as it has finally been made known through the Prophet Muhammad.

As they are regarded as being outside the community of true believers this will profoundly affect the attitude and relationships that Muslims will adopt towards them. However, respectful religious and friendly contacts will often modify preconceived abstract attitudes. To a large extent the nature of the relationship will depend on their common history, on educational background, and on the social, economic and political conditions in which they happen to co-exist.

In our time, in spite of the well documented tensions, it is heartening that there are prominent Muslim scholars who are drawing on another series of Quranic texts which support a more 'pluralist' position such as the verse which indicates that it is the divine will that different religious communities should co-exist until the end of time.

> To each among you we have prescribed a law (*shari'ah*) and a path. If God had wanted to he could have made you one community but (it was his will) that he might test you in what has reached you. Be competitive with regard to good works; altogether you are returning to God and he will inform you of those wherein you differed. (Surah 5:52)

We know from the *Sirah* or life of the Prophet[9] that Muhammad once received a group of Christians in Mecca where they discussed their doctrinal differences and that at the end Muhammad allowed them to pray in the mosque before they departed.

In the new pluralist world in which we live many Muslims and Christians are coming to realize that an over-emphasis on the theological issues can cause division and tension and there is need for a greater spirit of cooperation between all religious believers for the sake of our world. I will conclude by once again quoting Syed Z. Abedin.

> As I see it, the current form of dialogue has so far been rather overly burdened with theological content. Why do we have to necessarily start with ponderous issues like Jesus in the Qur'an and Jesus in the Gospels, or the Christian estimation of the Prophet of Islam or their views on the divine origins of the Qur'an? What immediate purpose would be served? We come together, if my understanding is correct, under the constraints of not theological but mainly extra-theological factors; human-

ity is threatened by extinction, planet earth has become or is likely to become the arena of perpetual strife. Those who subscribe to the belief in a higher life and have faith in the transcendent potential of human nature owe it to themselves to join hands and stem this drift toward extinction.[10]

NOTES

1 Cf. Norman Daniels, *Islam and the West: The Making of an Image,* Edinburgh, 1960
2 Cf. Syed Z. Abedin, 'The Role of Believers in Promoting Mutual Trust and Community', a paper read at a colloquium organized by WCC, Kolymbari, Crete, 27 September – 1 October, 1987, on the theme of *Religion and Society,* pp. 49–64
3 Cf. Surah 7:18–24.
4 Cf. *Epistle to the Romans.* chap. 5.
5 Cf. R. Caspar, 'The Pursuit of Salvation in Islam', *Religions: fundamental themes for a dialogistic understanding.* Editrice Ancora, Rome, 1970. pp.113–114; also Christian Troll, 'Islam and Reconciliation', *Reconciliation in India,* edited Kuncheria Pathil, St. Paul Publications, Bombay, 1985. pp. 42–44.
6 Cf. the original *mithaq* (covenant) when in Adam the whole human race submitted to God – Surah 7: 171.
7 Cf. W. Montgomery Watt, *Companion to the Qur'an,* London, 1967. pp. 35–36.
8 Surah 5:116.
9 Cf. *Sirah al-Rasul Allah,* translated by A. Guillaume as *The Life of Muhammad,* Oxford, 1955. pp. 270–271.
10 Syed Z. Abedin, 'The Role of Religion in Promoting Mutual Trust and Community', p.62

RECONCILIATION IN HINDUISM

Ginnie Kennerley

Reconciliation is not a leading concept in any of the major Hindu streams of thought, and with the memory of the shocking demolition of the Ayodha mosque and the subsequent riots still fresh in our minds, one might query whether Hinduism could now offer any light regarding reconciliation at all.

Yet we should remember that Hinduism at its best is hospitable to truth and divine revelation from any quarter; and that from the ancient sages of the Himalayas down to Mahatma Gandhi the great souls of Hinduism have preached respect for all people, whatever their religious tradition. And do not Irish Christians seem as bankrupt after Warrington, as do Hindus after Ayodha?

For the Hindu, God-realisation and truth are the highest values, so implicitly reconciliation *in the fullness of truth* is something all human beings are required to work towards; and Hindus in general – religious rioters and terrorists excepted – are more willing than most to accept that the truth they possess is only partial, always provided that their partner in dialogue does not claim omniscience.

The idea of reconciliation in traditional Hinduism is most commonly expressed in that of the personal *forgiveness*, which sinful human beings seek from God and to a lesser extent from each other. The theme runs from the early Vedic literature[1] through the Bhagavad Gita[2] down to the later devotional lyric poets of our era.[3]

Forgiveness may be sought for personal offenses, ritual errors, or most often sins committed through the ignorance (*avidya*) which Hinduism sees as the root of all moral failure. The subsequent reconciliation would be both with the god offended and with the person or people damaged; and the means of expiation would generally be public confession and repentance, and according to the more juridical documents, ritual ablution, fasting and sacrifice.[4]

The question of the need for *inter-community* reconciliation, caused by conflict between social, political or religious groups, is not much found in Hindu thought before the late 19th century and early 20th century, in the work of religious thinkers such as Ramakrishna, Vivekananda, and Radhakrishnan. It blossoms most visibly and fully in the life and thought of *Mahatma Gandhi,* the Hindu most admired in the West, which I will explore shortly.

But first, if we are to seek out whatever useful contribution Hindu thought and practice may have to offer us in the West regarding reconciliation, we need to become aware of the distinctive world-view of Hinduism. For most Hindus, the material, sensible world is '*maya*', illusion, or at most it is the visible clothing of the invisible and ineffable reality, 'the body of God' (Ramanuja). In this *maya* human beings are trapped in a series of incarnations which will continue until they learn to discern the true reality underlying the epiphenomenal world – Brahman, the Absolute, or the Godhead.

Thus sin is seen chiefly as the result of ignorance, as indicated above, and the evil that befalls individuals, whether its source is personal or impersonal, is held to be the result of their past misdeeds, often in a previous life, their *karma.* Suffering therefore is not an unmitigated evil, since through undergoing it individuals 'pay off' their *karma* and come closer to release, *moksha,* from the troubles of this illusory world.

Penitence and the desire for forgiveness and reconciliation with God come about through increased understanding, as is the case in the Bhagavad Gita when Arjuna, after being granted the great theophany of Ch. XI., begs Krishna's forgiveness for having treated him as a fellow mortal.[2] Hindu thinkers differ on whether such reconciliation means that the individual is released from the demands of justice. According to some authorities, sinners must still pay with suffering of their own for the hurt they have inflicted on others in the past, and continue doing so until every debt is paid. Others point to a 'fast route' to salvation through the mystical experience of God or the Absolute.

Because the Hindu regards the world as illusory, quarrels between individuals, whatever suffering they may cause, are not generally viewed with the seriousness found in Christianity. They are seen as the inevitable result of *avidya* (ignorance), to be transcended when both parties have developed sufficiently to see their own error, or at least to admit that their vision can only be partial. But the reconciliation cannot be forced. In the meantime, the wise person will be forbearing and not allow themselves to harm the one who stands against them. To do so would create bad *karma*.[5]

Reconciliation between ideas, to the Hindu way of thinking, will also be transcended when each person's *avidya* is overcome through their spiritual progress, which results in a fuller apprehension of truth, (*satya*).

When it comes to political reconciliation, matters are less simple, partly because the evil resulting from ignorance is both more damaging and harder to correct in a whole community than in an individual. In the opening chapter of the *Bhagavad Gita*, the hero Arjuna shrinks from the prospect of killing his kinsfolk, many of them innocent, in the coming battle between his family group and their evil cousins, who have seized power by underhand means. In the following chapter he is scolded by Krishna, the incarnate god acting as his charioteer, who reminds him that as all souls are immortal, no one can really be killed; it is his sacred duty, his *dharma*, to fight this righteous war, in which, win or lose, he cannot fail to be blessed, provided he does his duty and leaves the results to God. The implication is that bad *karma* is not produced by dispassionate acts of justice, even if these involve killing innocent people.

This passage had been much used in Hinduism in support of the just war, and understandably so. However it is to be noted that Gandhi, for whom the Bhagavad Gita was a major source of inspiration, refused to read the passage in this way, remarking instead that the destruction in this great battle of the Bharata clan was so great that it demonstrated only the futility of war.

Following the Gita, Gandhi to some extent reconciled the three alternative ways to God and to enlightenment proposed by Hinduism, the way of knowledge (*jnana*), the way of devotion (*bhakti*), and the way of right action (*karma*); the first as one who holds to truth (*satyagrahi*), the second as a devotee of the loving Lord (*bhakta*), and the third as one so acutely aware of the process of karma that he insists on *ahimsa*, a strict non-violence which has much in common with Christian *agape* love.

This value he deliberately adopted in response to his reading of the Sermon on the Mount, but he found it also in Hindu tradition and in the related thinking of the Jains. It has been observed that he took it so far in his own life as to approach the Christian idea of vicarious suffering, and to make this accessible to the Neo-Hinduism of this century.[6]

As already mentioned, it is chiefly in Gandhi's work that we find principles developed from Hindu tradition for reconciliation between communities, whether between castes and sub-castes, or between the different religious groupings. From the early 1920s on, and most especially in the years leading up to independence in 1947, and his death in 1948, both before and after the decision for partition was taken, he dedicated himself wholeheartedly to fostering mutual respect and friendship between Muslim and Hindu communities, and also between Hindus and the Sikh and Jain minorities.[7]

His major instruments were *satyagraha*, the force of truth, the term he lit upon for his early struggles in South Africa, and *ahimsa*, loving non-violence. Gandhi saw the two as aspects of the same reality, since he saw Truth as God and love of all creatures as a central value of all religion.

The terms were used almost interchangeably to refer to his campaigns of civil disobedience against British rule, which built him up as a respected spiritual and political leader, and also his demonstrations against inter-community rioting. He insisted that both were much more than tools or techniques; they were spiritual attitudes, rooted in prayer, and essential for those who aimed to bring about justice and communal harmony through non-violence. They were the means for the brave and the mentally strong, for those who do not fear death, to overcome communal conflict.

In conjunction with them Gandhi developed a further resource, which he used sparingly but to great effect: the personal fast, sometimes announced as a three-week fast, sometimes as a conditional 'fast unto death'. He presented his fasts as 'doing penance' for the sin he must have committed for community relations to have deteriorated to a nadir of violence and hooliganism. Some have accused him of using them as coercion. If he did, it was coercion in a good cause, since it led people of both sides to come to him to confess their own sins of hatred and intolerance, and to promise in future to respect and protect those of other communities of faith.

The tragedy was, as we all know, that this man who did not fear death fell victim to an assassin's bullet, and no one of like stature and moral authority has emerged in India to work effectively for communal reconciliation with his non-violent methods.

If we strive to emulate them in the West – (I wonder would a fast by our key spiritual leaders bring our extremists to their senses?) – we must remember that at the heart of Gandhi's non-violence was his prayer, and his refusal to take decisions without the leading of his 'inner voice' – not an infallible precaution, it's true, but an important caution. Gandhi's inner voice, and his prayer, always led him to have and to display total respect for the religious views and experience of others. May we too display that total respect, both personally and communally, that deep and lasting reconciliation may be realised, in our country and in God's world.

NOTES

1 In Pannikar, *The Vedic Experience*, DLT, 1977, see 'Sin and Mercy' anthology, pp.482–529.
2 *Bhagavad Gita* XI.38–40, most conveniently found in Swami Prabhavananda and Christopher Isherwood, *The Song of God, Bhagavad Gita*, Phoenix House, 1947, pp.124–5.
3 See especially the poems of Manikka Vachakar (10th century), Tukaram (17th century) and Dadudayal (17th century) collected in *Temple Bells*, ed. A. J. Appasamy, Y.M.C.A., Calcutta, 1930.
4 A useful exploration of ideas of sin and its removal in the spiritual literature of Hinduism is to be found in *Religious Hinduism*, ed. R. V. De Smet, St. Paul Publications, Allahabad, 1968, pp.126–135.
5 A good illustration is to be found in *Ramana Maharishi* by T. P. Mahadevan, Unwin Paperbacks, 1977 p.57–8.
6 This is suggested by M. M. Thomas quoting Dr. A. G. Hogg in his *The Acknowledged Christ of Hinduism*, SCM, 1969, pp.234–6.
7 A wealth of detail regarding his activities in this sphere over three decades, culled from the publications *Young India* and *Harijan*, is collected in *Communal Unity* by M. K. Gandhi, ed. Rajendra Prasad, Ahmedabad, 1949.

RECONCILIATION IN BUDDHISM

John D'Arcy May

Reconciliation – bringing people or their viewpoints together (again), helping people to be of one mind – certainly has a place in all strands of Buddhist tradition. The Buddhist canon is full of examples which show the Buddha doing this, whether between quarrelling monks, warring kings or fractious laypeople. The Buddhist practice of reconciliation includes mutual forgiveness and it is implicit in the ethical principles whose observance forms the basis of all spiritual progress. But in Buddhism reconciliation takes place in a mental framework so different from what Christians are used to that there is ample scope for misunderstanding and even a certain condescension towards the supposed 'negativity' and 'individualism' of Buddhism.

The difference in mental background can be illustrated if we agree that reconciliation presupposes two people or groups whose interests, attitudes or opinions have become opposed. In the West, we assume that the personal relationships involved have become skewed and need to be rectified, or that there is some objective contradiction in the individuals' viewpoints that needs to be discovered and resolved. In the East, however, the premise itself is not accepted: *there are no two opposites* if one adopts the standpoint of reality as against the illusions upon which we normally base our daily lives; reconciliation consists, not in overcoming difference, but in transcending it. The one approach is moral, the other ontological.

Rather than lose ourselves in the intricacies of doctrine, let us turn to some examples of Buddhist practice to help us understand where the Buddhist equivalent of what Christians mean by reconciliation lies. There are three modern Buddhists who could be said to have practised reconciliation to an outstanding degree:

The Dalai Lama, who was born as Tenzin Gyatso into a peasant family in eastern Tibet in 1935, was yet to ascend the Lion Throne

as spiritual and temporal ruler of his country when the Chinese
invaded it in 1950. Their cruel destruction of both the traditional
culture and the natural environment led to open revolt in 1959,
forcing the youthful ruler to flee the country with 100,000 refu-
gees; he has been in exile in northwest India ever since. There are
now 7.5 million Chinese in Tibet compared with only 6 million
Tibetans; 1.5 million are estimated to have died under Chinese
oppression.

In 1989 the Dalai Lama received the Nobel Peace Prize in
recognition of his tireless and humane advocacy of his people's
right to self-determination. He has consistently urged non-violent
resistance to the intolerable provocation offered by the Chinese,
invoking Gandhi's renunciation of violence and the spirit of Buddhist compassion. No word of condemnation of the Chinese themselves has ever escaped his lips. 'Tolerance can be learned only
from an enemy', he says. 'Therefore, in a way, enemies are pre-
cious, in that they help us to grow'.[1] His stance is based on the
belief that 'compassion and love are necessary in order for us to
obtain happiness or tranquillity' (119). 'When you have fear, you
can think, "Others have fear similar to this; may I take to myself all
of their fears"' (108). Again and again he stresses the oneness of
human nature everywhere. 'When we return to this basis, all
people are the same. Then we can truly say the words *brother, sister*
. . . This gives us inner strength' (122–3). We are challenged to
develop not only 'a sense of universal responsibility', but also
'universal human and spiritual values' which can 'become the
fiber of the global family which is emerging' (113–14).

Sulak Sivaraksa is a Thai Buddhist layman, born in 1933 and
educated in Christian schools. After nine years in Britain he returned at twenty-eight to become one of his country's foremost
intellectuals and social critics, suffering exile and the destruction
of his bookselling business after the bloody military coup of 1976
and imprisoned for allegedly criticising the king in 1984. After the
most recent coup in February 1991 he again had to escape into
exile for confronting both civil and military governments with
their contempt for democracy and their exploitation of the people under the cloak of 'development', and he is currently standing
trial. He has been nominated for the 1994 Nobel Peace Prize by
Nobel laureate Mairead Maguire of Belfast.

Far from accepting the usual clichés about the a-social and a-
political nature of Buddhism, Sulak boldly asserts: 'Religion is at

the heart of social change, and social change is the essence of religion'.[2] 'Buddhism', he says, 'is primarily a method of overcoming the limits or restrictions of the individual self' based on 'the Buddha's doctrine of no-self, or interdependence' (66). His summary of this could not be more succinct: 'Religion means a deep commitment to personal transformation. To be of help we must become more and more selfless. To do this we have to take moral responsibility for our own being and our own society' (72). It should therefore come as no surprise that '(t)raditionally Buddhism has seen personal salvation and social justice as interlocking components' (67). The key to reconciliation is that we 'must come to see that there is no "other". We are all one human family. It is greed, hatred and delusion that we need to overcome' (116).

Thich Nhat Hanh is one of those Vietnamese monks who tried to keep open a 'third way' between communist revolution and capitalist domination during the Vietnam war. Together with a group of Buddhists – monks and nuns, laymen and laywomen – he founded the Tiep Hien Order in 1964. *Tiep hien* translates an expression from the *Heart Sutra* of Mahàyàna Buddhism and is translated in turn by Thich Nhat Hanh as 'interbeing'.[3]

After the self-immolation of monks and nuns had drawn the world's attention to the Buddhists' peaceful protest, Thich Nhat Hanh embarked on a speaking tour through Asia, Europe and America to explain the religious basis of the Buddhists' peaceful resistance. He revived the term 'engaged Buddhism', which had been used by reformist monks in the 1930s.[4] He was never allowed to return, and he has lived in exile ever since in a small community in northwest France.

Thich Nhat Hanh's is a Buddhism of the present moment, of 'mindfulness' in everyday life. 'Engaged Buddhism' connotes, not social activism, but bringing society and its sufferings with us into meditation. Nhat Hanh re-expresses Buddhist non-duality as *being* the other, even if this means identifying with the oppressor as well as the oppressed:

> I am the twelve-year-old-girl,
>   refugee on a small boat,
> who throws herself into the ocean after being raped
>   by a sea pirate,
> and I am the pirate, my heart not yet capable
>   of seeing and loving.

Please call me by my true names, so I can wake up
and so the door of my heart can be left open,
the door of compassion.[5]

'Interbeing means that you cannot be a separate entity. You can
only interbe with other people and elements'. If the flower is on its
way to the garbage, the garbage is destined to nourish future
flowers. 'To me, this is the most important Buddhist teaching
on non-duality'.[6] The Buddhist doctrine of the interconnectedness
of all things grounds a practice of universal reconciliation
which refuses to take sides because it transcends all possible parti-
sanship.

Each of these contemporary Buddhists has suffered exile at the
hands of particularly brutal oppressors of their peoples, yet each
holds steadfastly to the path of non-violence. Though they are all
familiar with Christianity and have participated in inter-religious
dialogues, each draws both his practice and his teaching from the
sources of Buddhist spirituality. The Dalai Lama belongs to the
tradition known as the 'Diamond Vehicle' (*Vajrayàna*), which has
been strongly influenced by the tantric Buddhism of India and the
indigenous Bön religion of Tibet. Sulak Sivaraksa is a Theravadin
or southern Buddhist who has learned much from the 'Great
Vehicle' (*Mahàyàna*) of northern Buddhism, the tradition of Thich
Nhat Hanh. Their collaboration in exile is itself a practice of
reconciliation, a precursor of Buddhist ecumenism.

As is usual when Christians try to come to terms with Buddhists,
the thoughts and example of these reluctant activists seem strangely
familiar yet profoundly alien. Each of them insists on the **interrelatedness** of all beings. We realise with a shock that the expression
'interbeing' is meant to be taken literally, as are 'universal responsibility' and the denial that there is ultimately any 'other'. We are
being presented with a spiritual ecology which acknowledges the
'rights' of all beings, not just the human 'other', to care and
compassion.

The complement of universal interrelatedness is the ultimate
emptiness of all beings, for this is the deeper dimension of
paticcasamuppàda, the 'mutually dependent co-origination' of all
things, i.e. without the intervention of a creator God. Only the
interrelationships 'exist', not 'things' which are in any way distinct
from them. Meditative insight into the illusoriness of the personal
'self' (*an-àtman*) is deepened to reveal the 'emptiness' (*shùnyatà*)

at the heart of all reality and of all attempts to speak about it. The Buddhist 'absolute' (*nirvàna*) is no exception to this: all form is emptiness, and emptiness is form.

The question with which the lives and philosophies of the Dalai Lama, Sulak Sivaraksa and Thich Nhat Hanh confront the Christian is how the equanimity of Buddhist compassion results from the radical realism of Buddhist wisdom. This is all the more difficult to understand in that, although there are varieties of Buddhism such as Pure Land (*Jodo Shin-shu*) which invoke the 'other power' (*tariki*) of Amida Buddha, the more prevalent versions are based solely on the practitioner's 'own power' (*jiriki*), appealing to the many sayings of the Buddha which stress the disciple's self-reliance and independence. Christians are also dismayed to find that Buddhist 'loving-kindness' (*mettà*), which the meditator is to radiate to all beings, is only the lowest in a series of spiritual states which rises through 'compassion' (*karunà*) and 'sympathetic joy' (*mudità*) to detachment from both joys and sorrows (*upekkhà*, 'equanimity'). This seems very different from the love (*agapê*) and self-denial extolled in texts such as 1 Cor 13:13 ('So faith, hope, love abide, these three; but the greatest of these is love') or Luke 14:26–27 ('Whoever does not bear his own cross and come after me, cannot be my disciple'), and it also seems far removed from the person-to-person relationships which are at the centre of Christian community.

Further reflection, however, gives us pause. In the testimonies of all three engaged Buddhists we detect the conviction that anger and aggression do more harm to the aggressor than to the victim. This is the deeper motive for their renunciation of violent resistance or even feelings of hostility and is the mainspring of Buddhist efforts at reconciliation. Christians practise renunciation by becoming **involved** in the alleviation of suffering, Buddhists by encouraging all, oppressors and oppressed, to be **detached** from the causes of suffering. Hard as this may be for Christians to understand, it opens the way to that complete **identification** with the evil-doer which gives Buddhist compassion its universal scope. Not the guilt attaching to individual actions, but the fundamental 'unsatisfactoriness' (*dukkha*) of existing at all is its object. In the light of this we can perhaps appreciate the Great Vow of the Bodhisattva, the 'being on the way to enlightenment', who turns back at the threshold of Buddhahood to work for the liberation of all beings from suffering. Universal reconciliation, including within its scope the natural as well as the human world, is the ultimate aim of Buddhist practice.

NOTES

1 The Dalai Lama, *A Policy of Kindness: An Anthology of Writings By and About the Dalai Lama*, ed. Sidney Piburn, Ithaca NY, Snow Lion Publications, 1990, pp. 105–6. Page numbers in the text refer to this publication.
2 Sulak Sivaraksa, *Seeds of Peace: A Buddhist Vision for Renewing Society*, Berkeley, Parallax Press, 1992, p. 61. Page numbers in the text refer to this publication.
3 Cf. Thich Nhat Hahn, *Interbeing: Commentaries on the Tiep Hien Precepts*, Berkeley, Parallax Press, 1987, Introduction by Fred Eppsteiner, pp. 5–8.
4 Cf. Thich Nhat Hanh. *Vietnam: The Lotus in the Sea of Fire*, London, SCM, 1967. p. 52.
5 From Thich Nhat Hanh's poem 'Please Call Me By My True Names', *id.*, *Being Peace*, Berkeley, Parallax Press, 1987, pp. 63–4.
6 Thich Nhat Hanh with Anne Simpkinson, 'Seeding the Unconscious: New Views on Buddhism and Psychotherapy', Sulak Sivaraksa, ed., *Radical Conservatism: Buddhism in the Contemporary World*, Bangkok, Thai Inter-Religious Commission for Development/International Network of Engaged Buddhists, 1990, pp. 48–57.

RECONCILIATION IN JUDAISM

Carmel Niland

The concept of reconciliation/forgiveness is strikingly true and basic in Judaism. While both Jewish and Christian traditions hold common ideas about this concept they also hold divergent ideas with different theological bases or emphases. Ultimately it becomes clear that in Judaism the concept of reconciliation is often more appropriate than that of forgiveness since it affords a greater ability to address some Jewish concerns especially regarding inter-group relations.

Within the framework of Jewish theology, the actual naming of reconciliation/forgiveness as a basic Jewish value appears much easier than its actual rootedness in practice. However, it is often the circumstances which bring reconciliation about which give it its definitive meaning. These can range from slight interpersonal hurts to the tremendous horror of the Shoah (Holocaust).

In the hierarchy of Jewish values forgiveness/reconciliation is based on its theological and psychological counterpart 'repentance' or 'teshuvah' (returning). There is a double movement within 'return'. The first is genuine remorse for the wrong committed: 'cease to do evil'; the second movement is 'to be active, learn to do good' (cf Is.1:17–18). This idea of making amends is the basic pre-requisite for forgiveness of sins and reconciliation between people. The next stage is to repent and confess one's sins before God. The medieval Jewish philosopher and Rabbi, Maimonides (1135–1204) summarised the tradition best in the following words:

What is complete repentance? It is when the same opportunity to sin presents itself and (the sinner) is capable of sinning the same way again but distances himself from it and does not do it because of his (resolutions and act of) repentance. It is that the sinner should leave his sin, removing it from his thoughts and resolve in his heart that he will not do it again. Moreover, he must have remorse for the wrong that he did . . . and call the Knower of all secrets (God) as a witness that he will never return to his sin . . . And he must admit his sin verbally and articulate these resolutions he has made.[1]

The concept of repentance has a prominent place in daily Jewish liturgy: 'Bring us back into Thy Presence in perfect repentence . . . Forgive us O Our Father, for we have sinned, for Thou dost pardon and forgive'.[2] The Day of Atonement focusses on this process. It is the culmination of a period of searching and repentance known as the 'Ten Days of Penitence'. Jewish tradition is confident that God forgives (Exod.34:7) and the Rabbis maintained that God's forgiveness exceeds God's wrath five hundred fold (Tosefta Sotah 1.4) While the search for forgiveness and reconciliation with God and people is the focus of the penitential season, it is not restricted to it. If one has physically injured another, Jewish law maintains that making compensatory payments is not sufficent. The assailant must also ask the victim's forgiveness (M.Fava Kamma 8:7; B.Yoma 85b; M.T. Laws of Repentance 2.9–10) Not only the injury must be repaired but also the relationship. According to Torah, retaliatory actions are prohibited 'You shall not take vengeance or bear a grudge . . . Love your neighbour as yourself' (Lev. 19:1–18). This does not mean, however, that the wrong should be forgotten. On the contrary, the perpetrator must remember it, so as not to commit it again.

Forgivenes then simply means that even though the wrong is not forgotten and even if it is not morally excused, nevertheless there is an agreement to be reconciled and to continue mutual interaction. The point of forgiveness is therefore to restore relations on a more or less even keel despite past wrongs. In such situations, both wrongdoer and victim confront each other and go through the process of repentance and forgiveness together.

What happens when victims are no longer alive? Need subsequent members of their family or nation extend forgiveness to the descendants of the perpetrators? Such is the complex situation confronting Jews when they consider their response to present day Germans after the horrendous event of the Shoah. Here the impossibility of human forgiveness in this circumstance is not because Jews and Judaism are by nature unforgiving – there is already ample evidence of Jews being merciful just as God is merciful – nor is it because contemporary Germans are insincere. On the contrary, it is precisely because of their goodwill that Jews are obliged to consider the question in the first place. For only those who have been wronged can forgive and conversely only those who committed wrongs need forgiveness. In the realm of human relations, people are responsible only for that which they themselves do (Deut.24:16). Forgiveness can only be given for their own actions. Forgiveness for wrongs suffered by those at another time and place at the hands of people who are no longer alive – such forgiveness can only be at the hands of God, the All Merciful.

It is clear that a blanket unconditional forgiveness of the unrepentant wrongdoer is not advocated in Judaism.[3] Such forgiveness is of itself productive of evil and condones evil. Further the determination to forgive anything and everything promotes injustice since priority is given to forgiving rather than investigating the circumstances of the crime. Empty words of forgiveness will not effect change while the pursuit of justice is the best way of helping those imprisoned in their evil actions.

According to a leading Rabbi[4], the work of reconciliation is now in process among contemporary German Christians who teach many fellow Germans remorse and the building of moral values. He poses the question 'Would not a blank cheque of forgiveness handed out blindly to these students have destroyed the quest for the truth and wholeness among this group?' Such people who feel the need to repent should not be interrupted in the healing process by those who blithely hand out pardon in the name of God. True love, according to Torah, does not shield others from understanding the consequences of their actions.

Furthermore blanket forgiveness to unrepentant Nazi criminals with their heinous crimes would weaken rather than strengthen their quest for reconciliation:– 'calling for forgiveness for such people', notes Rabbi Solomon,[5] 'is merely saying to aggressors eg. Saddam Hussein, the Serb and other Balkan warlords, that they can commit any vile atrocities they like because all will be unconditionally forgiven as soon as it is all over. This is undoubtedly a grossly immoral point of view'. On the other hand many Jews including Rabbi Solomon want to help victims including the victims and potential victims of new genocides, such as the Balkans, and want to thwart all action and talk which might encourage such crimes.

While Judaism holds a rich theology of forgiveness and reconciliation, any attempt to apply the concept of forgiveness to the

Holocaust or to the Jewish-Christian tragedy presents many difficulties which have to be confronted. One such example is reflected in the pain both of the dying SS soldier who sought
absolution for his crimes and of the Jew who was unable to grant
forgiveness on behalf of his murdered fellow Jews.[6]

The question is often asked whether the term 'forgiveness'
might be used to characterise certain 'collective actions' of the
Jewish people – the return of Jews to countries where they were
persecuted – to Spain or Germany. According to Jewish standards,
however, such actions would not characterise forgiveness since
'collective forgiveness' presupposes 'collective guilt'. According to
Hyam Maccoby, it was the presumption of collective guilt of the
Jews which was at the heart of two thousand years of the 'teaching
of contempt'. Churches have now repudiated the murderous myth
of the Jews as collective 'Christ killers'. Furthermore a generation
has now passed since the Holocaust. According to Torah and the
prophets, children should not be held responsible for the sins of
their parents – let alone earlier generations (Deut. 24:16; Ezekiel
18).

From a Jewish point of view, therefore, the concept of reconciliation is far more appropriate than the concept of forgiveness.
With regard to the matter of inter-group relations, reconciliation
means overcoming hostilities rather than accounting for and par-
doning specific interactions. Rabbinic writings offer copious advice on the process of turning swords into ploughshares (Is.2:4).
Rabbi Natan[7] asks 'Who is a hero'? and responds 'someone who
turns an enemy into a friend'. The commentator clearly points out
where the process of turning enemies into friends must start.
According to the dictum of Ben Zoma: 'Who is a hero? someone
who subdues his own passions' (Ethics 4:1). Here the biblical text
is recalled 'He who is slow to anger is better than the mighty and
he who rules over his own spirit than he who conquers a city'
(Proverbs 16:32).

Events rejected as examples of forgiveness can serve as illustrations of reconciliation. For example, the Jews who returned to
countries where they had been persecuted had to overcome their
own resentment and hostility before they could become useful
citizens and potential friends of their neighbours. Even though
self-interest may appear to play a part in the process it does not
make it any less an act of reconciliation. Further examples of
working towards reconciliation is 'The model of Non-Violent Com-

munication' initiated by Dr Marshall Rosenberg who is making this model widely available throughout the world. The model, writes Dr Rosenberg, 'can best be understood as a tool to support our efforts 'to live compassionately': it calls our attention to characteristics about ourselves and others that must be understood for compassion to flourish'. This model is used effectively in professional and political activities resulting in reconciliation.

Perhaps one of the clearest examples of Jewish reconciliation is the pilot project initiated in the early sixties in London by Jewish Rabbis and Lutheran Pastors of the German Church to heal the relations between Germans and Jews. It entailed Jewish families reaching out to Germans and receiving German Christians into their homes ... 'the first interchange between an English Synagogue and a German Church ... no facts, no hostilites were suppressed and the first steps in reconciliation were honest'.[8] Eventually these encounters towards reconciliation resulted in the Bendorf Conferences – Jewish/Christian Bible Studies and later the J.C.M. – Jewish, Christian and Muslim students and scholars, coming to study together at the Bendorf Centre, now an annual event since 1967.

Apart then from theological considerations the concept of reconciliation seems to be far more helpful than that of forgiveness both in current dialogues such as the Jewish – Christian Dialogue and those between Israelis and Arabs. In contrast the statement 'I forgive you' often intones a ring of self-righteousness and is burdened by memories of the past. For the Jew, memory and its proper use must be guided by the well known repetitive event of 'the redemption of our people from the land of bondage'.

Finally basic attitudes leading to positive inter-group relations and the promotion of reconciliation with all peoples and nations can be summed up with this important Jewish text:

'The stranger who lives with you shall be to you as one born among you and you shall love him as yourself; for you were strangers in the land of Eygpt' (Leviticus 19:34).

NOTES

1 Maimonides, 'The Book of Knowledge': Mishneh Torah (Feldheim Publishers, N.Y., Jerusalem) 827.
2 Joseph H. Hertz, The Authorised Daily Prayer Book, rev. ed. (New York; Bloch Publishing Co., 1955) 139.

3 Hyam Maccoby, 'Forgiveness and the Nazis' in *European Judaism*, Vol.19, No.2, (Spring 1985) 12–13.
4 Rabbi, Dean, Leo Baeck College, London, *European Judaism*, Vol.19, No. 2, (Spring 1985) 9.
5 Rabbi Dr Norman Solomon, Interview on 'Reconciliation in Judaism' February 1993
6 Simon Wiesenthal, *The Sunflower*, (New York, 1973).
7 Rabbi Natan, Commentary to the Mishnaic Tractate, Pirke Avot (Ethics of the Fathers).
8 Rabbi Lionel Blue, 'Practical Ecumenism: Jews, Christians, and Muslims in Europe', *Journal of Ecumenical Studies* Vol.10:No.1, 1973 18–27.

EUCHARIST AND RECONCILIATION

Roisin Hannaway

'I have come that they may have life and have it to the full' (Jn 10:10). It is because of my personal experience of these gospel words in the context of the Eucharist that I stand here before you this evening. I give testimony of something I have heard and seen with my own eyes; that I have watched and touched with my hands: the Word who is life (cf 1Jn 1:1), the living bread which has come down from heaven (Jn 6:51) – that is my subject. I have known something of the agony and the ecstasy of life drawn from the bread of life. My earliest spiritual memory is the anticipation of my First Communion at the age of six when I wondered if I too might die of joy at the moment of reception like the little boy saint of whom the teacher spoke. The predominant memory over the ensuing twenty years as an almost daily communicant is of quiet consolation. It was at a Mass during an educational workshop organised by the Irish Commission for Justice and Peace in the early seventies that the pain of division struck me forcibly. I can still recapture the shock and the horror, as we filed to the altar rail, of having to abandon to the loneliness of a long empty seat, an Anglican man whom I had grown to love. It was through that pain that I heard the call to work for the unity of the Church; it is through the persistence and intensification of that pain that my desire for reconciliation continues to grow.

For the past five years I have lived as a member of the Columbanus Community of Reconciliation. Although attendance is optional there is a celebration of the Eucharist in the house on six days of the week. Because in Columbanus we have made the choice of remaining faithful to our individual Church traditions we forgo the luxury of inter-communion and suffer daily the pain of separation. We live as a close – knit, interchurch family, working, eating and praying together; but at the moment of communion we face the reality of the brokenness of our Churches. You find this an absurdity? So do I. The situation angers me, makes me scream out inside. I complain to the Lord that it is dreadful, intolerable, unbearable and unchristian, that it is not what God desires. My heart cries out that there must be an end to this alienation because it hurts; it hurts people who want to love one another and to be at one. Reflecting morning after morning I allow my feelings and my intuition to instruct me. There are days when it is my sense of justice which is offended: I look around the Community Chapel aware of the haves and the have-nots, those who are fed and those who are hungry; and I wonder if we are not sometimes celebrating the Eucharist with bread taken from the poor.

Another set of thoughts and emotions surface when the celebrant is a woman; for who is better able to do what Christ did, namely to feed and to bleed, to give life to and for others, than the one whose body is equipped for mothering? I cannot forget the strength of my reaction on the morning the young Presbyterian minister, the mother of two, stood before me with the plate and I had to refuse the offer of the bread of life. At that moment she stood for every mother who had ever sacrificed herself to provide and to prepare food for her hungry children; and I was insulting her. Yet there was also that great day when I shared the happiness of a woman ordained for the Church of Ireland. I had known her as a deacon and we had shared together the cup of sorrow. But on the occasion of her first celebration of the Eucharist in Columbanus my joy knew no bounds; my heart sang its Magnificat as we embraced and were nourished by the communion of womanhood. Isn't there in reconciliation that element that recognises the sacredness of the other, that knits together what is most deeply held in common? For in what unites us, 'There lives the dearest freshness deep down things', as the poet Gerard Manley Hopkins[1] would express it.

As I see it reconciliation necessarily involves conversion, changing things for the better. I have seen the change for good in myself, the transformation brought about through the experience of participating in Communion Services in Churches other than my own. I have on occasion sensed so strongly Christ's eucharistic presence among his people that I could not doubt the priestly character of the presiding minister. I have watched the profound reverence with which the sacred elements were handled and have heard the depth of meaning and the fervour with which the words of institution were spoken. It is often with tears and great restraint that I pass the unshared bread or refuse the invitation to 'draw near and receive'. Never were the feelings more distressing than on a particular Holy Thursday evening. For two years in succession, forgoing my own deeply cherished Roman Catholic ceremony, I accompanied my Presbyterian friend to the Communion Service in Rosemary Church Hall. The room was set up as for a meal, with a large white-draped table in the centre, decked with silver plate, cup and glassholders, with chairs arranged around it, suggestive of the Upper Room. On the first occasion I had many negative feelings, sensing a formality, a lack of warmth and intimacy, the emptiness which comes from the stripping away of the secure and the familiar. I consoled myself by reflecting that letting go of the known is part of the sacrifice demanded so that the Churches may move forward together. As I chose to attend the Lord's Supper there the second year I felt I knew what to expect. Yet I was totally unprepared for the heart-break experienced as the bun moved from hand to hand and I had to pass it unpartaken. The moment was made all the more poignant for me when Margaret, with whom so much of my life was shared in Columbanus and who was normally so undemonstrative, grasped my hand for an instant. I knew then that her pain was akin to mine, a real sharing in the Agony of Jesus on the night on which he was betrayed and the true price of Church unity.

During Holy Week of this year I joined in the combined services of the four Protestant Churches in the Cavehill area. I feel very 'at home' usually in St Peter's, the local Church of Ireland Church, where the services were held. But when I found myself sitting alone as my friends and neighbours went forward to receive the elements, to be in communion, I felt like an alien. Suddenly I knew what it was like to be conspicuous, to stand out, to experience being different. I entered into solidarity with the outsider, the marginalised, the crippled, the mentally handicapped; and it was exceedingly painful. I wished I could disappear and not be noticed, that I could melt into my surroundings; and the wish made me shrivel up inside. Then someone, a woman, grasped my shoulders from behind and said, 'Roisin, peace be with you'. I answered, 'Amen', and turned to look sidewards at her in relief and thankfulness. It was one of our Presbyterian neighbours. I wanted to cry out my appreciation. It was as if she had done what Jesus did that night; she had washed my feet: an act of reconciliation. My joy and my gratitiude were overwhelming as the seats around me began to fill up again.

As well as the evolution in my own attitude and faith I have seen the change which is sometimes wrought in others. Two summers ago we had an American couple staying at Columbanus. Bob, a Presbyterian pastor, willingly accepted the invitation to take a Communion Service but found that he was quite unready for the face to face encounter with the scandal of Church division. With the help of his wife he worked through the bitterness of the first experience and at a subsequent Communion Service he introduced us to the *antidoran*, a custom in the Orthodox Church of sharing bread which has been blessed, not consecrated, among all who are present. The purifying effect of eating together the bread of tribulation on that morning was most salutary, not only for Bob, but for all of us. We learned the lesson that reconciliation involves a change of heart, a radical transformation; that it includes dialogue, making amends, seeking new and creative ways of restoring harmony in a relationship; and that it is not an easy option.

In the Columbanus Community of Reconciliation we try to build structures for our life together based on accommodation and mutual agreement. Yet we acknowledge that 'our tribes', our tribal Churches, are at odds, that they do not get on together and have not done so for centuries. We want to lay aside the ancient quarrels and animosity, not by papering over the cracks, not by making do with facile solutions, but by seeing the situation for what it is, by engaging in sincere dialogue and by celebrating the good which we hold in common. We want to care rather than be apathetic; we want to reject the luxury of pretending that unity exists where it does not. So we fast, we weep, we mourn. Firstly we fast from eucharistic sharing. This is not unlike Jesus's own avowal of abstinence. Modern exegetes such as Jeremias[2] suggest that Jesus fasted completely at the Last Supper, that he made a twofold declaration of intent to abstain from eating the passover lamb and from drinking the cup until all would sit down together at the Messianic banquet (cf Lk 22:14–18; Is 25:6; Ps 23:5). I find it consoling to take my stance alongside Jesus fasting, declaring my intent to make amends for the deep disagreements and rifts within the Church. Aware of the gravity of the alienation and of the estrangement which can exist between the Churches I take seriously the injunction of Christ to 'go and be reconciled . . . first and then come back and present your offering' (Mt 5:24).

Secondly we weep and we mourn. Indeed it is not unusual to see moist eyes in the course of the Lord's Supper at Columbanus

House. I am often reminded of Jephthah's daughter (Jg 11:30–40), who, knowing she was to die a virgin, went to the desert with her companions to mourn over her unfulfilled life. I too feel the need to bewail what is unconsummated, what is incomplete in the Church, the Bride of Christ. Sometimes my tears are those of repentance when I weep with shame over the superiority and the exclusiveness of my own Church which refuses to recognise the ministry of other Churches and fails to practise eucharistic hospitality. At other times I weep for need of forgiveness as I sit, after the distribution of the elements, with bowed head longing for the consoling touch, for the outstretched forgiving hand which pardons my rudeness in refusing to participate in the eucharistic meal.

In conclusion, I find that I can enter into life most fully through the Eucharist in a spirit of reconciliation:

- a reconciliation which transcends dogma and doctrine and which embraces all Christians in the unity for which Christ prayed;
- a reconciliation which involves mutual forgiveness and pours the oil of compassion on the wounds of humanity;
- a reconciliation which deprives no one of bread or of work but which brings all to the table of life;
- a reconciliation which gathers all of creation with the bread and the wine into the web of life to await the final liberation.

Let us not then be deaf to the call to 'choose life' (Dt 30:19). Let us rather break the bread of sorrow and drink the cup of suffering in memory of Christ who prayed, 'That they may be one' (Jn 17:23) – so that his prayer may be fulfilled and our joy may be complete.

Notes

1 G M Hopkins, *God's Grandeur* (poem)
2 J Jeremias, *The Eucharistic Words of Jesus*, London, SCM, 1966, p. 207.

EUCHARIST AND RECONCILIATION

John Petty

I will never forget it. It was a remarkable Eucharist. If we had planned it, it would never have happened. It defied all the barriers thrown up by denominational pundits who tell us we should know better. For a moment the Holy Spirit prevailed and love transcended law.

The way for this particular Eucharist was paved by another Service of Reconciliation that had happened two days earlier, on 14 November 1990, in Coventry Cathedral.

Fifty years to the day before that, on 14 November 1940, the German Luftwaffe had invoked a new word, to 'Coventrate'! In a massive air raid, disregarding all civilian life, they had decided to wipe-out the City of Coventry. The first wave of bombers brought fire bombs so that, with the City kindled and ablaze, there would be enough light to pin-point, for explosive bombs, the heart of the manufacturing industry.

The fire bombs penetrated the roof of the Cathedral, the organ caught alight and soon the whole building was an inferno. Provost Dick Howard, in a personal gesture of courage, rescued the cross and candlesticks from the high altar and placed them in the Police Station nearby, which had already been hit with the loss of a Police Sergeant's life. Later, the ornaments were returned to the Cathedral and can today be seen in the Undercroft.

From the bombing of that Cathedral emerged two important crosses. The first was large. From two of the mediaeval beams that had fallen burning to the ground across each other. Wired together, they were placed behind a stone altar, built from the rubble, by the stonemason Jock Forbes. Behind this charred cross, on the walls of the Cathedral with its gaping windows, Dick Howard had two words emblazoned

'FATHER FORGIVE'

– not the full sentence of Our Lord on the Cross 'Father forgive them for they know not what they do', but just the two words, to remind us that, as St Paul said to the Romans 'All have sinned and fallen short of the glory of God' (Romans 3 : 23), so we need to remember that, whatever the situation, we all need forgiveness, a concept that remains at the heart of reconciliation.

The other cross was the result of a Vicar, Arthur Wales, walking in the smouldering ruins and seeing at his feet hundreds of nails that had fallen from the roof. Hand-forged, with flattened heads, some were immense. He took three of them, a symbolic number, and wired them into the shape of a cross. 'This cross of nails will be our symbol of peace and reconciliation', said Provost Dick Howard.

To fulfill his Christmas broadcast in 1940 of 'trying to make a kinder, simpler – a more Christ-child-like sort of world in the days beyond the strife', Dick Howard took crosses of nails to Germany, Russia, Poland, Czechoslovakia and to many other places where there was hurt and the desperate need for reconciliation.

This ministry of the Cross of Nails continues vibrantly today; it has taken me to Nicaragua during the Sandinista/Contra confrontation; it is guiding German pastors to Bratislava to help relationships between Czech and Slovak in their new respective countries; it has reached out to Corrymeela and this City of Belfast, and brings me back to the Service of 14 November 1990.

(Yes, I have done a Ronnie Corbett! Sitting in his comfortable leather chair, he starts a story and then immediately goes off at a tangent to, in his case, the laughs of his TV audience. A sense of humour is a pre-requisite of reconciliation, but not its raison d'être. A pulpit is not an armchair, nor I imagine, are you sitting as comfortably; so, back to the Service).

The Queen Mother and the President of Germany, Richard von Weizsäcker, at the fiftieth anniversary of the bombing, exchanged symbols of peace and reconciliation. Her Majesty, who had accompanied her husband, King George VI, in a survey of the bombed ruins half a century before, gave the President a Cross of Nails. He gave her a Bell of Peace with 'Peace' and 'Friede' cast on it and it now hangs on the wall of the Nave and is rung every day before the Midday Prayer in the Chapel of Unity. So it was that, in that Chapel, two days later, gathered some of those who had attended the Reconciliation Service.

There were eighty Lutheran Choir Boys from Dresden, the most bombed city in Europe. Because of the size of the Chapel they sat on the floor while, sitting in the Bishop's chair was Archbishop Pimen, the Orthodox Archbishop of Volgograd, formerly Stalingrad who had, at the Service with the Queen Mother, made a personal gesture of reconciliation in dedicating, with the Bishops of Berlin and Coventry, a poignant picture called the Stalingrad Madonna, created by a priest/surgeon and sent to his wife, before he died in the Siege of Stalingrad.

At the round altar in the middle of the circular Chapel of Unity, were two clergy co-presiding. The Dutch Catholic Dominican priest from Rotterdam which, like Coventry and Dresden, had been flattened in the war, and our own International Director Canon Paul Oestreicher. So, a Catholic Priest and an Anglican Canon concelebrated, using the Church of England Service, but saying it in German. With the Lutheran boys singing and the Archbishop, accompanied by his Archdeacon and his Chaplain, giving an orthodox blessing in Russian (they also sang it!) we had a total amalgam of four nationalities and four denominations.

I would hope that this instance exemplifies the title of this Sermon 'Eucharist and Reconciliation.' I will return to another example later but I would like to think about the Eucharist itself.

Thousands of books have been written about what is fundamentally two simple gestures. Our Lord took the food that he knew would continue to be made as long as there are human beings, he took bread, broke it and shared it with his friends saying 'This is me, eat it and in this way remember me'; it was dramatic, simple and meaningful, as was his second gesture as, avoiding the danger of water that can be contaminated, he took a drink that, like bread, would continue to be available throughout the ages, he shared wine with them; 'This is my blood, my life-blood; drink this and remember me.' And we have remembered; to the extent that we can think of no better way to mark the special moments in our lives, nationally and individually. So amidst much panoply, kings and queens receive communion at their Coronations. Popes and pastors celebrate communion at the consecration or inauguration of a new Cathedral, or place of worship. But, more simply, the last gesture of a person before, as Teilhard de Chardin expresses it, God penetrates to the very marrow of our substance to bear us away within himself, that last gesture of a person before death is to receive bread, with an intinction of wine, quietly, with the priest or minister kneeling by the bedside.

The Service surrounding the central features of sharing the consecrated bread and wine became global in its recognition for, whatever the country, it was said in Latin. This could be seen as transcending barriers but, perception does not necessarily admit understanding and the 17th Century 'hocus-pocus' was a pejorative word for those who, according to Brewer's Dictionary, did not understand '*hoc est corpus*'.

So now the Eucharist is in different languages and can be shared with anyone with a modicum of understanding. On Ash Wednesday, I was on the Atlantic East Coast of Central America for a Eucharist in English in the morning, and was able to follow the identical service in Spanish on the Pacific side in the evening – although I am a hopeless linguist and don't speak Spanish.

And this is where we see the Eucharist becoming an agent for reconciliation. When the disciples first encountered Jesus, they were disturbed by his remarkable ability to bring the 'unlike' into relation to each other. Difference was for him the beginning of reconciliation.

Jesus knew that one of the most powerful steps towards reconciliation is to value the differences, which means stepping into the shoes of the other person to understand. This vision is never easy, for vision and vulnerability go together and so, to quote Robin Green, 'Reconciliation always involves someone in a step too far. For God, it meant stepping outside the city wall.'

But that 'step too far', the title of Robin Green's book, was taken by Our Lord only after he had ensured, as is so graphically described in St Luke's Gospel, that he remains with us in the breaking of the bread. There we meet him in penitence and love, neither of them easy but both ingredients of reconciliation. In practical terms, Canon Heather Wallace, the Director of our Cross of Nails ministry, described reconciliation as 'disagreeing with a smile'!

And, in practice, this found me one morning in the office of the Lord Mayor of Coventry. He had asked me to join him and his wife for coffee. David Cairns, with fresh complexion and blue eyes, looked at me and said, 'We belong to the oldest ethnic minority in Coventry'. I said, 'Come off it, David, what are you talking about?' He said, 'We're Irish(!) and, in August, we're having an Irish week and wondered if we could launch it with a Catholic Mass in your Anglican Cathedral?'

'Certainly' I said, and so it was that Maurice Couve de Murville, Archbishop of Birmingham, came to co-preside over a Mass, with the Cathedral so packed to the gunwales with Catholics that they sat on the steps of the Chapel, and anywhere else they could find.

In our Cathedrals the Dean or Provost, by tradition, is last in procession entering for worship, unless his Diocesan Bishop is present. Wondering what we should do with a visiting Catholic Archbishop present, about to preside at a Mass, we took a simple expedient and had the Verger lead the Provost and Canons in a special group at the front of the procession, so that I could be seen to be in the Cathedral first to welcome the Archbishop and all Catholics present.

Some, on learning about what we did, will say that that was a step far too far, but I would counter that the Eucharist, with Our Lord revealing himself in the breaking of the bread, must be a moment for our valuing our differences so that the hand that reaches for the bread, also reaches out in reconciliation and love, but in the humble recognition of the barriers that still remain, so that we continue to say, in penitence,

'FATHER FORGIVE'

RECOMMENDED READING

I History and Reconciliation

John Bossy, *Christianity in the West 1400–1700*, OUP 1985 pb.
C E J Caldicott, *The Huguenots in Ireland. Anatomy of an Emigration*, Dublin 1987 hb.
Patrick J Corish, *The Catholic Community in the 17th and 18th Centuries, Dublin 1981 pb.*
A T Q Stewart, *The Narrow Ground. The Roots of Conflict in Ulster.* Faber and Faber 1989 pb.

II Bible and Reconciliation

Leonardo Boff, *Faith on the Edge, Religion and Marginalized Existence*, Harper and Row, San Franscisco 1989.
Donal Dorr, *Integral Spirituality*, Oasis Books, New York, 1990.
R P Martin, *Reconciliation: A Study of Paul's Theology*, Grand Rapids, Zondervan, revised ed. 1989.
Neil Ormerod, *Grace and Disgrace. A Theology of Self-Esteem, Society and History.* E J Dwyer Publishers, Australia, 1992.

III Justice and Reconciliation

W Brueggemann, *Hope in History.* John Knox Press 1987.
A Falconer, ed. *Reconciling Memories.* Dublin, Columba, 1989.
E McDonagh, *The Gracing of Society*, Dublin, Gill and Macmillan, 1989.
A Macintyre, *Whose Justice? Which Rationality?* London 1988.
R C Solomon and M C Murphy ed. *What is Justice? Classic and Contemporary Readings.* Oxford, 1990.

IV Ecumenism and Reconciliation

S Arokiasamy, SJ., ed. *Responding to Communalism* (Jesuit Theological Forum Reflections, 6), Anand: Gujarat Sahitya Prakash, 1992.

Alan Falconer, ed. *Reconciling Memories*. Blackrock, The Columba Press, 1988.
Brian Frost, *The Politics of Peace*. London, Darton, Longman and Todd, 1991.

V Ecology and Reconciliation

D Carroll, *Towards a Story of the Earth*. Dublin, Dominican Publications, 1986.
F. Capra, *The Turning Point*. London, Flamingo, 1982.
D. Edwards, *Creation, Humanity, Community*. Dublin, Gill and Macmillan, 1992.
IUCN/UNEP/WWF, *Caring for the Earth. A Strategy for Sustainable Living*. Gland, Switzerland, 1991.
S McDonagh, *To Care for the Earth. A Call for a New Theology*. London, Chapman, 1986.

VI Politics and Reconciliation

Brian Frost, *The Politics of Forgiveness*. London, Darton, Longman and Todd, 1991.
Kairos Theologians, *Challenge to the Church: The Kairos Document*, London, Catholic Institute of International Relations, 1985.
Terence P McCaughey, *Memory and Redemption: Church, Politics and Prophetic Theology*. Dublin, Gill and Macmillan, pb 1993.

VII Evangelicalism and Reconciliation

D W Bebbington, *Evangelicalism in Modern Britian, A History from the 1730's to the 1980's*. London, Union Hyman, 1989.
D Hempton and M Hill, *Evangelical Protestantism in Ulster Society 1740–1890*. London and New York, Routledge, 1992.
S Bruce, *God Save Ulster! The Religion and Politics of Paisleyism*. Oxford and New York, Oxford University Press, 1986.

VIII Gender and Reconciliation

Margaret Atwood, *The Handmaid's Tale*. London, Virago Press, 1987.
Lavinia Byrne, *Women before God*. London, SPCK, 1988 and *The Hidden Tradition*. London, SPCK, 1991
Melanie A May, ed. *Women and Church*. New York, Eerdmans, 1991.

Elizabeth Moltmann-Wendel and Jurgen Moltman, *Humanity in God*. London, SCM Press, 1984.

Letty M Russell, *Household of Freedom – Authority in Feminist Theology*. Philadelphia, The Westminister Press, 1987.

Sandra M Schneiders, *Beyond Patching*. New Jersey, Paulist Press, 1991.

IX Other Religions and Reconciliation

Buddhism

Sidney Piburn, ed. *The Dalai Lama, A Policy of Kindness: An Anthology of Writings by and about the Dalai Lama*. Itchaca NY, Snow Lion Publications, 1990

Thich nhat Hanh, *Being Peace*. Berkeley CA, Parallax Press, 1987.

Sulak Sivaraksa, *Seeds of Peace: A Buddhist Vision for Renewing Society*, Berkeley CA, Parallax Press, 1992.

Hinduism

R Pannikar, *The Vedic Experience*. London, Darton, Longman and Todd, 1977.

Islam

Norman Daniels, *Islam and the West: The Making of an Image*. Revised ed. Oxford, Oneworld Publications, 1993.

Christian Troll, 'Islam and Reconciliation' *Reconciliation in India*. ed. Kuncheria Pathil, Bombay, St Paul Publications, 1985.

Judaism

Louis Jacobs, *A Jewish Theology*. London, Darton, Longman and Todd, 1973.

Roseenzweig, *The Star of Redemption* (trans. William Hallo) New York, 1971.

Simon Wiesenthal, *The Sunflower*. New York 1973.

X Eucharist and Reconciliation

J Jeremias, *The Eucharistic Words of Jesus*. London, SCM Press, 1966.

M Thurian, *The Mystery of the Eucharist – an ecumenical approach*. London and Oxford, Mowbray, 1983.

J Vanier, *The Broken Body: Journey to Wholeness*. London, Darton, Longman and Todd, 1988.

INDEX